In The Wake Of Captain Cook
The Life and Times of Captain Charles Clerke, R.N., 1741-79

The only known portrait of Captain Charles Clerke which is now hanging in Government House, Wellington, New Zealand. It was painted by Nathaniel Dance in 1776 and was presented to Government House by The 8th Viscount Galway when Governor General of New Zealand in 1941. The painting of the Maori chief incorporated in the painting is the first known serious painting of a Maori chief and was reproduced by Dance from Captain Clerke's own drawing.

In The Wake of Captain Cook
The Life and Times of
Captain Charles Clerke, R.N., 1741-79

by
Gordon Cowley
and
Les Deacon

Richard Kay
80 Sleaford Road • Boston • Lincolnshire PE21 8EU
England

Gordon Cowley and Les Deacon have asserted their right to be regarded as joint authors of this book in accordance with the requirements of the Copyright, Designs, and Patents Act 1988.

© Gordon Cowley
The text was written by Gordon Cowley and approved by Les Deacon and is based on research carried out jointly by Gordon Cowley and Les Deacon.

First published by Richard Kay Publications 1997
ISBN 0 902662 49 X

Typeset by the publisher initially in Microsoft Word™ which was transcribed to PageMaker™ on an AppleMacintosh™ and output in camera-ready copy which was then manipulated via Rank Xerox Media Server. Printed electronically, in Bookman typeface for the body of the text, at 420 dpi resolution at 135 pages per minute on a Rank Xerox DocuTech™ 135 Laser Production Publishing System by:

Foxe Laser
Enterprise Road • Mablethorpe • Lincolnshire. LN12 1NB

Acknowledgements

Thanks are due to the staffs of the libraries consulted during the research that was carried out in the preparation of this book, particularly those of the National Maritime Museum, the Guildhall, the Southwalk Local History Centre, Chelmsford Borough, the Royal College of Physicians and the Society of Antiquaries. The staffs of the Public Records Office at Kew and at Chancery Lane, the Essex Records Office and the Surrey Records Office have also been unfailingly helpful in offering guidance through the mass of material they have to offer.

No biographer of any person who took part in any of Captain Cook's three great voyages could succeed in his task without reference to the monumental works of Prof. J. C. Beaglehole. Without them the task would be well nigh impossible. N. A. M. Rodger's *The Wooden World* gives a vivid account of life in the Georgian Navy and has been of inestimable value.

Thanks are also due to Derek Norman for his help and advice with photography, particularly with the reproduction of the engraving of the town and harbour of St. Peter and St. Paul in Kamchatka.

The Government of New Zealand kindly provided a photograph, and authorised the reproduction, of the portrait of Captain Charles Clerke shown as the frontispiece.

Finally, my thanks are due to Dr. M. Duffy, lately consultant physician at Broomfield Hospital, Chelmsford, for his advice on the probable progress of Charles Clerke's tuberculosis.

CONTENTS

MAPS AND ILLUSTRATIONS

CHRONOLOGY

1741	22nd August	Born Wethersfield.
1754		Entered Royal Naval Academy.
1756		Beginning of Seven Years War.
1758	February	Joined *Dorsetshire*.
	30th April	Action against *Reasonable*.
1760	27th March	Joined *Bellona*.
1761	13th August	Action against *Courageaux*.
1763		End of Seven Years War. *Bellona* paid off in January.
	27th June	With John Gore attended wedding in Wethersfield.
1764	3rd July	Sailed with Lord Byron in *Dolphin*.
1766	3rd May	*Dolphin* returned.
	10th June	Passed examination for Lieutenant.
1767	12th February	Letter to Royal Society.
	20th February	Joined *Romney*.
1768	11th February	Left *Romney* on American Station.
	26th August	Sailed in *Endeavour* as Master's Mate.
1771	22nd May	Promoted Lieutenant.
	13th July	*Endeavour* returned.
	12th October	Attended wedding in Wethersfield.
	28th October	Received commission to *Drake*.
1772	13th July	*Resolution* sailed.
1775	30th July	*Resolution* returned.
	26th August	Appointed Commander *Favourite*.
1776	10th February	Appointed Commander *Discovery*.
	29th July	Released from Kings Bench Prison.
	1st August	Sailed in *Discovery*.
1779	14th February	Took over command of expedition following death of Captain Cook.
	22nd August	Died off Kamchatka.

Preface

On the north wall of the church of St. Mary Magdalene in Wethersfield, in north-west Essex, is a family memorial plaque, similar to many others throughout England. It commemorates Joseph Clerke, a local squire, who was no doubt a worthy man but long since forgotten, and tells of his being a Justice of the Peace and of his misfortune in all his sons predeceasing him. When it comes to his fourth son, Charles, the reader is told that he went round the world with Captain Cook. This is believed to be the only memorial to one of England's great explorers.

Fate determined that, except for a short time, Charles Clerke was to play the part of second in command and, as is so often the case for men in this position, his achievements have been forgotten, even in his native village.

A man who served in the Seven Years War, circumnavigated the world before going on each of Cook's three epic voyages to the Pacific, took over when his commanding officer was killed and carried on to the end even when he knew he had but a short time to live, surely deserves to have some record of his life. This, however inadequate, is an attempt to accord to Charles Clerke something of the recognition he surely deserved.

Whenever possible his own words have been used, partly because he wrote well and partly because there is no better way of getting to the essence of the man, particularly his humour. Charles Clerke's life was closely bound up with that of James Cook and a large part of his story must inevitably overlap that of the great man. However, this is not an attempt to write another biography of Cook, there are already many excellent ones, and it would be mere presumption to add to their number. Neither is it intended to relate in detail every step Clerke ever took, for this would become tedious. The object of this book is to describe the events with which Clerke was most closely involved and to try to set them in the context of his times.

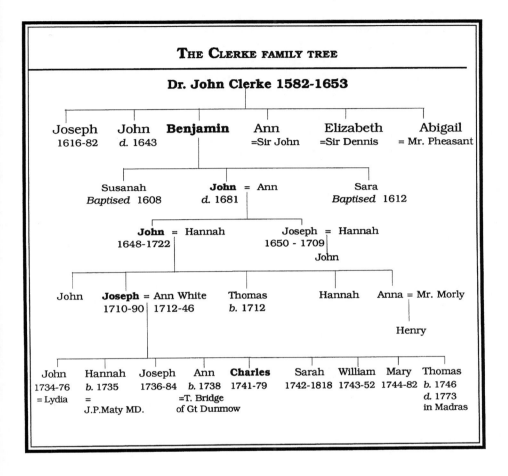

THE CLERKE FAMILY TREE

Dr. John Clerke 1582-1653

Joseph	John	**Benjamin**	Ann	Elizabeth	Abigail
1616-82	d. 1643		=Sir John	=Sir Dennis	= Mr. Pheasant

Susanah
Baptised 1608

John = Ann
d. 1681

Sara
Baptised 1612

John = Hannah
1648-1722

Joseph = Hannah
1650 - 1709

John

John	**Joseph** = Ann White	Thomas		Hannah	Anna = Mr. Morly
	1710-90	1712-46	b. 1712		

Henry

John	Hannah	Joseph	Ann	**Charles**	Sarah	William	Mary	Thomas
1734-76	b. 1735	1736-84	b. 1738	1741-79	1742-1818	1743-52	1744-82	b. 1746
= Lydia	=		=T. Bridge					d. 1773
	J.P.Maty MD.		of Gt Dunmow					in Madras

2. The monument in Wethersfield church which aroused the authors'
interests.
[Transcription given in Appendix 1.]

CHAPTER ONE

THE EARLY YEARS

ON THE WINDING ROAD between Braintree and Saffron Walden in Essex lies the village of Wethersfield, a pleasant place with a street of mainly old houses. Overlooking the village green is a flint-faced church with a square tower which Pevsner dates to the thirteenth century. The settlement is on a small rise in the valley of the River Pant and is surrounded by a gently rolling landscape, quite unlike the flat lands which are characteristic of much of the county. The countryside is a mixture of cultivated fields and woodland which is not high enough to intrude upon the wide sweep of the East Anglian horizon.

People have lived here for more than a thousand years, since Wutha brought his tribe across the North Sea in the ninth century. They followed the river now called the Pant until coming upon a clearing in the forest—a feld—in which they could make their home.

On the southern outskirts of Wethersfield is Brook Farm, one of the oldest houses in the village and the birthplace of Charles Clerke, Georgian sailor and explorer. He was born on 22nd August 1741,[1] the sixth child, and fourth son, of Joseph and Ann Clerke. He was to have an adventurous, active life. The world was then both a smaller and a larger place because, while most people never ventured far from the village except for the very occasional visit to a nearby town, when they thought of the outside world it seemed to be almost without limit. Today, when people are able to travel in but a few hours to every corner of the earth, it is difficult to believe how little of the geography of the globe was known to even the best educated Europeans just over two hundred years ago. They were familiar with the outline of most of the continents but knew virtually nothing about the Pacific region and the very existence of a Great Southern Continent was a matter for speculation. When Clerke died thirty-eight years later many of the mysteries of that great ocean had been solved and he had played no small part in their resolution.

Charles was born into an ordered society, but one on the verge of the Industrial Revolution. The old rural way of life which had evolved over many centuries and seemed to be immutable was soon to end for ever, to be replaced in a relatively short time by a world which had discovered ways of harnessing the power of steam. George II was on the throne, ruling over a population of about seven million. There were few large towns and most people lived in the countryside making their living, directly or indirectly, from the land. Only London, Bristol and Norwich could lay claim to be called cities. The capital was by far the largest, with about 500,000 inhabitants, and it owed its prosperity not to industry but to being a port and distribution centre. This was not all for it was growing in importance as a financial centre with power moving there from Amsterdam. Trade was the essence of life in the cities, and although their inhabitants had little awareness of a class structure they lived in a stratified society with successive layers of unskilled workers, shopkeepers, artisans and merchants.

The King was a Hanoverian, one of the House which had come from mainland Europe in 1714 to rule England. The sovereign had less influence than had his predecessors because the House of Commons had gained the power to dissolve Parliament and to form ministries. While it was not a system of government that would today be described as being democratic, by the standards of continental Europe at that time it was positively enlightened. The English Parliament consisted of about 550 members who were elected by men (women were excluded) who had to qualify by ownership of a freehold over a certain level to get on the electoral roll. The assembly was dominated by a small number of powerful families— about seventy— the heads of which sat in the House of Lords with their nominees in the Commons, 'representing' the Rotten Boroughs which they controlled. Candidates frequently gained their seats by purchasing the votes of the electors— often at high cost. Patronage was all-important and, despite the limited degree of democratic influence ordinary people were able to exert, there was little animosity between the various strata of society and no rigid class barriers. Even though few of them had a vote, Englishmen were proud of the freedoms they enjoyed and in comparison with the rest of Europe they had something to boast about. They were free to express an opinion on any subject without let or hindrance and the Press was unfettered, often descending to scurrility. Visitors from abroad coming to England at the time of an election were often amazed at the sight of common people heckling Parliamentary candidates who were often drawn from the aristocracy.

Robert Walpole was coming towards the end of a period of twenty-one years as Prime Minister. The members of the Parliament in which he sat were loosely formed into two main groups— Whigs and Tories— which were far removed from today's rigidly drawn party lines with M.P.s often moving between the two. Whigs were usually Low Church and involved in business; Tories were High Church and often owned land. Walpole was a Whig but, even so, he was regarded as being the representative in Parliament of the landed class, men such as Charles Clerke's grandfather and later his father. The Clerke's belonged to the group which provided the Justices of the Peace who carried on the daily government of the country at a local level. Walpole was now 65 years old, a landowner from Norfolk and M.P. for King's Lynn, fond of food and drink and possessed of a sense of humour which could be described as being 'broad'. The giving of bribes and their being taken by politicians was considered to be part and parcel of the political system and Walpole was not above the practice. On the face of it he was a man unlikely to be a reformer but it was he who introduced into the system of Parliamentary government a feature which survives to this day. He established the principle of rule by Cabinet in which a group of men, dependant on the support of Parliament, accept collective responsibility for their decisions and become the link between the legislature and the executive. He may thus be credited with the creation of the party system and all that has flowed from it, for better or worse.

Ten years after the turn of the eighteenth century the government granted the South Sea Company a monopoly of English trade in the Pacific and on the east coast of South America. Slave trading was at the core of the business. When the company collapsed in 1720, following feverish speculation, thousands of investors were ruined and Walpole was brought to power in the following year to restore public confidence. This he succeeded in doing through policies which brought about stability and internal peace to the extent that most people regained about one third of their capital.

Walpole had a strong aversion to war and his foreign policy was based upon a genuine desire to avoid conflict, in stark contrast to many of those in power on the Continent. He managed to prevent England's involvement in the 'War of the Polish Succession' and in 1734 was able to say to Queen Charlotte, entirely truthfully, that 50,000 men had been killed in Europe that year and not one had been English.

Despite this, Charles Clerke was born at a time when the country was at war. The long peace had come to an end in 1739 when Walpole's policies were undermined and, against his better judgement, he had to give way to public clamour and allow England to embark on a mainly maritime war with Spain. The Spaniards had tried for years to prevent trade, other than their own, with South America but their policy was being increasingly challenged. A Captain Jenkins was one who was prepared to defy them and he indulged in trade which the Spanish authorities declared to be illegal. When Jenkins appeared in the House of Commons one day in 1738 and produced one of his ears which he said had been torn off by a Spanish customs official, the mob in London erupted. Against all Walpole's instincts the country was drawn into the War of Austrian Succession, with France coming in on the side of Spain in 1744.

The fighting on the Continent, which was not well conducted, went on for four years. In the middle of it Charles Stuart, the Young Pretender, thought he saw an opportunity of displacing the Hanoverians from the English throne and of re-establishing the House of Stuart while most of the English troops were campaigning in the Netherlands. Charles Clerke was only four years old when 'The 45'— the Jacobite Rebellion— began. A Scots army of 5,000 men, mainly Highlanders, crossed the border and marched south. It had high hopes of attracting support in England as it moved towards London but it was met with almost universal indifference, almost the sole exception being a small number of Catholics in the north-west of England who rallied to the Stuart cause. News of the Scots' arrival in Derby reached London on the 6th December, 'Black Friday', and caused panic in the city. The inhabitants need not have worried because the rebellion had run out of steam and was turned back towards the north by its commanders before all momentum was lost.

As a small child Charles Clerke would have been unaware of what was going on but the failure of the Jacobites, and the collapse of their cause after the defeat at Culloden in 1746, meant that he was to spend his life under the rule of a Protestant, Hanoverian, king rather than a Stuart, Catholic, monarch. It is a matter of speculation what the effect would have been if the result had been reversed. Would alliances have been made with the Catholic rulers of France and Spain or would national interests have remained paramount? How would the Royal Navy have been used and how would that have altered the course of Charles' career? Might there have been another Civil War? The uprising against Charles I was less than a century into the past and had been fought on issues which were mainly religious. The only thing that is reasonably sure is that the Hanoverian victory brought about a more stable regime than would otherwise have been the case.

When Charles was born his family had already lived in Wethersfield for over 400 years. They had originally been called Youngman and there are references to them going back to the fourteenth century. The name was changed about two hundred years later for reasons now lost to history but it was not an unusual thing to do at that time and was often associated with the inheritance of property.

His early ancestor, Dr. John Clerke, was born at Brook Farm in 1582, and acquired the Manor of Wethersfield from Thomas Allen of Finchley. John studied at Cambridge University, qualified M.D. in 1615 and became a Fellow of the Royal College of Physicians in 1622. He practised medicine in his native village and in London, revised the pharmacopœia and refereed a treatise on rickets.

One of his contemporaries was William Harvey, the most eminent medical practitioner of his day and the first man to describe the circulation of the blood. He was educated at Cambridge and various Italian medical schools and came from Hempstead, a village only some ten miles from the Clerkes' home. The village has a more dubious claim to fame for it was the home of the notorious highwayman Dick Turpin who ended his days on the scaffold at York. Harvey was a Royalist at a time when political convictions were held very intensely and was physician to the court of Charles I, an appointment which meant he had often to be away from his position at St. Bartholomew's Hospital. At that time he and Clerke must have been on good terms, for Harvey was a man of influence and agreed to his colleague's appointment as second physician at the hospital.

From then onwards their paths diverged and their personal relationship deteriorated to the point of bitterness. They disagreed on politics, for Clerke supported the Parliamentary cause in the Civil War and organised its army's medical services. This was not the only thing to upset Harvey. Despite his support of the King he still had a huge reputation but this did not prevent the House of Commons trying, unsuccessfully as it turned out, to have Harvey replaced at 'Barts' with Clerke's son-in-law, Sir John Micklethwaite.

John Clerke prospered and became Treasurer and later President of the Royal College of Physicians in 1645, to the great resentment of Harvey who refused to attend meetings if Clerke was in the chair.

John seems to have been an argumentative fellow because he was involved in another dispute, this time with a Dr. Lawrence Wright who had a neighbouring practice in Wethersfield. The cause of the disagreement is long forgotten but it is not surprising that the more influential man emerged the victor. Clerke had bought more land in the area before he died, a wealthy man, in 1653. Dr. John's funeral was a fine affair with the cortege being escorted to the church of St. Martin Without, Ludgate, by the berobed Fellows of the College but not, it may be presumed with some confidence, by Harvey.

John had three sons one of whom, Joseph, inherited the Manor but spent most of his time at Lincoln's Inn. The other two, John and Benjamin, were both doctors. When Joseph died in 1682 he left the Manor to Benjamin's son, another who was called John. The son of this John Clerke also carried the family name of John and when he died in 1768 the Manor went to his son Joseph, the father of Charles Clerke. By the time Joseph Clerke came into his inheritance he had been a widower for twenty-one years and only eight of his children were still alive. This is a large number but Joseph and his wife Ann (née White) had twelve children before she died in childbirth in February 1747, aged 35 years, when Charles was only 5 years old.

There were five boys in their family. John, the eldest, followed a naval career, was knighted and had risen to the rank of Post Captain before he died in Madras in 1776. Joseph came next; he became a lawyer in Ipswich after being articled to a firm of solicitors in London and died in Abington, near Cambridge, in 1784. William came after Charles but failed to reach adulthood, dying in 1753. The fifth son was Thomas who was born in 1746. He took Holy orders, secured the position of curate in Hempstead, Harvey's home village, and occasionally took the road to Wethersfield church where he officiated at weddings, funerals and christenings. He seems to have been smitten with the same wander-lust that gripped his brothers, John and Charles, because he left England to become vicar to the Factory (as the colony was known) at Surat, in India, where he died in 1773.

Ann Clerke married Thomas Bridge of Great Dunmow to whom the Manor passed on Joseph's death in 1790. Sarah was the last surviving child of Joseph and Ann when she died in Castle Hedingham in 1818.

When Charles Clerke's eldest brother, John, decided upon a career at sea he was taking an unusual step since, as the eldest son, he could expect to inherit both his father's property and his position. John's move was significant for Charles because it set the precedent he was to follow for the rest of his life. The Clerke family had no history of service in either the Royal or Merchant Navies and, unlike counties such as Devon, Essex does not spring to mind as a place with a long maritime tradition. This is a misconception because reference to a map shows what a long coastline the county has. Its southern boundary runs along the length of the north bank of the Thames, turns north at Southend, passes the estuaries of the Crouch and the Blackwater and ends at Harwich. For centuries, many seafaring men have had their homes there— the fishermen of Leigh and Mersea, the bargemen of the great rivers who traded as far away as Spain and the Baltic, and the distant water sailors of Harwich. Both the *Mayflower*, the ship which took the Pilgrim Fathers to America, and her commander, Captain Jones, were from Harwich. Both before and during Charles Clerke's time, Essex men were in the crews of many a Royal Navy ship and in the future would be included in ones which fought at Trafalgar and Quiberon Bay.

It was unusual for the eldest son of a landed family to go to sea as did John Clerke. Rodger[2] goes so far as to say: 'It may be taken as axiomatic that a first born son in the Navy must have come from an impoverished family'. This was not so in his case for he was a man with prospects. John's father, Joseph, was a 58 year old farmer when he inherited the Manor in 1768 together with the property and an income of £500[3] a year that came with it. Although by this time John was thirty-four years of age and well embarked on a naval career he could have expected to have succeeded his father in the fullness of time. Because of the prevailing system of primogeniture he knew that he would not have had to share his inheritance with his brothers and sisters because it was rare for estates to be divided. John had expectations of a fair sized fortune and poverty was not the reason for his going to sea. The way in which his later life developed suggests that he was high spirited and adventurous, given to risk-taking to the point of recklessness. For him the Royal Navy, with its chances of danger and prize money, had an irresistible attraction.

It must have been apparent early on that Charles was a bright child. Where and from whom he received his early education is unknown but whoever it was produced a boy who had a good grounding in grammar and a wide vocabulary which he used in a flowing, fluent style, always laced with humour. His teacher also gave him a good foundation in mathematics which he was able to build on in later years to become a first class navigator. Charles is unlikely to have been sent to one of the local 'Dame's schools' because the ladies who taught in them, being themselves barely able to read and write and with only a rudimentary knowledge of mathematics, catered mainly for the children of small farmers. His father and his uncle Thomas attended Colchester Grammar School and his younger brother, also called Thomas, went to Felsted School. Since Charles' name does not appear on the roll of either establishment it is probable that he was educated privately, possibly under the tuition of Rev. Ridlington, the then vicar of Wethersfield.

Charles had lost his mother when he was only a small child and was coming towards the end of his schooling when a second tragedy came into his life: his elder brother William died on the second day of the year 1753.

At the age of 13 years and almost certainly influenced by his eldest brother John, whom he dearly loved, Charles decided that he, too, would make a career in the Royal Navy. One morning in 1754 he gathered together his possessions, said good-bye to his family and took the road to London and on to Portsmouth where the Royal Naval Academy awaited him, leaving behind for ever the rural life of his childhood.

4. The Youngman – Clerk(e) memorial. See also the caption below for Fig. 3.

3. Wethersfield church as it is today, doubtless still recognisable as the church known to Charles Clerke two and a half centuries ago. It contains both the Clerke family memorial shown facing page 1. and the memorial tablet illustrated here, which shows the name change from Youngman to Clerk (before the final 'e' was added) half a century before Charles was born. [see also the text on page 4.]

CHAPTER TWO

LAND AND SEA

IT IS BEYOND DOUBT THAT LIFE AFLOAT in the mid-eighteenth century was a hard business, but it was no less so for the majority of people living in the villages of England. True, country folk did not have to face the everyday dangers which confronted the seafaring man, and they were certainly unlikely to be killed by an enemy cannon ball, but they had plenty of other problems.

Life outside the towns, with the exception of mining and fishing communities, was nearly always based on agriculture which was recovering from the depression of the 1730s. When Charles walked the short distance from Brook Farm into Wethersfield he was surrounded by a way of life that was typical of countless villages the length and breadth of England where all the people gained their living from working the land and in the trades which supported agriculture. In the fields surrounding Wethersfield, the usual crops were grown, the farmers using a system of rotation, together with more specialised produce such as hops. In the spring the countryside would have been a blaze of colour from the millions of crocuses which were grown to produce saffron, to be used in dyes and medicines. Its cultivation went on until cheaper imports from Spain and the Middle East made its production uneconomic.

There was a secondary, but important, cottage industry. Although it was going into a slow decline by the late 1740s, weaving was the second most important industry in England and East Anglia was its centre. English woven products enjoyed a good reputation in Europe and much of the produce of the looms was exported, particularly to the Iberian Peninsular. Near to Wethersfield, weavers were working in Braintree, Halstead, Bocking and the Hedinghams, bringing employment to many other people. In Braintree alone more than eight hundred men and women were engaged in the trade and each weaver required six spinners to keep up the supply of prepared wool. This work was done by the wives and daughters of the farm labourers in the nearby villages and it brought much needed extra income to the agricultural communities.

The village was almost self-sufficient and the main street was the focus of activity. All kinds of trades went on there; butchers and bakers, publicans and tailors, cobblers and harness-makers all earned a living from the shops and workshops lining the road. Each could make a case for being important but the blacksmith went further— he claimed to be indispensable because all the other tradesmen depended on him for making and maintaining their tools.

Most people lived in Wethersfield's main street in thatch covered dwellings built in lath and plaster on a timber frame. In the surrounding countryside there were scattered farmhouses and cottages, sometimes grouped together to form hamlets. This pattern of settlement came about because the land around the village had been enclosed since the Middle Ages but not very far away, particularly in the direction of Cambridge, the landscape then, as now, looked different. There the age-old strip farming system was still in use, although enclosure was beginning to take place, and it had an effect on the rural scene. Only a few people lived in isolated houses beyond the village boundary and most had their homes in the village street. Each day they went out to till their strips in the communal fields, sometimes walking several miles each way to and from work. There are few old houses now to be seen outside these villages and the fields are larger, even allowing for the recent loss of so many hedges, since they were not divided up by enclosure. In Charles's time about half the land in England was enclosed and by 1800 another three million acres had been taken into the new system.

Although not from the aristocracy, Charles Clerke came from a relatively privileged background. When Joseph succeeded his father to become Lord of the Manor other advantages came with the title; he was now a Justice of the Peace, a local landowner of substance and consequently more affluent. A movement to improve the land had begun in Norfolk and was gaining strength in Essex and Suffolk. Men in the position of Joseph Clerke were to the forefront because they had either the necessary capital, or access to it, to bring into use the new techniques. Farms were being amalgamated to form larger units, a new system of crop rotation was introduced with a four year cycle replacing the previous one of three years; more efficient drainage was put in and new types of seeds came into use. All combined to bring about greater productivity of the land. A rich and ready market for the produce was provided by London, which was not far away and had an expanding population waiting to be fed. The city had yet to intrude into the Essex countryside, its eastern boundary did not extend beyond Stratford and places like East Ham, Leytonstone and Romford were merely villages.

Getting goods to the market offered by London was becoming easier because the roads were much better than they had been only a few years earlier. A turnpike had been built in 1726 connecting Castle Hedingham to Chelmsford via Braintree. There it joined another which had been finished in 1722 and followed the route of today's A 12, or rather the line it took until the various post-war by-passes of the twentieth century were completed. Such roads were the exception, for nearly all the others were of a much lower standard, making it difficult for the majority of the population to travel more than a short distance. Country people tended not to go far from their native village and most spent their entire lives within a few miles of home. Those who had to travel because of business were often obliged to use unmetalled roads with surfaces that were nearly always in poor condition. Travellers going on a long journey were embarking on a major expedition; the journey from York to London, for example, usually took a week. The winter rains turned the roads into quagmires and it was a common sight to see a wagon bogged down, sunk up to its axles in mud. As a consequence, for much of the year it was impossible to move goods over long distances in wheeled vehicles and most were carried on the backs of pack animals that crept slowly forward in long trains.

Water transport was sometimes an alternative and much of the produce of Essex was taken to London through the then thriving port of Maldon. Inland waterways seemed to offer a solution and at the time of Charles' birth the great era of canal building was about to begin. The 'navigations', as they were called, made possible the quicker and more efficient movement of goods and the fuel that was needed for their manufacture. Later, during the reign of George III, the building of canals was stimulated by the need to move coal, a bulky cargo, which was replacing the dwindling supplies of wood.

For people in the position of the Clerkes a good income brought more than just access to the comforts and luxuries of life; it also gave status and influence. The ordinary farm worker had a very different existence. His life was one of unremitting toil with only occasional relief for him and his family, although they were often unrestrained during their leisure time. Most men were paid by the day and those in Essex earned, on average, about seven shillings a week. They had no guarantee of year-round employment and if there was no work there was no pay. Things changed during the few busy weeks of harvest time when there was plenty to do and wages went up accordingly. During the summer the usual hours of work were from 6.00 a.m. to 6.00 p.m. and in the winter the labourer toiled all the hours of daylight.

The women of the family made a substantial and probably an essential contribution to the budget by spinning wool for the weavers in the nearby towns. Wives and daughters between them could make as much as 3s 6d a week if they worked hard but at the time of Charles' youth earnings were tending to fall. When they were old enough, small children were expected to do their part by earning a few pence picking up stones in the fields, generally helping at the harvest and gleaning when the crops were safely in. After a rudimentary education at Wethersfield's charity school, older boys began work on the farms or, if they were lucky, were apprenticed to a local tradesman. Girls often became domestic servants, earning about a shilling a week.

Each labourer's cottage had a garden which grew products to supplement the food bought by wages but even during better times the diet was monotonous. Breakfast was bread and cheese, dinner consisted of mutton and vegetables and at supper time it was back to cheese and onions. In most cottages beer was the usual drink. This was just as well because water drawn from the village pump or local springs was often contaminated. Beer was a safer drink because the bacteria which caused so much disease were killed by the boiling process which was part of brewing. At the time of Charles' youth, standards of living for the working class were under pressure because prices were rising, largely due to the influence of London, but wages were being held down. It was a poor living. The squeeze meant that something had to give and it was often the family diet that had to be cut back; a previously staple food like bacon became a rarity and the price of cheese made it almost a luxury.

Larger farmers were becoming more prosperous but smaller ones and tenants, although better off than the labourers, had to work hard for long hours. They had but little machinery to help them and all their efforts could give them little more than a bare existence.

In 1750 it took about £10 an acre to set oneself up in farming but, despite this, ambition was not dead in the countryside. An intelligent young man who was prepared to work even harder than his peers and who had a little luck could improve his lot and move up the economic and social ladders, the first stage being to obtain a tenancy.

The only commodity the farm worker had to sell was his labour but if he tried to improve his standard of living by using the market he immediately came up against an almost insurmountable barrier. His problem lay in the way the village was administered.

The day to day government of the community was carried out by a small group of men who in previous times had met in the church and were collectively known as the Vestry; in Wethersfield they gathered in public houses, 'The Dog' or 'The Lion' in the village, or 'The Bull' in nearby Blackmore End. The most important members were the local

Justice of the Peace (in Wethersfield, Joseph Clerke was a member at the time of Charles' birth) followed by the Anglican clergyman and various prominent farmers.   One of their main functions was to administer 'Poor Relief' which was given when a parishioner fell on hard times; it was funded by a parish rate. A typical example of its activity occurred in 1745 when the Wethersfield Vestry, with Joseph Clerke present, awarded William Johnson's boy ' . . . a waistcoat, a pair of Breeches and a Pair of Stockings'. Robert Sains' daughter had died and he was given ten shillings towards the cost of burying her. In practice it was an efficient system because, while no one was allowed to starve, neither was there abuse. Every applicant for relief was known to the members of the Vestry and, while the genuine were helped, the undeserving were soon weeded out.   Samuel Beal, for example, was given two shillings a week because his wife was ill; he not only had help in overcoming his immediate problem, he was also given a shilling towards buying himself a spade to allow him to make his own living. On the other hand, Mary Crisp was thought to be an undeserving case because her application was refused.   Francis Willmore was not allowed to escape his responsibilities.   He was ordered to ' . . . pay into the hands of the Overseer for the time being one shilling a fortnight towards the support and maintenance of his Daughter otherwise the Overseer is desired to make Complaint thereof to a Justice of the Peace.'   In the following year Thomas Phillips, son of Andrew, was the subject of an Order of Bastardy. It was issued: 'For the maintenance of a female child begotten on the body of Mary Stammers of this Parish a single woman.'[1]

There was even a rudimentary health service for the Vestry paid the village doctor a retainer.   The practice of medicine was unsophisticated but in return he gave whatever treatment he was capable of, without charge, to those parishioners who could not pay his fee. Joseph Clerke was present at the Vestry meeting which gave Dr. Robert Harrison eight guineas ' . . . to be paid on Easter Monday next to carefully look after all the poor in the said Parish . . . in respect of Physick, Man-Midwifery and Chirurgery . . . the Small and French pox only excepted'.

The Vestry administered the workhouse, the last refuge of the very poor and destitute.   These institutions were usually run in an humane way and inmates often found themselves warmer and better fed than they had been for most of their lives. Margaret Davies, Mary Spleen, Widow Hatley, William Harvey and Robert Passfield probably considered themselves fortunate when, in the summer of 1745, the Wethersfield Vestry ordered that they be admitted to the workhouse because it meant they would not have to face the following winter with only their own resources to support them. A few years later, when a young boy, Charles Clerke would know some of these people. It was only in the next century when workhouses from adjacent parishes were amalgamated and became known as the 'Union' that they earned their evil reputation. As a deterrent to those seeking sanctuary, the Masters of the new institutions were told to ensure that conditions were kept worse than those endured by the lowest working labourer.

There were many positive aspects to what was essentially an humane system but the main drawback in Charles Clerke's time, and indeed right up until 1795, was that if a man wished to move to another parish to find a better job he had either to be invited by the new parish or take with him a certificate from the vestry of his home village. This said that if at any time in the future either the man or his family needed 'relief', the cost would be borne by the parish from which he had come. Not surprisingly, vestries were reluctant to make such undertakings because they did not wish to be landed with the costs of moving back destitute families if the worst came to the worst. In December 1744 Joseph Clerke was present with Samuel Plumb when such a certificate was issued, enabling Samuel Stammers and his family to move to the nearby village of Little Yeldham.

For a man to go to a new place without either an invitation or a certificate took a deal of courage or foolhardiness. In effect, the system all but destroyed the free market for labour in the countryside and goes some way to explain how wages were kept down during a period of rising prices.

Charles' father was a major local figure in this order of things and Joseph would have had the final say in the business of the Wethersfield Vestry. His authority did not end there. He had been appointed a Justice of the Peace on the recommendation of the Lord Lieutenant of the County and this position gave him wide powers. Sitting with his fellow Justices he heard all but the most serious cases at the quarter sessions, played a part in setting the county finances and helped administer the running of roads, bridges and gaols.

Religion played a large part in village life and was centred, in the case of Wethersfield, on the church of St. Mary Magdalene. Levels of tolerance were rising but not to the point of including Roman Catholics— there was still much prejudice against them. Nonconformism was a rising force and played an increasing part in local affairs; in Wethersfield the church was well supported, having been established in the second half of the seventeenth century.

Added to the doctrinal differences between the churches was a growing awareness of what were seen as deficiencies in the Anglican Church to which all tithes were paid. In the country at large there were all too many cases of rectors who had more than one living and enjoyed lives of considerable comfort but had their homes many miles away from the parishes for which they were responsible. They delegated their responsibilities to vicars or curates (who had a much more spartan existence) and appeared before their congregations no more than three or four times a year. Tithe payers were beginning to wonder if they were getting value for money.

For those other than the strongest it was not a very healthy life. small pox, tuberculosis and even scurvy were commonplace. Untreated water was taken directly from springs and wells and made water-borne diseases frequent visitors to many a cottage. Infant mortality was high— in the cities, where health was worse than in the countryside, nearly half of all children did not reach two years of age.

Most people accepted things as they were, for the majority had never known anything else, but for most folk living in rural England it was a life of almost unceasing toil. They were trapped into a low standard of living about which they could do little and for some there was only the workhouse to look forward to at the end of their days.

This, then, was the lot of most people, other than those fortunate enough to be born into a higher station in life, and one with which Charles Clerke would have been very familiar when he left Wethersfield in 1754 and took the road to London and on to Portsmouth. There is no evidence of a great flood of boys rushing to leave home and join the Navy but for an adventurous youth wondering what to do with his life, seeing the world around him and knowing what to expect, a career at sea had its attractions.

Since Charles was the fourth of Joseph's sons it would seem to him that he had but little chance of inheriting his father's property; he was not to know that Joseph was to outlive all his boys. Charles was faced with a choice of what he was to do with his life but when the time came for him to make up his mind— a decision in which his father must have played a major part— there were not many opportunities for a young man with his background.

Commissions were bought and sold in the Army and promotion was dependent more on a family's financial situation than on an individual's own ability. Ever since the Civil War the men in authority, the King and the politicians, had had a deep seated mistrust of a standing army and tried to keep control by placing it under the command of officers who had the most to gain from stability—men drawn from the upper classes. Wealthy officers spent months away from their regiments because they could, and did, take very long leaves. The common soldiers were usually drawn from the dregs of society and were often the victims of a corrupt system in which quartermasters took for their own use the men's supplies and rations. Such a situation was not likely to appeal to young Charles.

Charles' eldest brother John, whom he adored, was then twenty years old and making his way in the Navy where commissions were not traded and the standards of professional skills were higher. John was now a Lieutenant on the *Kent*, about to sail for the West Indies, and it is not difficult to imagine conversations between the brothers. John would tell Charles of life in the Georgian Navy, the adventures to be expected, the possibilities of promotion and, not least, about Prize Money which could make him a wealthy man if luck came his way. All this was likely to be very exciting to the young man, particularly when set against the other options. As Charles' later exploits were to show, his personality and a career in the Church made less than a perfect match. The Law and Medicine, where the family had connections, were possibilities to be considered, but both were rejected. Perhaps almost inevitably he chose the Navy.

In the middle of the eighteenth century life in the Royal Navy could scarcely have been more different from that of rural England. Sailors lived in a world apart, and could be easily distinguished from their fellow countrymen when ashore because they dressed differently, spoke their own language, and even walked as though they were still on a rolling deck. To the inhabitants of a village, a sailor could as well be a creature from another planet. Other than John Clerke, it is doubtful if a single person in Wethersfield had ever seen a ship of the Royal Navy.

For many people alive today any vision they might have had of the Georgian Navy has been distorted by Hollywood's depiction of it; the truth is that the film makers' efforts bear but little resemblance to the reality. Britain was then a nation of about seven million souls and more money was spent on the Navy than on any other arm of government. In return, it was expected to be both efficient and effective, and, despite corruption in the Royal Dockyards, it probably was. How else could its consistent success, year in and year out, be explained?

Despite the dangers of seafaring, the peacetime Navy never had any difficulty in getting enough recruits. There has always been a romance associated with the sea and Charles lived in a time when the power of the maritime magnet was reinforced by a growing curiosity about far-away places.

For a young man embarking on a seagoing career the Royal Navy had several advantages over the Merchant Marine. For a start the work was less hard. Ships had no powered machinery, everything had to be worked by human muscle and it was always in the interests of a commercial owner to man his vessels with as small a crew as possible. The Navy, on the other hand, had to have far larger complements because the ships had not only to be sailed, they had to be fought. Although the watch-keeping system in warships at sea meant that a sailor never had more than four hours sleep in any one spell, opportunities for rest were greater in the government service. Warships spent, on average, less than half their time at sea whilst merchant ships, wind and weather permitting, had to be sailing to be profitable. In addition to this when naval ships were in port or, more commonly, lying at anchor outside a harbour there was plenty of leisure time.

Nevertheless, the work was hard even when shared between many men. Although battles were few and far between, life in the Royal Navy was often dangerous—the sea alone was hazardous enough—and living conditions were not good. Navy ships were always crowded but so too were the tiny cottages of farm labourers with their large families. A 74 gun ship, for example, normally had a crew of between six and seven hundred men who were packed into a space of about 165 ft by 45 ft. When not on deck during a watch the men's home was on the gun deck where they ate, slept and spent their free time. At night their beds were hammocks slung with but little space between them and used turn and turn about by two men. It was nearly always damp down below and clothes were rarely dry except after they had been put in front of the galley fire. There was no other means of heating in cold weather and when the ship was in a hot climate 'air-conditioning' was provided by a scoop made from an old sail set over the hatchway. In short, there were not many creature comforts on offer.

When he first went to sea the young Clerke was following the well beaten path towards becoming a commissioned officer but this did not give him the right to any more living space than that allocated to a rating. He did what all future officers had to do—he started in the ranks—and it was only after he became a Midshipman and later a Master's Mate that he was allowed to live in a separate, scarcely more secluded, space at the aftermost end of the gun deck. As the years went by and he rose to the rank of Lieutenant on *Resolution* he had a small cabin to himself. This gave him space for a bunk instead of a hammock, room for a sea chest and, much more importantly in such a crowded world, a degree of privacy. Much later, when he had his own command, his accommodation was, of course, in the Great Cabin.

Charles Clerke came from a well-to-do background and would therefore be used to a good diet but a rating in the Royal Navy, coming as he nearly always did from lower down the social scale could expect to eat a good deal better than he would have done ashore., Few labourers in either town or country could anticipate a weekly fare which included four meat meals, six ounces of butter and twelve of cheese. Every day the sailor had a pound of bread or biscuit and no less than a gallon of beer. The only known means of preserving food was by pickling or salting it in casks and the Navy always took care to buy in supplies of a good standard; even so, the quality deteriorated during a long voyage. When a ship sailed it usually took with it fresh meat on the hoof, a miniature farmyard of cattle, sheep, pigs, hens and geese. Goats, taken to provide the officers with milk, were often permitted to roam freely about the deck and frequently became the pampered pets of the sailors. When in port, vegetables and fruit were usually available. The discovery of Vitamin C was still many years in the future but the relationship between scurvy and diet had been recognised and most captains on long voyages used every means then available to combat it. James Lind had published his *A Treatise on the Scurvey* in 1753— the year before Charles Clerke entered the Navy. The cuisine of the service may not have been cordon bleu but by the standards of the day seafarers in the employ of the Crown ate well.

Huge quantities of alcohol went down sailors' throats and drunkenness was commonplace. The careers of many officers, some of them promising, came to an abrupt end because of the demon drink; Pickersgill, who sailed with Clerke on *Resolution*, was one. Despite the heavy drinking that went on, being drunk was not, in itself, regarded as a crime. There were two caveats to this; the first was that the man must not be troublesome and the second was that he must be ready for duty when required, particularly if the ship was at sea.

Pay tended to fall behind during the War of American Independence but rates were usually quite good. After various stoppages an ordinary seaman had about 88 pence a lunar month, an able seaman earned £1-12d and a landsman, the least skilled, had 82d. When expressed in terms of today's money they seem very poor rewards, but by the values of the time it was not bad pay. Most of the men were unmarried so their money was available to spend. In addition to this, and in contrast with the farm labourer who never knew from one day to the next whether or not he would have work, Navy wages were guaranteed although they were sometimes in arrears. There were other financial attractions because during wartime volunteers had the inducement of a £5. bounty on enlistment, a small fortune in those days.

All sailors, high and low, and ratings no less than officers, lived in the fervent hope of prize money and fortunes were sometimes made in this way. Some of the great estates of England were bought with the proceeds from the sale of captured ships and cargoes. When an enemy ship was taken the whole value went to the victorious crew and to certain senior officers, even if the latter were not physically present. It was divided according to a strict formula: one eighth went to the Commander-in-Chief (and some became very rich men indeed as a consequence), a quarter to the ship's Captain, an eighth to the Master and Lieutenants, another eighth was divided between the Warrant Officers, a further eighth between the Petty Officers and the remaining quarter to the seamen. As a result, lucky officers could become wealthy and ordinary sailors very comfortable. This presupposes they had sense enough to look after their money but one suspects that all too often the cash quickly evaporated at the first brush with temptation.

Men at sea lived in close proximity to each other, in conditions which made the transmission of infectious diseases very easy; tuberculosis seems to have been particularly prevalent. Despite this the Navy's health in general was much better than that of the civilian population, as was to be expected with such a preponderance of young men making up most of its work force. There was more to it than that. Most naval officers were well aware of the importance of maintaining good health in their crews and they enforced high standards of personal and communal hygiene. Capt. Cook and the men he trained, and who later became commanders themselves, were particularly scrupulous in matters of cleanliness; they were forever cleaning their ships, fumigating them and ensuring that they were properly ventilated.

While he was attending the Royal Naval Academy at Portsmouth the young Clerke could hardly have failed to see the Navy's own hospital being built at Haslar since it was at that time the largest brick building in Europe. It was constructed between 1745 and 1761 and showed the commitment of the Service to the health of its men. Previously there had been an unsatisfactory system in which sick or wounded sailors lived in hired accommodation that was frequently unsuitable and with attention that was often of a low standard. The new hospital was one of the most advanced of its time and allowed sailors to be treated as well as the limited knowledge of the day permitted.

Very few landsmen of any class, and certainly no country labourers, had access to anything remotely resembling such a facility.

The Navy had no difficulty at any time in recruiting officers and in peacetime there was always an adequate flow of ratings but lower deck sailors became hard to come by when war broke out because wages then shot up in the Merchant Marine. The Navy had to meet its increased commitments and this was when it was necessary to resort to impressment. Today this means of recruitment is thought of as being very disagreeable, and so it is, but it should be recalled that National Service and conscription, resorted to during the 1939-45 war and for a relatively short period afterwards, was the 'Press' by another name. In most of Clerke's time impressment was only used as a method of last resort, when all others had been exhausted.

There are no surviving records of men from Wethersfield joining the Navy at this time and a search of the ship's musters of the various vessels in which Clerke served has failed to unearth any names which are extant in the village today. Nevertheless, because officers in Charles Clerke's time were often encouraged to send home for likely volunteers it is quite possible that he tried to persuade young men he had known from his own boyhood to come forward and take the Bounty. In the same way, lower deck sailors serving in good ships would send messages to their home districts recommending that old friends join them.

Prisons were another source of men. They supplied debtors and smugglers (the latter were not regarded as being really criminal and were often good seamen) and, in theory at least, no one else. Some seamen and water boatmen, usually engaged in essential traffic such as the collier trade, were entitled to certificates of exemption from the Press. During the period of Clerke's service, according to the strict letter of the law the Press was permitted to take only men who held no such certificate but in fact the rules were often stretched and 'recruiting parties' were not as particular as they might have been when they went looking for men ashore or afloat. On land they usually set up shop in public houses where drunken men made easy targets. At sea, press gangs would sometimes board incoming merchantmen at the end of long voyages, with the coast of England in sight, and forcibly recruit prime seamen. To counteract this tactic a 'service' developed which sent out men holding exemption certificates to a homeward bound ship when it reached the Downs, off the Kent coast. The new men then brought the vessel to harbour while the incoming sailors made for the shore, often, it must be suspected, for them to be picked up by the Press in the first tavern which caught their eye.

The fact that volunteers could go to the ship of their choice, while pressed men went where they were sent, prompted many last minute decisions to sign on, more or less willingly, in order to avoid having to serve with an unpopular captain.

Once in the Navy there was no discrimination in that all men, no matter how their services had been come by, were treated equally and had the same chances of promotion.

Discipline is the part of Georgian naval life which now most often attracts attention and it is usually assessed by the values of the present time. Each age has its own code of what is considered to be acceptable behaviour, together with a matching system of sanctions for those who are judged to have broken the rules. To people living two hundred years later, the eighteenth century ways of punishment often seem barbaric but they, and the system of discipline in the Navy of which they were a part, should be judged by the values then deemed to be reasonable.

In the civilian world at that time hanging was the penalty for quite minor offences. Contemporary maps of the north bank of the Thames show that it was lined with gibbets at frequent intervals, the bodies left hanging from them to act as deterrents. Deportation (to America, since most of Australia had yet to be discovered) was commonplace and even branding was not considered to be unreasonable.

The necessity for firm Naval discipline was dictated by the need of ships and crews to survive and it was not considered to be unduly harsh by the standards of the times. Flogging was the standard means of punishment and sailors accepted it provided it was used fairly and consistently. Team work was necessary for survival and if a man was punished for not pulling his weight his chastisement was often welcomed by his fellows who would have to make up any deficit. A largely unspoken code of behaviour had developed and there was an accepted idea of what was right and what was wrong. In general, there was little awareness of a class structure and this was reinforced by an expectation that officers would support legitimate grievances, which they nearly always did. Sailors individually or *en masse* could complain directly to the Captain and, if that did not bring about a satisfactory result, to the Admiral. They could do this knowing that an alleged wrong would be taken seriously, properly investigated, and corrected if it was found to be justified. It was not unknown for captains to be dismissed the Service following proven cases of unwarranted brutality.

Even mutiny was tolerated provided that it took place in harbour, that the ship was not put at risk and that no violence was involved. But as soon as the anchor was up it became another matter; the safety of the vessel and its crew took precedence over everything else and discipline became much tighter.

The Captain was the unquestioned ruler of his floating empire and although his word was law his powers were not unlimited. No commander could award a punishment of more than twelve lashes on his own authority and cruelty, as defined by the mores of the time, was not tolerated. He could send an offender to be tried by court marshal but the Navy usually did its best to avoid going down that particular route. In those cases that did, the verdicts were nearly always just, the innocent were rarely found guilty and the officers sitting in judgement frequently went to extremes to accept the most unlikely stories.

Some crimes were considered to be beyond the pale and were dealt with harshly. Theft from shipmates was despised and when courts marshal awarded punishment of between two and five hundred lashes, which they often did, it was considered to be justifiable. Both buggery and murder were intolerable and in these cases the death penalty was applied. Otherwise, hanging was not much used except when there were aggravating circumstances or the offence of which the accused had been found guilty had been repeated several times before.

Throughout his life Charles Clerke had the reputation of being a jolly fellow and good company but he was also a firm disciplinarian. When he eventually had his own command and became both judge and jury he nearly always stayed within the limits of his powers, even though he was operating on the other side of the globe, many thousands of miles outside the Admiralty's immediate bailiwick. On only a very few occasions did he go beyond the normal bounds as, for example, when he awarded the persistent Polynesian thief forty lashes. In mitigation, it must be said that he was very unwell at the time and had endured one theft after another for months on end. He was usually a good natured man, well aware of the rules, and for him to so overstep the normal limits of punishment his patience must have been completely exhausted.

When, at the age of thirteen, Charles entered the Royal Naval Academy at Portsmouth he was embarking on the first stage of a naval career which would last the rest of his life. The school had opened in 1729 for the education of 'forty young gentlemen, the sons of noblemen and gentlemen'.

It was a radical departure from the usual way of entering the Navy because until then a young man hoping to progress to commissioned rank had first to become an Officers' Servant. The term did not have the same meaning as it does today, it was more akin to the word apprentice. Ranks in the Georgian navy were much more blurred than they were later to become and the young sailor would hope later to progress through the levels of Able Seaman, Master's Mate, and Lieutenant, with appropriate examinations along the way, and then, if good fortune was his, become a Captain and perhaps even hoist his Flag.

At the Academy the boys were placed in the care of the Master, three ushers and a number of instructors. They were taught drawing, fencing and the use of the firelock. The arts were not neglected, for they also had lessons in French, Latin and even dancing. These may seem strange ingredients in the tuition of boys who were destined to spend their lives at sea but the Navy took the view that what distinguished officers from the men of the lower deck was education— and that was what they were going to get.

More than anything else, they had to be good seamen. Early on they were sent aloft with the ordinary sailors to take part in the heavy, and sometimes dangerous, work high above the deck. The boys were not left alone because it was the usual practice for each to be assigned a 'Sea Daddy', a reliable and experienced sailor who supervised his early progress.

Each year Charles' father had to find the not inconsiderable sum of £25 to pay the school's fees, as much as it would have cost if he had sent him to Eton.[2] In return he was to board with the Master who was to provide: 'a decent and proper table and to find him in washing, fire, candles, table and bed linen and the messing utensils of the house'. A suit of blue cloth, to a pattern supplied by the Master, was to be worn on the King's birthday and cost £5.

It sounds hard enough but the school's discipline was not as strict as it might have been and there were soon complaints that the boys were talkative when under arms. They were supposed not to leave the dockyard, where the Academy was situated, without permission but it became commonplace for the rule to be ignored. The students enthusiastically applied themselves to more congenial activities than their studies and they quickly fell in with undesirable company; soon there were reports of drunkenness and visits to 'bawdy houses'.

Neither the Academy nor the College Volunteers (as the young men were called) were well regarded by serving officers because they saw the new way as a potential threat to the privileges they enjoyed under the prevailing system of patronage. Under the 'Captain's Servant' method of apprenticeship a young man would try to attach himself to a senior officer who he anticipated would have a successful career. As the older man rose in rank and influence the younger would hope to follow him. A good officer attracted followers readily enough and when he went up in the world he tried to take his best people with him. The other side of the coin was that a less competent, or less popular, officer had difficulty in finding able men to go with him.

* * * * *

Charles graduated from the Academy at about the time of the beginning of a war with France. He had grown into a tall, fair haired young man with slightly sharp features, a characteristic of his family, and a manner that was both cheerful and friendly. He was convivial—'social', he called it—and developing an ability to entertain by spinning a good yarn. His proficiency in getting on well with people from any walk of life made him a popular figure and was a useful asset in a world where men had to live cheek by jowl for months on end. Both Charles Clerke and James Cook, the sailor and explorer with whose life the Wethersfield man was to become closely connected, were heavily engaged in the Seven Years War. Victory in this conflict was to lead to the laying down of the foundations of the British Empire.

The years preceding 1756, when hostilities officially began were, at least nominally, a time of peace but in reality an undeclared state of conflict had existed since 1748. In India a vacuum had been created by the disintegration of the Mogul Empire and the East India Company, which had been granted a charter by James I, had come to dominate trade on the subcontinent, far outstripping the efforts of the French, by building forts and employing troops to defend its interests. The French tried to reverse the situation by raising Sepoy armies under the command of officers brought out from France. At the same time they courted influential rulers to enable them to make alliances with various native powers. The East India Company was not prepared to give in without a struggle against the threat to its position and found its saviour in Robert Clive. He was the son of an impoverished Shropshire squire and had emigrated to Madras, arriving in debt, to find employment as a clerk with the Company. After leaving his desk to join the army at the beginning of the fighting his rise was meteoric. His colourful career involved the making of numerous political deals, not all of them above suspicion, and winning a whole series of military victories which, by 1754, left the French position in India in a state of terminal decline.

The conflict which began formally on 16th May 1756, two years after the actual fighting first began, was fought mainly on the

Continent and in Canada. The European campaign started badly when Admiral Byng was sent from Gibraltar to raise a French siege of the British base on the island of Minorca. He failed, the island's garrison was left with no alternative to surrender and Byng was court marshalled and executed, probably to encourage his peers.

William Pitt the elder, 'the Great Commoner', had come to power in England mainly because he had the trust of the middle and working classes, a confidence based upon his being one of the few politicians who was honest in a time of systematic corruption. He had many qualities, not least of which was an ability to inspire the people, rather as Winston Churchill did in 1940. Pitt was an excellent strategist and had an ability to think beyond the boundaries of Europe; he had a clear understanding of the strategic need to prevent North America falling under the control of France and knew it could be done by the combined use of land and sea power.

At the beginning of the Seven Years War in 1756 there was a real threat of invasion and Pitt sought to divert the French forces threatening England by keeping them engaged in fighting the armies of Frederick the Great of Prussia. A small expeditionary force under the command of the Marquis of Granby was sent to the Continent to support the Prussian left flank where, despite its modest size, it distinguished itself at the Battle of Minden. Pitt also sent indirect aid by giving Frederick large subsidies to help pay for the Prussian war effort, but at high cost to the British Treasury.

An interesting diversion at this point is the view set out by Paul Kennedy in his book *The Rise and Fall of the Great Powers*. Even two hundred and fifty years ago wars were expensive enterprises and required more money than current revenues could provide; during the Seven Years War expenditure outstripped the taxes collected by £60 million. This money had to be borrowed (from creditors at home and abroad, particularly Holland) and Kennedy believes that Britain's ability to bear not only its own costs but at the same time to subsidise its allies, a tactic used time and time again, was due to her higher credit worthiness as compared with that of France. Britain had an efficient system of collecting taxes, which were mainly indirect, and compared well with the French methods. Tax farming was used on the other side of the English Channel, with successive layers of revenue gatherers buying and then subletting the rights of collection, each taking a commission and stimulating a culture of evasion in the process. This was not the only problem, because the tax burden was carried almost exclusively by the poorer sections of French society; whole categories, notably the aristocracy and the clergy, were exempt from taxation. Despite having a population of between only one third and one half that of France more tax was raised in Britain, so enabling three-quarters of the extra money needed to fund the war to be raised as loans—and at a lower rate of interest than paid by the French.

In Canada and North America the colonists of British descent lived mainly in settlements along the eastern seaboard. The French, only about 55,000 strong in Canada, were concentrated mainly in or near a series of military posts running along a line which followed the St. Lawrence River, past the Great Lakes, through the Ohio Valley and on down the Mississippi to the Gulf of Mexico. Acting in concert with some of the Red Indian tribes, the French intention was to appropriate all of North America north and east of the Appalachian and Allegheny Mountains, thus pinning the far more numerous settlers of British ancestry against the coast.

Pitt understood the meaning of sea power and realised the key to victory lay in starving the French in Canada and India of reinforcements from the homeland. The blockade was carried out by increasing the size of the Royal Navy to over 400 ships. A crash programme of ship building allowed this to be achieved but the quality of the vessels was often not up to standard because both shipyard capacity and seasoned timber were in short supply. Nevertheless, the Navy succeeded not only in isolating France from her colonies but also in removing the threat of invasion of England from across the Channel. It won a series of victories at sea, culminating in Hawke's triumph at Quiberon Bay, the equivalent of Trafalgar in years to come.

On land it was a different story, for the British Army in North America got off to its traditional slow start. British settlers were dislodged from the Ohio Valley, the French built Fort Duquesne to prevent their return and when General Braddock's army was defeated the British were everywhere on the defensive.

The fate which befell Braddock's army was fairly typical of the way in which the early campaigns in North America were fought.

General Edward Braddock was a good natured but hot tempered man who landed in Virginia in command of 1,000 troops who had sailed from Ireland. Although neither he nor nearly all the other British officers held a very high opinion of colonial soldiers—and they had good reason for their prejudice—it was decided to recruit 400 Virginians to augment the British regiments, the 44th and 48th. The men of the former were recruited in Charles Clerke's home county of Essex and were later to become the First Battalion of the Essex Regiment. The British officers set about the task of trying to make the colonial troops as much like soldiers as possible in the time available to them before the campaign began.

Braddock's objective was the capture of Fort Duquesne and he began by assembling his force at Fort Cumberland. There he tried to recruit thirty Susquehannah Indians, warriors who arrived in full war dress and danced a war dance for the benefit of the General. The Indians declared war on the French, ate a bullock which the Army provided for them and went home. Not deterred, Braddock tried again with men from the Delaware and Shawnee tribes but their attitude corresponded precisely with that of the Susquehannas.

The force which set out from Fort Cumberland at first made slow progress. In the party, on the staff of the General, was a land and slave owner from Mount Vernon in Virginia, a man by the name of George Washington, and it was partly on his advice that Braddock decided to press on towards Fort Duquesne, one hundred and forty miles away, with 1,200 men, leaving the artillery and heavy baggage to follow on at the best speed they could make.

Shortly after the two regular regiments had crossed the River Monongahela, about seven miles from Duquesne, with bands playing and colours waving, they suddenly came under attack from unseen assailants who were concealed by trees and rocks. Casualties soon mounted, confusion spread, Braddock was wounded and Washington had two horses shot from under him. More than half the British soldiers were killed or wounded before they began the long, stumbling retreat to Philadelphia. Braddock died five days later.

Washington was never to know that the successors of the Essex men alongside whom he had fought would later, in a futile war with America in the early years of the next century, burn down the White House in the city named after him.

The situation changed when Pitt, the master strategist, decided to attack the French settlements on the St. Lawrence, using troops brought from England by the Navy. The approaches to the river were commanded by a powerful French fort at Louisburg which had to be taken before the main advance could begin. When this had been done the sailors were able to deliver General Wolfe and his soldiers to the Heights of Abraham where his victory enabled him to take Quebec. This marked the beginning of the end of French power in North America.

Pitt was commemorated when Fort Duquesne, captured after the Ohio Valley was eventually retaken, was given the new name of Pittsburg.

The success of British arms was not confined to North America, for in India Clive had secured a memorable victory at Plassey in 1757.

This led to the conquest of Bengal and, almost on the other side of the world to Canada, to the laying of the foundations of the British Empire on the subcontinent.

While all this had been going on Charles Clerke was continuing his studies at the Royal Naval Academy, preparing himself for his future career. Then, in February 1758, when he was 17 years of age, he graduated and went to war. He joined the ship's company of *Dorsetshire*, a third rate with a complement of 520 under the command of Captain Peter Denis, as a captain's servant.[3] His commanding officer was the son of a Huguenot refugee, had fought with Anson and was later to take part in the action in Quiberon Bay. Clerke's service with Denis is an early example of his ability to associate with people of importance for Peter Denis eventually rose to the rank of Vice-Admiral of the Red. When Clerke joined her, *Dorsetshire* was at Portsmouth working up and preparing to join the Channel Fleet in the blockade of the French coast. She sailed with *Dunkirk* and *Achilles* on 25th April, passed Portland Bill on the 26th and came up with the Fleet off Ushant a few days later.

She was soon in action. The last day of April was cloudy and the ship was on a SSW. course; Captain Denis's log tells of what then happened:

> The Commodore made the signal for the Achilles and we to chase to the SE. We made the signal that the Chase was an enemy at 1/2 past 5. The Commodore made our signal to leave off chase we made the signal that we could come up with the chase without losing company with the Squadron. At 7 pm the chase hoisted the French colours and fired her Stern Chasers at 1/2 past 7. We got alongside the Enemy within a half pistol shot and began to engage which continued till 10 minutes after 9 which time the enemy ceased firing and hove aback. We ported our helm and he did the same which brought us to leeward of him in which situation we lay 3 minutes and having discharged our Starboard broadside. We ceased firing and gave the Enemy 3 cheers. Came up the *Achilles* and sent their boat on board the Prize at 1/2 past 10. The *Achilles* boat brought on board the Commodore of the Prize who struck to us found her to be *Reasonable* of 64 guns with men belonging to the French King.

It is clear that Denis had the bit between his teeth and a team of wild horses could not have stopped him from chasing his quarry. His bald, factual account does little to convey what it must have been like to take part in a ship-to-ship engagement in the middle of the eighteenth century. At Jutland in 1916 the battleships exchanged fire at a distance of many miles and at Midway during the Second

World War the American and Japanese carriers never came within sight of each other. *Dorsetshire* and *Reasonable* lay within half a pistol shot of one another, blasting away for all they were worth. Each was a floating fortress; at Waterloo, Wellington had only about as many artillery pieces as their combined number of guns. The noise, the smoke and the gore are unimaginable. The casualty list, as reported, shows a remarkable discrepancy between the losses of the two sides: the English were said to total fifteen while the French were put at two hundred killed and one hundred wounded.

The normal method of fighting at sea was for two ships to lie parallel with one another and exchange broadsides at very short range. The French preferred to fire on the uproll and try to disable an enemy by destroying his masts and rigging while the English fired on the downroll and battered away at the opponent's hull. The power of a warship was measured by the weight of metal it could deliver in a given time and this was determined by the number and calibre of its guns and the rate at which they were fired. In general, English gunnery was reckoned to be superior, largely because of a higher rate of fire based on better discipline. This may help to explain the difference in the numbers of casualties in this engagement but does not seem enough to offer a complete explanation. *Dorsetshire* must have been placed in a position from which she was able to deliver far more punishment than she received in return— perhaps at right angles to the Frenchman's stern, from where she could fire her broadsides and have to face only the stern guns on *Reasonable*. If this is so, it shows a high standard of seamanship on the part of Captain Denis.

Dorsetshire came home after the action and arrived at Spithead on Saturday 13th May together with her prize. She was soon at sea again and Clerke stayed with her during the next two years which she spent as part of the fleet blockading the French coast. In February 1760 her entire ship's company was transferred to *Bellona* and Charles went with them in the rank of Midshipman. His Lieutenant's certificate shows him to have spent one year, eight months, two weeks and a day as a captain's servant and three months, three weeks and six days in the rank of Midshipman Ordinary. A tenuous link with Cook was established at this time for another of Denis' servants was Michael Lane who later served in *Antelope* and *Guernsey* (in the latter as Schoolmaster) before becoming master's mate to Cook in *Grenville* in 1766.

Bellona was a brand new 74, built in Chatham and launched on 19th February 1760.[4] Her keel had been laid down on a slipway close to the dry dock in which perhaps the most famous ship in the world,

H.M.S. *Victory*, was nearing completion. Denis took *Bellona* to sea on her first operational voyage on 9th May 1760 when she sailed from the Nore to her position off Ushant, going via Portland and Torbay. On the way she had occasional contact with other ships— one was a Dutch warship whose salute was returned with one of nine guns. She stayed on station for six weeks before coming back to Plymouth Sound, setting a pattern which continued until the spring of 1762. There was a major break in this routine in August 1761 when she was involved in one of the most lethal single ship actions ever fought.

Denis had been temporarily replaced by Captain Faulkenor and *Bellona* was cruising under his command in company with *Brilliant*, a frigate, off the northwest corner of Portugal near the city of Vigo. The two English ships were heavily outgunned when they came into contact with a French force of three warships consisting of *Courageux* a 74, *Malicieuse* and *Herminone*, the last two being frigates. At first the French commander decided to avoid an action but he then made the fatal mistake of thinking *Bellona* was a 50 gun ship. This was a crucial error because there was a huge difference between the perceived and the actual power of *Bellona*.

The Frenchman ordered his two frigates to close with and engage *Brilliant*, and a sharp engagement began. Meanwhile *Courageux* sailed to attack the English 74 and when the ships came within musket range the big guns of *Courageux* opened fire and sent *Bellona's* mizzen mast over the side - the French were using their usual tactics. Charles Clerke was stationed in *Bellona's* mizzen shrouds, one of the most dangerous positions in the ship, and he came down with the mast when it was shot away. He saved himself by climbing up the fore chains of his ship and found he was quite unscathed; he was reckoned to be the only survivor of all those who had been on the mast.

Captain Faulkenor succeeded in placing his vessel on the starboard quarter of *Courageux* from whence one broadside after another was poured into the French ship. Eventually, she struck her colours, just forty minutes after the action began. The carnage aboard her was dreadful; her 'butcher's bill' was 240 dead and 110 wounded compared with *Bellona's* six dead and twenty-eight wounded.

After the action *Courageux* was towed into Plymouth where she was repaired and taken into service with the Royal Navy, *Bellona's* crew pocketing the prize money due to them.

The capture of *Courageux* was a more significant event than merely the taking of a valuable prize. The design of French warships at this time had reached a more advanced stage than that of English

5. *This photograph of a mast and rigging was taken aboard the replica of the bark* H.M.S. Endeavour *in 1997 when in harbour. Although all her sails are furled or stowed it still gives some indication of how the mizzen mast would have been, with some of her canvas unfurled, when* Bellona's *mast was shot away with Charles Clerke stationed up the mast and being the only survivor.* [see page 30.]

6. *An early photograph of Brook Farm of uncertain date but thought to be late nineteenth century. It was probably much as Charles Clerke would have known it when he returned on leave from one of his voyages.* [and see overleaf.]

Facing page 30.

7.   *Brook Farm as it appears in the last decade of the twentieth century.   Although of course changed from Joseph Clerke's day it would probably still be recognisable as the family home to members of the eighteenth century Clerke family.*

Facing page 31.

vessels and many of the details included in *Bellona's* prize were incorporated in future ships of the Royal Navy.

Bellona was at Spithead again in May 1762 when a seaman called Stiles fell overboard and was drowned. Her next assignment was in marked contrast to the excitement of the previous year for she was to spend weeks on end at anchor— off the French coast. *Bellona* left Spithead on 17th June 1762, acting as escort to a convoy, and came to off the Isle de Ré, near the French port of La Rochelle. Shortly afterwards she moved to the Basque Roads. There she stayed for nearly six months and it was not until Sunday 12th December that she left again for Spithead. Nearly all the time she was off the enemy coast there was only the occasional pursuit of a foreign vessel to relieve the monotony. Something more exciting happened now and again as, for example, when seven French deserters came aboard on 11th June or a small prize was taken. One man, by the name of Charles Randall, was so distraught by the life he was leading that he committed suicide by hanging himself. Virtually every day the Parole Signal was flown. This was a sign to the watching French that *Bellona* was prepared to take off any English Prisoners of War who had given their word they would take no further part in hostilities between the two countries.

Charles missed Christmas at home for his ship did not reach Spithead until 28th December. She stayed for three weeks before being paid off on Wednesday 19th January 1763. He had been with her for just under three years; to be precise, two years, eleven months and six days.

* * * * *

The long war was coming to an end and, with the Navy being run down in size and ships paying off, it was not until the following year that Charles was able to find himself a berth. This time he was going to circumnavigate the world.

C harles Clerke was nearly twenty-two years old when the war with France came to an end in February 1763. He came home to a country now ruled by a new King because George III, then aged 22 years, had come to the throne in 1760 in the middle of the Seven Years War. The domestic politics of Britain for the next two decades were dominated by George's attempts to reclaim the authority his Hanoverian predecessors had lost to Parliament. He saw the Prime Minister and the Cabinet as being no more than the instruments of an absolute sovereign and, with the Tories in disarray and unable to form an effective opposition, the country came to be ruled by a combination of the Monarch and a group of subservient Whigs. It was only during the Napoleonic Wars at the turn of the century that the balance was restored by Pitt the Younger.

Charles Clerke left Portsmouth and went home to Wethersfield where, on the 27th of June, he and his brother Thomas acted as witnesses at the wedding of Gamaliel Keys and Hannah Tagelle in the village church of St. Mary Magdalene. Charles drew his friends from a wide circle and was able to relate easily to the wealthy and powerful, the well-to-do and the poor and humble. Hannah had received a little education, probably at the charity school, and was able to take up a pen to sign the marriage register but the groom was illiterate and had to make his mark with a cross.

The returning hero must have made a romantic figure as he stood in the churchyard, a young sailor who had helped defeat the French, been in two battles and barely survived the second. No doubt his presence attracted an audience of curious villagers, for weddings were commonplace but naval heroes were a distinct rarity.

Charles' career was in the Navy, his was not the life of a countryman, and the following year he was off again on another adventure, this time as a Midshipman in the *Dolphin* a ship displacing 500 tons and carrying twenty guns. Commodore Lord John Byron, 'Foul Weather Jack' as he was known, destined to be the grandfather of the poet, was her captain. The Admiralty had two good reasons for ordering her to the Pacific.

The idea of the existence of Terra Australis Incognita had long exercised the minds, and often the imaginations, of both the philosophers and the map makers who translated their ideas into charts which frequently owed more to fantasy than to fact. In the second century A.D. Ptolomy of Alexandria was the first of a whole series of thinkers to postulate the presence of the unknown continent. He believed the world to be a globe floating in space and he was aware of the great land masses in the northern hemisphere; surely, he concluded, there must be a corresponding continent in the southern half of the world to maintain the balance. The main purpose of Byron's voyage was to look for it. Ptolomy was correct, for there is a Great Southern Continent, but Antarctica is covered in ice, inaccessible to sailing ships and far removed from what he and others had predicted.

The Admiralty was always anxious to get the best possible value from any expenditure and the second task given to the expedition was even more ambitious. England was not the only country which was thinking about the Pacific when the First Lord of the Admiralty, Lord Egmont, another man with a good grasp of strategy, turned his mind to the question of who should control the northern and southern accesses to the great ocean and the markets which might lie there. Realising that if the Pacific was joined to the rest of the world by a Northwest Passage the nation which controlled it would be in a very strong strategic position, he ordered Byron to begin the search in latitude 38° N., in Drake's New Albion, and to follow the coast towards the north.

Egmont also understood that if that same nation also had control over the southern entrance to the Pacific—and he intended that it should be England—it would be even better placed. He considered the Falklands to be the key to the Straits of Magellan and he ordered Byron to take possession of them, realising that English sovereignty would have the additional benefit of her ships no longer having to use Spanish ports in South America. Byron was also ordered to look for any other islands which might lie between the Straits of Magellan and the Cape of Good Hope. As an added insurance, he was to look for Pepys' Island, the precise position of which was unclear. Ambrose Cowley had circumnavigated the globe between 1683 and 1686 and in January 1686 had come upon an island he had shrewdly named after Samuel Pepys who was then Secretary of the Admiralty. On his return, he reported it as being in latitude 47° 40' S. but the longitude, as was often the case at that time, was less precise—he merely said it was not far from the mainland. Egmont wanted the mystery to be cleared up and England to take possession of it.

Byron was left free to choose his route home which could be either by way of the Northwest Passage, if he had found it, or via China and the Cape.

By any standards it was a project conceived on the grand scale and carrying it out was a daunting task for any expedition because its objectives were at opposite ends of the Pacific. If it was to succeed it needed as its leader an outstanding man of the calibre of Cook, and Foul Weather Jack fell far short of this demanding standard. Nevertheless, Lord Byron had an impressive curriculum vitae and when he came to command *Dolphin* he had behind him a remarkable history. In the course of his life, Clerke sailed with many exceptional men but none could lay claim to having had experiences comparable to those of his new captain . His story is worth a little diversion.

Byron was born on 8th November 1723 and, as the second son of a noble family, had to make his own way in the world. He decided upon a naval career and in September 1740, when he was a young man of 17 years, he sailed in an old East Indiaman named *Wager* which had been bought into the Navy to act as the storeship for a small squadron bound for the South Atlantic. She was not a good vessel and it is clear that the Navy gave her a low priority when it came to finding her a crew because most of the men had either been pressed or had recently been invalids in Chelsea Hospital.

She managed to reach the tip of South America but when she arrived at the Straits of le Maire, not far from the Horn, *Wager* became separated from the other ships of the fleet. Her troubles were only just beginning, for shortly afterwards she struck a reef. Several sailors were drowned but the survivors made it to the shore and set about gathering whatever debris they could find from the shipwreck. Before long they had put up crude huts which, while not overflowing with creature comforts, at least offered them some shelter from the elements. It did not take the castaways long to fall out and split into two groups. Ships passing the Straits of Magellan were few and far between but one party, thinking they had a better chance of being picked up, made for there in some of *Wager's* boats. The other group, which included Byron and Captain Cheap, *Wager's* commander, made towards the north in the remaining boats. The reason why is unknown, but four men went with neither party, either from choice or because of a disagreement; they could hardly have been overlooked. Six men of the captain's group were lost together with the barge they were travelling in and shortly afterwards, for some obscure reason, Byron became separated from his companions. How he came to find himself on his own is also unknown— perhaps he made a conscious decision to leave them or he may have been rejected by the others and it is just possible that he wandered off and became lost. Whatever the reason, he found himself alone in the desolate land near the Horn until he fell in with a group of itinerant Indians who took him in. To them he was just another mouth to feed in a place where food was scarce so perhaps it is not surprising that their attitude towards him was subject to wild variations— most of the time they were kind, but there were occasions when relations were very strained and they offered him violence. During one crisis an old lady who was part of the group took pity on him and intervened to prevent his being killed.

Byron was eventually able to make his way to Isle Chiloe, where the treatment he received from the local people was a distinct improvement. He travelled on to Chaco and then to Valparaiso in Chile but if, after all his privations, he expected to be greeted with open arms when he arrived there, he was disappointed. The Governor promptly put him in prison. After some time he was released and went to a town called St. Jago where, on resources which by then must have been very limited, he lived for two years. Then his luck changed for a French frigate, the *Lys*, called in and took him back with her to St. Malo. He arrived there on 31st October 1745, five years after leaving England, and finally reached home in February of the following year.

His subsequent career was rather more conventional. Before being given command of *Dolphin* he had been the captain of various ships sailing in the Channel and off the Atlantic coast of France, as well as serving in Guinea and taking part in the capture of Louisberg. In later life he became Governor of Newfoundland and before his death in 1786 had attained the rank of Rear-Admiral of the Blue.

Clerke sailed from Plymouth in *Dolphin* on 3rd July 1764, bound for the Pacific. The *Tamar* was the expedition's second vessel, commanded by Captain Mouat whose son was later to serve with Cook and get himself into trouble in Polynesia. One of Clerke's shipmates in *Dolphin* was his friend John Gore who had served with him on *Bellona*. By September they were well down the South Atlantic and had reached Brazil where a month was spent in repairing the ships and resting the crews. The next stop was at Port Desire in Patagonia and it was in this remote part of South America that Clerke met the local inhabitants who, if his account is to be believed, were remarkable people. On his return to England he wrote from Wethersfield to the Royal Society and his paper was read to the Members by Dr. Matthew Maty, the Society's foreign secretary. They can be forgiven if they were just a little sceptical because Clerke had written: '. . . there was hardly a Man there less than eight feet; most of them considerably more; the women, I believe, run from $7^1/_2$' to 8'. He did at least have the grace to add: 'I will give it the embellishment of truth, and rely on your goodness to excuse a tar's dialect'.

His paper gives an insight into Clerke's personality at this time. It shows he was still high spirited and that the exuberance had not been knocked out of him by the fall from *Bellona's* mast. Above all, he was not overawed by authority and was not above indulging in a little gentle ridicule of the most learned society in the land. Dr Maty forgave him and twelve years later his son married Charles' sister.

Byron searched in vain in the area Cowley had reported Pepys's Island to be and went on to the Falklands where he arrived in January 1765. He carried out his orders and annexed them in the name of the King, as Cowley had done before him. Finding nothing more of interest in the Atlantic he passed into the Pacific through the Straits of Magellan and then judged his ship to be in too poor a condition to undertake the hazardous voyage to the north. The quest for the Northwest Passage was abandoned before it had begun and Byron set out westwards. He seems not to have been an enthusiastic explorer, perhaps because of his previous experiences in new places, and when he reached the Tuamotu group which lay just to the north of the Society Islands and was so much appreciated by those who followed him, he named them the Islands of Disappointment. Beaglehole judged him to be apathetic and wrote of him: '. . . he does not appear to have been activated by any curiosity to explore them'. Byron gave as his reason the ill health of his crew—they were suffering from scurvy—but, as Rolfe pointed out, if this was so it only added weight to the case for finding a haven where the men would have a chance to recuperate. Byron carried on across the Pacific, passed to the north of Samoa and the Marshall Islands, spent a month at Tinian and eventually arrived at Batavia on 27th November 1765 by way of the Philippines. He had followed a track too far to the north to offer a chance of making any discoveries of consequence.

Byron was now in a great hurry to get home and six months later, on 3rd May in the following year, *Dolphin* dropped anchor in the Downs.

Beaglehole was expressing a widely held opinion when he wrote: '. . . As a voyage of Pacific discovery it had been extremely useless . . . '. Not much had been achieved, certainly less than the objectives that had been set. The Falklands had been claimed but there had been no sighting made of the Great Southern Continent and Byron had not even begun to search for the Northwest Passage. On the other hand, since the voyage had taken only twenty-two months to complete, he could lay claim to having made the fastest circumnavigation to date, although ocean racing had hardly been the purpose of the enterprise.

Dolphin was turned round in remarkably quick time and only one month after her return she sailed again, in company with *Swallow*, on another journey to the Pacific. Charles Clerke, not surprisingly, did not go with her but his friend John Gore did, as a master's mate, and this after only a few weeks at home. Clerke spent the next nine months in England having some well earned rest, recuperating from his last voyage and, no doubt, going home to Wethersfield.

Captain Samuel Wallis, a 38 year old Cornishman, was the new commander of *Dolphin* and Philip Carteret was captain of *Swallow*. The latter had recent experience of the Pacific, for he had been Byron's lieutenant, but the ship he was given was a poor specimen and not in good enough condition for such a demanding voyage. The two vessels managed to stay together until they reached the southern tip of America but at the Straits of Magellan they became separated. With his ship leaking badly, *Swallow's* commander had every reason under the sun to turn back but he carried on. He was able to nurse his ship across the Pacific and complete a circumnavigation, making his way home by way of the Philippines, Batavia, and the Cape.

When Wallis reached home again, having taken a more southerly route than Byron, he reported a highly significant discovery— on 23rd June 1767 he had come across an island in Polynesia which was called Tahiti. On that day, *Dolphin* had dropped anchor in the black volcanic sands of Matavai Bay and Wallis spent a happy month there while his crew recovered from the trials of the long voyage. It had seemed to be a place of amazing fertility, its inhabitants blissfully happy and enjoying a life of uninterrupted peace and contentment. Tahiti was to become the centre of a romantic fantasy for this was the Age of Enlightenment, a time when philosophers such as Rousseau were seeking an alternative to the complex, and, in their view, corrupt ways of European societies. At the core of their thinking was the need to attain balance and harmony between Man and Nature; simplicity was to be the thing and its exemplar was the life led by the 'Noble Savage', a being who had escaped the debasement of the northern systems. It was a concept which attracted people who were disillusioned by the world around them and it eventually attracted a large following. The reality was somewhat different. Tahiti was certainly beautiful and the land *was* fertile but its society was not without flaws. Wallis' visit happened to coincide with a lull in the frequent civil wars which afflicted the island and the impression he gained was affected by the transient harmony he witnessed. He did not delve into the ways the Tahitians organised their community and was consequently unaware of their practice of human sacrifice or of the disturbing habit of the priests of strangling at birth any children they might sire. Wallis never knew that all was not sweetness and light in Polynesia.

The Captain was ill and much of the day to day running of the ship was in the hands of the First Lieutenant, Tobias Furneaux who was later to sail with Cook, and John Gore. Several of *Dolphin's* crew reported seeing mountains to the south of Tahiti which they thought could be the Great Southern Continent but the winds were contrary and the supposed lead was not followed up. Wallis achieved one thing of great significance at Tahiti— he accurately fixed the position of the island, using a technique developed by Nevil Maskelyne who had been made the Astronomer Royal two years earlier.

Dolphin came home via Batavia and the Cape and dropped anchor at Spithead on 20th May 1768. She was exactly one year in advance of Carteret in *Swallow*.

Ten months after Wallis left Tahiti a Frenchman named Bougainville arrived there. Like Clerke, Cook, and Byron he had fought in the Seven Years War, in his case at Quebec. His arrival in Polynesia, although unknown at the time by the policy makers in London, justified their apprehension of French interest in the region. Like his English contemporaries, he was looking for the Great Southern Continent and had received his orders before he left France in November 1766. On leaving Polynesia he sailed towards the west, but not as far as the east coast of Australia, before turning for home. As he came up the Atlantic, in all that expanse of ocean, he met Carteret before he, too, arrived home in 1768.

During this time Charles Clerke's career was following a different course. He spent the remaining months of 1766, following his return in *Dolphin*, at home before again making his way to Portsmouth. When he was there he would have seen his old ships *Bellona* and *Dorsetshire*, which were acting as guard vessels. Early in the New Year, on 20th February 1767, his name was entered as an A.B. in the muster of *Romney*[1], a 50 gun ship with a crew of 295. At first sight his sailing as an A.B., having been a Midshipman on his previous cruise, may seem like a backward step but in the Georgian Navy this was not always the case because the rank structure was not then as rigid as it was later to become. Ambitious sailors took the long view and were prepared to move sideways and even downwards in order to advance themselves, providing that the eventual route was upward.

Romney's captain was John Corner and he took her across the Atlantic to the American Station, sailing from England on 20th May 1767.[2] She was based at Halifax and spent her time cruising in the area of the mouth of the St. Lawrence River and off the coast of Nova Scotia, acting as flagship for the redoubtable Admiral Hood.

Clerke did not see out the whole of *Romney's* commission for he was discharged at Portsmouth on February 11th 1768 by order of the Admiral and pocketed two months advance pay which amounted to £2-5-0[3]. Why did he come home early? It may have been no coincidence that his homecoming was at the same time that Cook's expedition to the Pacific was being planned and it is probable that he was called home by the Admiralty. Men with knowledge of the islands and their inhabitants, their customs, capabilities and methods of trading were few and far between and the Admiralty could be expected to seek them out. Hugh Palliser was then Commander-in-Chief of the American Station and would know of Clerke's recent voyage with Byron; he may well have recommended him to the Admiralty and thus to Cook. John Gore was another to be recruited. He knew as much as anyone about the Pacific, having been there twice— the first time with Byron, the second with Wallis.

No matter how he had come to be selected, Charles Clerke's career was now to take a decisive turn for he was about to embark on one of the greatest voyages of exploration ever made.

CHAPTER FOUR

FROM 1768 UNTIL THE DAY HE DIED the life of Charles Clerke was inextricably linked with that of James Cook, the greatest navigator of his age and one of England's most famous explorers. Together, they made two heroic voyages of exploration to the Pacific, became firm friends in the process and died within a few months of one another while attempting a third. Yet their characters and backgrounds could scarcely have been more different.

Cook was a steady, determined, self-contained, serious man; Clerke had the first two characteristics in no less a measure and he pursued his career very seriously but to these qualities was added an unfailing cheerfulness. He could never be described as being self-contained for a sense of humour was never far from the surface and his lightness of spirit made him much sought after as a companion. Women found him attractive and over the years he built up a substantial reputation as being a man who was fond of the ladies.

Clerke's father was a farmer who inherited the Manor of Wethersfield in the same year as his son sailed in *Endeavour* and from 1768 Joseph enjoyed the pleasant life of a substantial landowner. Cook's father was a farm labourer from the Borders who moved to Marston in Yorkshire where he married a local girl. He worked hard and in 1736 moved with his family to the nearby village of Great Ayton. There he secured the position of farm bailiff to a local landowner, a Mr.Thomas Skottowe, and built himself a house. The building still exists, but in 1933 it was dismantled stone by stone and taken to Australia where it was re-erected in a Melbourne park.

James Cook was born on 27th October 1728 and by the time he was eight years of age had become familiar with hard work by helping on the farm. Mr. Skottowe was the first of several people to recognise that young James was something out of the ordinary and he paid the fees which enabled the boy to attend the village school. Cook's father was anxious to give him a better start in life than he had had and James was apprenticed to a shopkeeper when he reached the age of sixteen. His employer was a Mr William Sanderson who was in business as a grocer and draper in the coastal village of Staithes, about twenty miles from Great Ayton. He was a kindly man and he treated James well but after eighteen months the young man decided that shopkeeping was not for him. When Sanderson was asked to release him from his indenture far from standing in his way he arranged for a ship-owning friend, a Quaker, to take Cook on as an apprentice seaman.

James Walker operated ships trading out of Whitby, mainly to London and the Baltic. His vessels were of a type known as 'Cats', ships whose design had evolved over many years to meet the requirements of the east coast trade. They were bluff bowed, built not for speed but for carrying capacity, and had a remarkable amount of cargo space within modest dimensions. Perhaps more important, they were flat bottomed and could easily take the ground on the numerous and often shifting shoals of the North Sea. London had a voracious appetite for coal and each year one million tons of it was carried there from the Tyne in a fleet of over four hundred ships. Most of Walker's trade was on this route but his vessels also went to Flanders, Norway and the Baltic.

Cook moved to Whitby and learnt the mariner's trade along the treacherous east coast of England. In the time between voyages, or when bad weather prevented his ship from sailing, he lived in an attic in Walker's house and applied himself to the study of navigation. When his three year apprenticeship was over Cook sailed for a further two years for a relative of Walker's, mainly in the Baltic trade. By 1752, when he had completed his training and passed his examinations, he was back in the employ of James Walker in the position of Mate. Cook sailed for him until 1755 by which time he was 27 years old. Walker then offered him the command of one of his ships, the *Friendship*, but Cook declined. Although they parted on the best of terms and remained friends ever after his employer must have been amazed at the young man's decision for Cook left him to join the Royal Navy as an Able Seaman. He could not have been compelled to join because, as the commander of a vessel engaged in the coal trade, he was immune from the Press. Cook was finding the confines of the North Sea too restrictive; all his life he had a mind which needed wide horizons— as large as those of the Pacific. Even when in middle age he had been given a sinecure at the Royal Naval Hospital after his triumphant 1772-75 voyage, he could not tolerate for long the lack of stimulation that went with the position and longed to be away again.

At the time he joined the Navy trouble was again brewing with the old enemy, France, and soon afterwards the Seven Years War broke out. In the middle of June Cook made his way to Wapping and joined the crew of *Eagle*, a powerful 60 gun ship under the command of Captain Hamer who was soon replaced by Hugh Palliser, a capable

Yorkshireman five years older than Cook. Palliser was destined to rise to high rank and had a considerable influence on Cook's subsequent career. He, too, soon recognised the qualities of the new recruit and within a month Cook was made Master's Mate. A man with Cook's background and capabilities was a rarity in the Navy and he began to ascend the promotion ladder. After two years in *Eagle* in the Channel, on his twenty-ninth birthday he was promoted Master of the almost new 64 gun *Pembroke*, under the command of Captain John Simcoe. Like Palliser, his new commander was a perceptive man and he took him under his wing. Simcoe encouraged him in the study of advanced mathematics, navigation, and charting, all subjects in which he had previously been unable to get first class instruction.

Cook saw action in *Pembroke* during the time she was engaged in the blockade of the French coast where both he and Clerke were part of a force trying to prevent the enemy sending men, supplies, and food to their garrisons in Canada and India. There is no record of their having met at this time.

One of England's main war aims was the elimination of French influence in Canada and the key to achieving this was seen to be the control of the St. Lawrence River. *Pembroke* was sent across the Atlantic and arrived in Canada at a time when it was realised that the existing maps of the waterway were too inaccurate to be relied upon. A plan had been drawn up which called for the capture of the French fortress at Quebec but the inadequacies of the charts meant that the Navy could not carry an army there in safety.

Cook made the acquaintance of an army engineer named Samuel Holland who taught him to survey and by 1758 he was using his new ability in helping to make new and precise charts of an important part of the seaway. Cook had to work quickly because he knew that the river would freeze over with the onset of winter, but he completed the task in time to allow the Navy to bring a force to Quebec. General Wolfe's army climbed the Heights of Abraham, defeated the French army, took Quebec and brought to an end French rule in Canada.

Cook then went as Master of *Northumberland*, the flagship of Lord Colville, the C-in-C of the American Station. After the war he was given his own command, the schooner *Grenville*, and spent the summers of the years leading up to 1767 surveying the coasts of Nova Scotia, Labrador and Newfoundland. In the winters he came home and worked on his observations, making them into accurate charts of the coastlines he had seen. His work had not gone unnoticed by Hugh Palliser, who was now the representative of H.M.

Government in the area. Although Cook was not then to know it all this experience, and particularly the charting of unknown coasts, was preparing him for what was to be the centrepiece of his life's work.

Cook's improving skills and the increasing breadth of his experience came at a time when England was taking a growing interest in the Pacific, partly for political, partly for scientific reasons. The former were the more important for underlying all the naval activity in the Pacific, exemplified by the voyages of Byron, Wallis, and Bougainville, was an awareness in both England and France of the changing strategic situation.

France's position had been much weakened by defeat in the Seven Years War for she had lost her possessions in Canada, Nova Scotia, and Florida at the same time as the British Navy, now the most powerful in the world, controlled the sea lanes of the globe. There was a growing suspicion in the minds of the policy makers in London that France might now turn towards the Pacific, perhaps gaining access through the lake and river system of North America where she still had a presence.

Their fears were justified for the French, finding themselves displaced and humiliated and seeking to redress the equilibrium, had begun to think in terms of expansion into the Pacific region. It did not take long for England to appreciate that control over the resources of the area, with the opportunities this would bring for trade and perhaps settlement, would affect the balance of power in Europe. For centuries this had been the very cornerstone of her foreign policy, the means by which her continued existence as an independant power had been achieved, and the decision was taken to establish a position in the Pacific.

The recent English and French expeditions of Wallis and Bougainville were far from being the first incursions into the region. The Portuguese sailor Magellan was the first European to go there when he broke into the Pacific in 1520 and he was soon followed by others, including Drake in 1578. In 1642 Tasman discovered the land now named after him but which he called Van Diemen's land in honour of his patron who was Governor General of the Dutch East India Company. Nearly two hundred years after Drake's time, Anson was another Englishman to sail across the Pacific during the circumnavigation he made between 1740 and 1744. The purpose of his voyage was to try to stir up opposition to the Spaniards who had a long established presence there as well as a trade route between Manila and Mexico which went via Guam.

The scientific reasons for an expedition to the Pacific added weight to those provided by the political ones for the Board of Admiralty had a concern which could best be satisfied in that Ocean. Naturally, the Navy had an interest in navigation and in any research which might increase knowledge, particularly if it had to do with the fixing of longitude. Navigators had long been able to calculate latitude and set their position north or south of the equator but the setting of longitude, which told them where they were east or west of the meridian, was a problem yet to be solved. When it was brought to the notice of the Admiralty that there would shortly be a fleeting opportunity to increase understanding of the solar system, and thus be of help to navigators, they immediately showed interest. The value the Navy placed on the expedition is shown by its finding resources at a time when England appeared to be drifting towards war with her American colonies.

The time was soon coming when it would be possible to make an accurate calculation of the distance between the Sun and the Earth and between the Earth and Venus, thus enabling the dimensions of the Universe to be established and longitude to be more accurately fixed. Halley, the astronomer, had died in 1742, a year after Charles Clerke was born, and one of his legacies was an opinion that the calculation could best be done by observing the passage of the shadow of Venus across the disc of the Sun. In November 1767 the Royal Society set up a special committee which successfully approached the King with requests for money and the use of a naval vessel to observe the 'Transit'. There being a common interest, the Navy agreed that a combined expedition be mounted.

Such astronomical events were rare. An attempt had been made to observe the one of June 1761, but it was not a success. The next passage was due to take place in 1769 and when 1768 came round there was a degree of urgency to get something organised. The transits were far from being everyday occurrences and the next, in 1874, would be well beyond the lifetime of anyone then alive. The following one was not due until 1882 and there would be no more until the 21st century— in 2004 and 2012. It was known the transit would last for only six hours so, when the proposed joint exploration became a reality, it was realised nothing could be left to chance. The Admiralty and the Royal Society agreed it should be viewed from widely spaced stations at North Cape, Hudson's Bay, and in the Pacific. The choice of a site in the Southern Ocean, where the planet's passage would be well above the horizon, was made in the hope that there would be no cloud to obscure it. Wallis came home at just the right time because Maskelyne, who had been on St. Helena during the 1761 Transit, had predicted that the best place in the Pacific from which the observations could be made was in Polynesia. Wallis' accurate fixing of the position of Tahiti placed it in the heart of that region. It was upon the recommendation of these two men that the island was chosen to be the place to house the Pacific observatory.

There was soon a difference of opinion between the Navy and the Royal Society about who should command the expedition. The Society sought the advice of Maskelyne and it was upon his recommendation that the civilians put forward the name of a Scot, Alexander Dalrymple. He had no formal sea training and had never commanded a ship but, not being unduly afflicted with an inclination to underestimate his abilities, he pressed his claim with enthusiasm. He was 31 years old and in his youth had gone to Madras to work for the East India Company. While there, he had gone on a voyage which whetted his appetite for exploration. Dalrymple was a member of the Ptolemy school of thought and became obsessed with that philosopher's concept of the Great Southern Continent. Dalrymple read everything he could find about the discoveries that had already been made and extrapolated them to an amazing degree. He predicted where the land mass lay, produced supporting charts, forecast its size and even prophesied that its population would be 50 million. The aspiring discoverer was only too eager to fall in with Maskelyne's wishes but only on the condition that he was placed in undisputed command. This was anathema to the Navy and the Admiralty refused to countenance even the thought of a civilian being in charge of a Navy ship.

At the time when all these factors came together— political, scientific and personal— James Cook had attained the rank of Lieutenant. He was now a married man, having wed 21 year old Elizabeth Batts of Barking in Essex in St. Margaret's church three days before Christmas 1762. He was living in the riverside town of Shadwell and George Downing, the Vicar of Little Wakering, a village near to Southend, was the officiating clergyman. Marriage had not caused Cook to give up the sea and Hugh Palliser, now a man of influence, recommended in May 1768 that he be given command of the forthcoming expedition. Dalrymple was not pleased and quite unable to understand his rejection. He never forgave Cook.

It would have been difficult in the eighteenth century to think of more exciting projects than the search for the Great Southern

Continent, the exploration of the Pacific, the circumnavigation of the South Pole, and the quest for the Northwest Passage. The scope of these undertakings leaves the observer lost in admiration but, while the three classic voyages Clerke made with Cook were conceived and executed on a grand scale, they were carried out with minimal resources. The gains made in various fields of knowledge; natural science, health, navigation and geography were out of all proportion to the material inputs to the expeditions.

It says much for the Royal Navy that it recognised the abilities of a labourer's son from Yorkshire and a farmer's son from Essex and sent them on such stupendous ventures. The choice of Cook as commander of the expeditions was inspirational for he was to prove himself one of the world's greatest explorers. Clerke was fortunate to be involved with him.

A ship had to be obtained which was capable of taking a mixed group of sailors and civilians to the Southern Ocean. She must be a good sea keeper, large enough to carry over a hundred people and their supplies for several years and yet have a sufficiently shallow draught to enable her to get close inshore when engaged in charting new coastlines. The Admiralty found her in a 368 ton vessel called the *Earl of Pembroke*. She was almost new, having been built less than four years earlier in the Fishburn yard in Whitby for a Mr. Thomas Milner. Her name was not one to appeal to the Navy and she was quickly renamed *Endeavour*. She was a Cat and therefore of a type of vessel well known to Cook from his days in the East Coast trade. Not even their most enthusiastic proponents could claim that these ships were greyhounds of the seas but their other qualities made up for a lack of speed. *Endeavour*, in common with all her kind, offered a remarkable amount of space within comparatively modest dimensions which, in her case, were 106 ft by 29 ft. with a draught of 14 ft.

When the Admiralty bought her she was valued at £2,300. She was taken to Deptford where she was given extra protection against the Teredo worm, a pest which was a particular hazard in the tropics because it damaged ships' hulls by boring into them below the water line. *Endeavour* was given a second outer skin into which were driven thousands of flat-headed copper nails. When the refit was complete, including work to her masts and spars, the total cost had risen to over £8,000. She was not expected to meet any serious opposition and was given a light armament of six 4-pounders and twelve swivel guns.

Few members of her crew were over 30 years of age. Clerke,

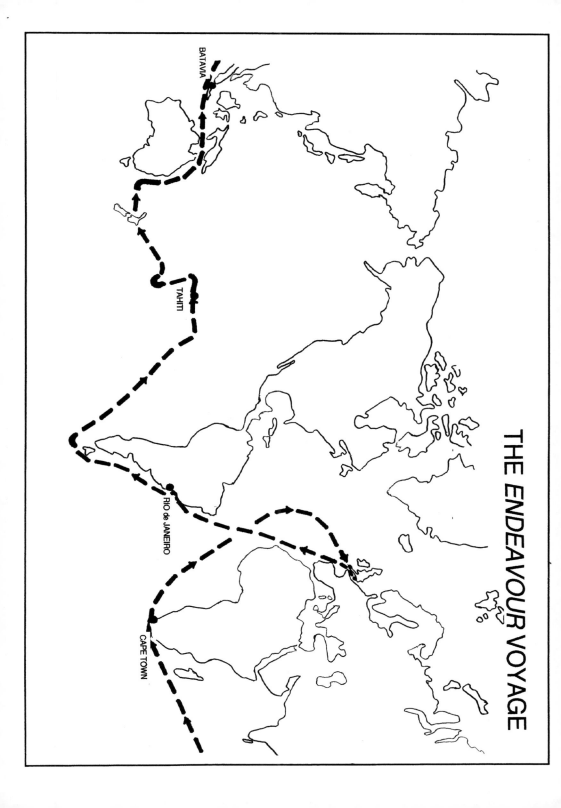

THE ENDEAVOUR VOYAGE

BATAVIA

TAHITI

RIO de JANEIRO

CAPE TOWN

9a. Charles
Clerke's
Lieutenant's
certificate

CHARLES CLERKE'S LIEUTENANT'S CERTIFICATE

In pursuance of the direction of the Right Hono^{ble} the Lords Comm^{rs} of the Admiralty signified to Us by Mr Stephens's letter of 30th May 1776, We have Examined Mr Charles Clerke who by Certificate appears to be more than Twenty two years of Age, & find he has gone to Sea more than Six Years in the Ships and Qualifys under-mentioned (viz)

Ships.	Quality.	Time			
		Y.^{s}	M.^{s}	W.^{s}	D.^{s}
Dorsetshire.	Captn Servt	1.	8.	2.	1
	Mids Ordry	0.	3.	3.	6
Bellona	Mids	2.	11.	0.	6
	Ables	0.	1.	2.	5
Dolphin	Mids	0.	6.	3.	3
	Ables	0.	0.	3.	6
	Mids	1.	4.	0.	5
		6.	11.	1.	4.

His not producing a journal for the Dolphin is to be —
dispensed with by their Lordship's Order of the 30th May 1766.
He produceth Journals kept by himself in the Bellona,
and Certificates from Captains Denis, Ulys, Norbury &
Byron of his Diligence, Sobriety, & Obedience to
Command, he can Splice, Knot, Reef a Sail, Work a
Ship in Sailing, Shift his Tides, keep a Reckoning
of a Ship's way, by plain Sailing, & Mercator, Observe
by Sun or Star, find the variation of the Compass, and
is qualified to do the duty of an Able Seaman and
Midshipman. Dated at the Navy Office the 10th June
1766.

Chas. B Man   Abra.^{m} North:

9b. This transcription of Charles Clerke's Lieutenant's certificate is fairly straightforward except for the first signature which is uncertain. Commissions were granted following: (a) an oral examination in seamanship and (b) at least six years service in the Navy as either Midshipman or Master's Mate.

recently home from the American station, was a member of a small group each of whom had recent experience of the Pacific. He was reunited with his friend John Gore, and Robert Molyneux, Richard Pickersgill, Francis Wilkinson and Francis Haite, all from Byron's *Dolphin*, were the others. Gore must have found a singular attraction in the forthcoming cruise because he had been home only two months between his return in *Dolphin* under Byron and his departure in the same ship with Wallis. Now he was off again on another three year voyage, having been in England for only a few weeks. Another earmarked for the long voyage was also an experienced sailor. Wallis' goat from *Dolphin* was signed on to be the milk supplier to *Endeavour's* officers.

At 27 years of age Charles Clerke was now a very experienced seaman. He had passed the examination for his Lieutenant's certificate and put together an impressive curriculum vitae since going to sea ten years earlier. His voyage with Byron had been a major turning point in his career because he then became one of a small band of Englishmen that had rounded the Horn to enter the Pacific. Clerke had been to islands never before seen by Europeans and consequently knew as much as anyone then alive about the geography and peoples of Polynesia. When Clerke sailed with Byron he had been at a cross-roads in his career because the path he then chose took him away from the one usually followed by most naval officers into the unknown world of the explorer. James Cook had been made aware of Clerke's capabilities and experience and he knew of the younger man's reputation for good humour, a quality which would be a bonus in a voyage scheduled to last several years. Cook chose him for the post of Master's Mate, a responsible position and a step up the promotion ladder because it was the Master, Robert Molyneux, who had the responsibility for sailing and navigating the ship. Both ranks were classified as Petty Officer but holders of them were recognised as being potential officers and enjoyed various privileges, including being allowed to walk the Quarter Deck.

Clerke was to sail with a group of eight civilians who were going on the voyage on behalf of the Royal Society. The most prominent was the botanist Joseph Banks who is now most remembered for the array of plants which bear his name. Banks had developed a deep interest in natural science at an early age and, while at Eton, he regretted having to learn Latin and Greek, in order to please his father, rather than discover the world of Nature. Banks was a wealthy landowner with an estate at Revesby, near Boston in Lincolnshire, and enjoyed an enormous income which was said to be over £6,000 a year. He needed it because it was rumoured that preparations for the voyage cost him £10,000. He was destined to have a long life and one full of honours because for nearly fifty years he was President of the Royal Society and eventually became, in effect, George III's advisor on all scientific matters. Banks was two years younger than Clerke and in him Charles found a kindred spirit for Banks, too, was fond of adventure, had a similar ability to get on well with people from many walks of life, and was not averse to the occasional amorous dalliance. The two young men struck up a friendship which was to last all of Clerke's life; almost his last letter was one of fond farewell to his friend. In his relationship with Banks, Clerke straddled the divide between the Navy men and the civilians in a way none of the other members of the crew seem to have done. Banks' association with Cook was on a different level; while he had great respect for the Captain his behaviour before the first *Resolution* voyage suggests that he regarded Cook as being no more than in charge of the travel arrangements. With Clerke he had a genuine and lasting friendship.

Banks' deputy was Dr. Solander, a 35 year old Swede who had studied under Linnaeus and was later to work at the British Museum. He was an affable man who made himself popular with the crew, particularly Clerke, who had a special liking for him.

An important member of the civilian group, the man who would be at the centre of the observation of the Transit, and later of help to Clerke as a teacher, was Charles Green. He was the 33 year old son of a Yorkshire farmer and had been trained as an astronomer by Maskelyne.

Clerke was now in the company of men of importance in a navy where advancement was much influenced by the system of patronage. Banks, in addition to his eminence in the world of science, had other useful connections— he had secured his passage in *Endeavour* through his friend Lord Sandwich, the First Lord of the Admiralty. The civilians Clerke was sailing with were all intelligent and learned men; Banks and Solander were reckoned to be two of the best scientific minds in Europe. He met them at a critical period of his life, a time when the impetuosity of his youth was beginning to wane and needing to be replaced by a more mature approach. He could hardly fail to gain from spending the next three years in the close company of such men; from Green he learnt improved methods of navigation and Banks and Solander taught him the value of careful observation. Beaglehole described Clerke's early journals as being disappointing and it is striking how the later ones record so much more about the animals, plants, people and customs that he had seen.

Charles Clerke left his home in Wethersfield and went to Deptford on the Thames where *Endeavour* was fitting out in the dockyard. The work was being closely supervised by Cook who was certain of two things; that the voyage would be long and that the shipyard workers would get away with whatever they could.

The captain took great care that all the work carried out on his ship was done to a high standard and it was only when he judged her fit to leave that the pilot came on board. John Blackburn took her round to the Downs, where she dropped anchor on 7th August. Bidding his family farewell, James Cook left Elizabeth and his home in the small town of Mile End; at that time it was a place little more than a village surrounded by fields, on the outskirts of London. He set out for Deal where he joined his ship and sailed her to Plymouth where *Endeavour* took on the final supplies which would enable her to be largely self sufficient for a period of almost two years. Finally, more sailors were taken out to join the crew, bringing her complement to ninety-six men.

At 2.00 p.m. on Friday 26th August 1768, with a breeze from the northwest to set her on the way, *Endeavour's* great voyage began.

Charles Clerke's commanding officer had been given his orders a month earlier. It was common knowledge that *Endeavour* was going to the Pacific to observe from Tahiti the Transit of Venus which the astronomers had predicted would take place on 3rd June the following year. On that day Venus would pass between the Sun and the Earth and throw its shadow on the Sun. Clerke and the rest of the crew were aware that Cook had been given a second set of orders. They were sealed, and the Captain had been directed to open them only when *Endeavour* was safely at sea and there was no longer any risk of their existence becoming known.

These secret instructions— which were not published until 1928— opened up a whole new set of interesting opportunities because, after the celestial observations had been made, the expedition was to sail in waters to the south of Tahiti, looking for the peaks Wallis' men had reported seeing. Cook was to go as far as 40° S, and try to solve the mystery of the Great Southern Continent— Terra Australis Incognita. If he did not come upon the continent by the time he had reached this latitude he was to turn west and accurately fix the position of New Zealand, the presence of which had been reported by Tasman over a hundred years earlier, in 1642.

Cook had profound doubts as to the existence of the Southern Continent but his opinion was not shared by many influential men. The Admiralty had its share of true believers and even Joseph Banks had been converted to the Ptolomy school of thought which said that it must be there to balance the northern land masses. Cook's orders were widely drawn and gave him the opportunity of filling in some of the many blank spaces on the map of the world as it was known in the 1760s. The outlines of most of the world's land masses were already known, including the west coast of Australia, but those of the rest of the continent and all of Antarctica were uncharted. Although it covered nearly one third of the Earth's surface, few Europeans had been to the Pacific by the middle of the eighteenth century and, other than the trade routes established by the Spanish, little was known of the geography of the region. The voyage was a considerable venture and Charles Clerke was to play his part in an expedition which would answer many questions.

It is strange that the Admiralty was sending only one ship because previous expeditions, most recently those of Byron and Wallis, had each had two. The risks to the crew of a single vessel were much increased for once they entered uncharted waters the risk of disaster went up and the hopes of rescue went down. If anything happened to them— and *Endeavour* was to come as near to shipwreck on the Great Barrier Reef as it was possible to be— they had to rely entirely on their own resources.

Cook's intention was to enter the Pacific via Cape Horn. *Endeavour* passed Cape Finisterre early in September and arrived in Madeira (always known in the Georgian Navy as 'The Island') on Tuesday the 14th. Fresh supplies of wine, water, and meat on the hoof were taken aboard. It was here in Funchal Roads that the first man was lost. A quartermaster called Weir caught his leg in a buoy rope and was taken to the bottom by the anchor, his body entwined in the rope. The thirteen American colonies were still ruled from London and their seaman were considered to be eligible for impressment. There happened to be an American ship at anchor in Funchal harbour and the loss of Weir was made up by taking one of her crew.

Endeavour's stay in Madeira lasted less than a week and she sailed at midnight on September 19th to begin the voyage down the North and South Atlantic oceans. Five weeks later she crossed the Equator, with the usual ceremonies to afflict those who had not previously been over the line, and came to Rio de Janeiro. Rio at that time was owned by Portugal, England's long standing ally but, despite this happy relationship, *Endeavour's* reception was not friendly. The Portuguese suspected that she might not be a King's ship and could be engaged in either trade or privateering. This was not completely unreasonable because *Endeavour* did not have the appearance of a typical Royal Navy vessel and privateering, and even piracy, were not activities entirely unknown in previous English visitors to the area, including Drake.

On Sunday, 13th November 1768, Clerke was sent ahead in the pinnace with Lieutenant Hicks with instructions to tell the Viceroy, Dom Antonio de Moura, the purpose of their visit. Barely had the two men set foot on dry land when they were put in gaol. Shortly afterwards, a boat filled with Portuguese officers came out to tell Cook that it was the custom to detain the first people to land, pending the captain presenting himself. Clerke and Hicks were soon released but the Portuguese never quite overcame their suspicions. No one was allowed to live ashore and when Cook tried to buy provisions he was obliged to employ an agent. *Endeavour* was always under guard and the Viceroy refused to believe that the ship's mission had anything to do with an observation of the Transit of Venus. The authorities tried to insist that one of their sentries always be on duty wherever the ship's boats went and this led to an incident when Lieutenant Hicks would have none of it. His boat's crew were taken to prison under armed guard but a furious Cook soon made the Portuguese release them.

Clerke's incarceration may have been an object lesson to him because it put him on the receiving end of the art of hostage-taking, a technique he was often to see used during his voyages in the Pacific. Cook, and no doubt Clerke too in view of his experiences there, was heartily pleased to leave Rio on 7th December. On 11th January in the New Year they landed on Tierra del Fuego and met the local people who bore not the slightest resemblance to the giants Clerke had described seeing on his last visit to the area. Cook's opinion of them was succinct '. . . in a word they are perhaps as miserable a set of People as are this day upon Earth'.

Clerke's friend Banks came close to tragedy during the stay in Tierra del Fuego. In the middle of January he took a party ashore to collect specimens but left his return so late he could not get back on board before nightfall. Two Negro servants were in the group and they had charge of a supply of alcohol. The temptation was too much for them to bear and they became so drunk that they either could not or would not move and, lying down several hundred yards away from the other men, both died from exposure.

Endeavour enjoyed fair weather when she entered the Pacific through the Straits of le Maire on 25th January 1769. She had been lucky, for it was not uncommon for vessels to battle for long periods to make the passage from the Atlantic into the Pacific. In 1788 Captain Bligh in the *Bounty,* who in his younger days had sailed with Cook and Clerke in *Resolution,* tried for several weeks before giving up and making his way into the Pacific by going round the Cape of Good Hope.

Endeavour was now in the southern ocean and had reached the point when her crew had only themselves to rely on for survival. Any supplies had to be won or traded for the goods they had on board; any repairs that became necessary had to be done with their own skills, for there was no dockyard within hundreds of miles. The officers were uncertain of the reception the expedition could expect to receive on arrival in the Pacific islands and in mid-March the crew began exercising in small arms. At the same time, the swivel guns which had been placed in the hold for the passage round the Horn were brought up and placed in position.

The ship followed a north-westerly track and at the end of March, as she neared her destination, Clerke witnessed a strange incident. William Greenslade was a quiet, twenty-one year old Marine— 'a raw young fellow,' thought Cook— who had been caught in possession of a piece of seal skin, the significance of which is obscure. At about 7.00 p.m. on the evening of the 26th he was being brought between decks to Cook when he broke free. Avoiding his pursuers, he ran to the forecastle and was not seen again. It was never established whether he fell overboard or committed suicide but Banks thought his fellow marines had driven him almost mad.

Early in April *Endeavour* made landfall at some islands of the Tuamotu group and at 6.00 a.m. on Tuesday the 11th, an unsettled, rainy day, Cook and his men had their first sight of Tahiti. Two days later, very early in the morning, she dropped anchor for the first time in Matavai Bay after a passage from England which had taken a little under eight months. The bay made a splendid haven and both the anchorage and the people were to become well known to Clerke in the years to come for he was to return several times during this and later voyages.

At that time Tahiti had a population estimated as being about 40,000, living in an area of some 400 square miles. However, when Charles Clerke landed in a party made up from men who had been there before, all they found were a few people and many abandoned houses. The Tahitians were hospitable folk and by the next day news of the ship's arrival had spread and a host of canoes put out from the shore. Before long, trading was under way with each group of bargain hunters being as excited as the next. Most of the crew made their first acquaintance with that ever recurring feature of contact between Europeans and the inhabitants of most of the Pacific islands—thieving. 'It was a hard matter to keep them out of the Ship', wrote Cook, 'they clime like Munkeys, but it was still harder to keep them from stealing but everything that came within their reach, in this they are prodiges expert.' A particularly audacious practitioner of the art took Cook's stockings from under his head while the Captain was asleep in his bed: one of the Monkhouse brothers was relieved of a snuff box by a pickpocket and Dr. Solander lost a spy glass. A local chief insisted the goods be returned. There was a much more serious incident a few days later when an islander was shot dead while trying to steal a sentry's musket.

Theft was a constant and recurring cause of friction between the indigenous people and their uninvited visitors, for each group had a different concept of ownership. It was the same all over the Pacific for this and all subsequent expeditions and in the end it led to the clash in which Cook lost his life. The pattern of the relationship which was to evolve between the sailors and the Tahitians was epitomised the following day. It was spent in an atmosphere of the utmost goodwill but all the time the Europeans were trying to prevent the disappearance of their belongings.

The Tahitian women were very attractive, perhaps the more so to young men who had been months at sea. On his return to England, Wallis had given them the reputation, rightly or wrongly, of being free with their favours. The crew of *Endeavour* began enthusiastically to put the theory to the test and Charles Clerke, if his renown was well founded, no doubt entered into the spirit of enquiry. Banks busied himself with botany and spent some of his spare time in making the acquaintance of several young ladies. Clerke seems not to have been much concerned with botany. Parkinson was one of the artists taken on the voyage to record flora, fauna, events, and places, and he noted that most of the crew took what he called 'temporary wives'. Cook was worried because 'the women were so liberal with their favours' and he had the doctor examine the entire crew. Cook wrote:

> Chastity indeed is but little valued especialy among the middle people, if a wife is found guilty of a breach of it her only punishment is a beating from her husband, the men will very readily

offer the young women to strangers even their own daughters and think it very strange if you refuse them but this is done meerly for the lucre of gain.

When the doctor had finished his mass examination he found that twenty-four seamen and nine of the eleven marines were suffering from venereal disease. Only a short time before *Endeavour's* arrival he had pronounced the entire ship's company to be free of it and the infection was blamed on a Spanish ship which was thought to have called at the island between ten and fifteen months previously. The evidence was flimsy. When pictures of various national flags were shown to a local chief he picked out that of Spain and one of his fellows pointed out to Cook the anchorage the Spaniards were alleged to have used. The matter became even more obscure when *Endeavour* reached Batavia and Cook was told that two French ships under the command of Bougainville, a frigate and a store ship, had also called at Tahiti. In fact, the English doctor had made an understandable misdiagnosis because the condition eventually proved to be another sexually transmitted disease called yaws. This infection frequently occurred in the Pacific and often presented with signs and symptoms which were similar to those of venereal disease. Both were treated in the same way with the use of arsenic.

Charles Clerke lost another shipmate on 17th April when Alexander Buchan, one of Banks' landscape technicians, died of a 'disorder of his Bowels which had more than once brought him to the Very point of death'. If Banks was overwhelmed by grief he managed to conceal it well for he wrote of the passing of his servant: 'His loss to me is irretrievable, my airy dreams of entertaining my friends in England with the scenes that I am to see here are vanished'.

The expedition arrived in good time, about seven weeks before the Transit of Venus was due to take place. Before leaving England Cook had been warned that the islanders could be treacherous and the need to protect the irreplaceable astronomical equipment brought all the way from home was now obvious. Men were set to work building a stockade called Fort Venus, inside which were placed some tents and the observatory. To be extra careful the main instruments were kept on the ship and not brought ashore until nearer the time of the Transit and a sentry was always on duty. Even this was not enough, for on May 2nd an astronomical quadrant made by John Bird, stored in an 18" square packing case, was taken from the fort while Cook himself was there— he saw nothing of the theft. Banks and Green went off in pursuit and retrieved it four miles away.

As had been hoped in England all those months ago before the expedition sailed, June 3rd 1769 was a clear, bright day. To be sure of making the most of the conditions, in addition to the main group at the observatory, two parties were sent to other locations. Clerke went in the ship's pinnace with Hicks, Pickersgill, and Saunders to an islet off the eastern side of the island and there they set up their instruments. The day grew hotter and a dusky shade round the body of the planet did nothing to help the accurate taking of observations. Nevertheless, and despite some discrepancies between the sightings taken by Cook, Solander, and Green, the measurements were judged a success.

The next six weeks were spent enjoying Tahiti and in preparing *Endeavour* for the next stage of her voyage. Among other delicacies, Clerke was introduced to the delights of eating dogs: 'a meat not to be despised'.

After such a long passage there were repairs to the ship which must be done. The hull, sails, and rigging had to be mended and the accumulation of weed on the ship's bottom had to be removed so that she could slide more easily through the water. Large amounts of food and drinking water had to be taken aboard; the collection of the latter was a laborious business since it had to be taken from a spring, put in barrels and manhandled aboard.

Many men must have wondered if they preferred life on Tahiti to that in an English port. On Monday 9th July, just before the ship was due to sail, two marines, Clement Webb and Samuel Gibson, were found to have deserted. Each had found the pleasures of Tahiti to be irresistible and had taken unto himself a 'temporary wife'; they were said to have made off into the mountains. This was something Cook could not ignore for if the deserters were allowed to succeed other men would follow their example. He was determined to have them back and for the first time he used a device he was to employ many times in the future, he took hostages. A local queen and four chiefs were seized and detained on *Endeavour*. Midshipman Monkhouse and a corporal of Marines were sent in pursuit of the deserters and during the evening of the next Monday, the 10th, Webb was brought back by a group of natives. They told Cook that Monkhouse and his corporal had been disarmed and seized by another party of islanders and that Gibson was with them. Lieutenant Hicks was now sent off with a strong party and by 7.00 a.m. next morning he was back with the other runaway. Each deserter was given two dozen lashes when the ship was at sea.

Endeavour got under way just before noon on Thursday 13th July

1769. After the joys of the island her crew might have had a different opinion but Cook took with him an impression that Tahiti contained little of any intrinsic value and that its worth would be confined to use as a haven for shipping.

Banks had recruited a Tahitian called Tupia. Clerke's friend seems not to have been moved by purely altruistic motives:

> I do not know why I may not keep him as a curiosity, as well as some of my neighbours do lions and tygers at a larger expence than he will ever put me to; the amusement I shall have in his future conversation . . . will I think fully repay me.

Endeavour went exploring other islands in the archipelago and visited Huahine, Ulietea, Borabora and Rurutu and claimed possession of them all in the name of the King. Cook had carried out that part of his Admiralty instructions that were public knowledge and he could now concentrate on the secret orders. He turned the ship's head towards the south and began his search for the Great Southern Continent. The weather soon deteriorated, the temperature dropped and heavy rain squalls made conditions uncomfortable. There was a long swell from the south which strongly suggested there was no large land mass lying in that direction to break up the movement of the water. The ship followed the Admiralty's orders and went as far as 40° S without sight of land before Cook turned her northward again, his scepticism as to the existence of Terra Australis Incognita now stronger than ever.

It was about this time that Clerke witnessed the outcome of an outburst of heavy drinking. The Navy was not unaccustomed to the use of alcohol but this binge on the part of a twenty-five years old sailor was something out of the ordinary:

> Monday 28th August 1769:
> At 10 am departed this life Jno Radon Boatswain's Mate his death was occasioned by the Boatswain, out of good nature, giving him part of a Bottle of rum last night which it is supposed he drank all at once, he was found to be very much in Liquor last night, but as this was no more than what was common with him when he could get any, no farther notice was taken of him than to put him to Bed when this morning at about 8 o'Clock he was found speechless and beyond recovery.

How had the kindly Boatswain come by the rum? Banks said that the gentlemen on the ship often found that their personal casks had been broken into (drinking was not confined to the lower deck) and all or part of the contents stolen, the deficiency being made up with salt water. Radon had obviously drunk a great deal of rum; Hicks said that he had consumed a pint and a half of the spirit and he probably died by choking on his own vomit.

On Saturday 7th October *Endeavour's* crew had their first sight of New Zealand when land was seen from the masthead. By the next day the ship was sufficiently close inshore for houses and people to be seen and on the following Monday, when the ship had been at sea for over eight weeks, a party went ashore at a place they called Poverty Bay. The people they met were very different from the friendly folk of Tahiti. Their relationship got off to an inauspicious start for soon there was a violent clash and the first Maori was killed. The sailors thought they were being menaced by the natives and when one of them appeared to be about to throw a spear a shot was fired into the air. This had no effect and the man was then killed by a musket ball. Next day a large group gathered near the same place— Gore said that they were over a hundred strong— and performed what seemed to be a war dance. Jumping first to the left and then to the right, lolling out their tongues and singing a hoarse song (all reminiscent of the All Blacks) they were meant to be, and were, an intimidating sight. The Marines were called ashore and Tupia spoke to them in a language they understood. Despite his efforts, relations got worse as the Maoris made several attempts to snatch the Marines' weapons from their hands and when Green's hanger was taken Cook gave the order to open fire. Monkhouse hit a man with a ball from his gun and the fellow died soon after. Pickersgill, in particular, was impressed by the Maoris' courage and the fact that they had not run away when fired upon, as the island people usually did.

Two or three more men were killed soon afterwards at a time when Cook was trying to make contact with a party of men in canoes. Three survivors were picked up from the water and became quite cheerful when they found they were well treated. Banks had considerable qualms about these early contacts:

> . . . thus ended the most disagreeable day my Life has yet seen.
> Black be the mark for it and heaven send such may never return
> to embitter future reflections.

Cook, who was usually sympathetic towards native people, was more sanguine, giving as justification for his actions the possibility of damage to his men.

A week after this incident *Endeavour* had sailed south to reach a place they called Cape Turnagain. The lie of the land was beginning to look less promising and it seemed to Cook that it was unlikely that any interesting new discoveries or a harbour would be found. The route to the north looked more promising— and so the Cape got its name.

As they went anticlockwise round North Island the sailors met with a mixed reception from the Maoris. They often followed the ship in canoes and sometimes showed an eagerness to trade but this was marred by an equal willingness to steal anything moveable when they came aboard. At other times they showed overt hostility. Stones were often thrown at *Endeavour* as she sailed by and in early November Clerke reported that a man in a canoe had flung a spear at one of the crew, fortunately without harming him. Several times Cook ordered grapeshot to be fired, not to injure but to deter, but on each occasion this was met with unexpected defiance. On the 9th of the month Gore shot and killed a man who refused to give up a cloak which Gore thought he had traded for a piece of cloth. This was an uncharacteristic action on the part of Clerke's friend and it is tempting to believe that Charles, who was a fair man with a liking for most Pacific people, would not have approved. Cook certainly did not, and thought that it was unwarranted for a man to be killed for such a trivial reason. Gore seems to have tried to do something to make amends for when the victim was buried the cloth was used as his shroud.

Fortunately not every day was as gloomy because at about this time the opportunity was taken to observe the Transit of the planet Mercury.

Auckland is one of the world's great natural harbours but Clerke was destined never to see it; *Endeavour* probably sailed past the entrance at night and it remained undiscovered until 1820. Strangely, a similar thing was to happen at Sydney.

Sailing in unknown waters was always a hazardous business and Cook was the most careful of men. He could only minimise risk, he could not eliminate it, and when, in the first days of December, *Endeavour* arrived at the Bay of Islands, just below the northern tip of New Zealand, she struck a rock. A group of Maoris was on the nearby shore watching the ship go by, and when they saw what was happening they thoroughly enjoyed the spectacle. They were to be disappointed because *Endeavour* was not firmly aground and the swell took her clear, to the relief of her crew. They felt no pressing desire to meet the reception committee which awaited them.

Just before Christmas, the astronomer Charles Green gave Clerke and two of his friends a lesson in advanced navigation. He had reservations about the improvement that could be expected.

> ...I lent my Quadrant to Mr Clark, Mr Saunders and Monkhouse
> ... this is the first Attempt of the kind these hopeful Youths have
> made and I wish they may not grow worse instead of better.

It is a strange thing to say of Clerke who at 27 years of age was hardly a youth. Green was teaching his pupils a method for fixing longitude which he had learnt from his tutor, Maskelyne, which compared the known position of the moon relative to a fixed star as it was seen from Greenwich with what was observed at a particular place.

They rounded the North Cape of North Island at Christmas time and celebrated the festival by eating goose pie and getting drunk. It had seemed a good idea at the time but next day the bill had to be paid and Banks wrote that everyone had a sore head.

Endeavour set off down the west coast quite unaware that a French ship was not far behind her on the opposite side of the island. She had come from Pondicherry in India and was commanded and part owned by Jean Francois de Surville, a member of a profit-seeking syndicate. Unlike Cook's expedition this was a purely private venture without government support. The two ships were never to meet, for the Frenchmen were suffering badly from scurvy and sailed away eastward to escape the hostile reception they, too, had met from the Maoris.

In mid-January 1770 *Endeavour* was being careened and her bottom cleaned when there was another brush with the Maoris, who Clerke recorded, 'behaved very insolent'. As happened all too often, the situation degenerated into violence and 'the Captain shot one of them in ye knee'. Luckily for the unfortunate man, painful as his injury no doubt was, Cook had used small shot and not ball.

It was at this time that the explorers found the first positive evidence they had come upon in New Zealand of the practice of cannibalism; Clerke would remember it when he came back in *Resolution*. A group of Maoris offered them a bone from the forearm of a woman who, they said, had been killed a few days before when she had been with a party of their enemies. While this meeting was going on the Englishmen were approached by another woman who had fresh cuts on her arms and legs, a sign of mourning for her husband who had been eaten by his enemies. There was more proof a few days later when a canoe was seen with four heads in it. Cannibalism seems to have been a widespread practice for, on 30th January, a party of about twenty men, women and children landed near the ship and the women scarified their bodies because, the sailors were told, their husbands had been eaten. Unruffled, the Maori men went about their business while the lamentations went on.

On the last day of the month *Endeavour* reached Queen Charlotte Sound, on the northern coast of South Island and came to anchor in

Ship Cove, as fine a harbour as Matavai Bay. A clan of particularly fierce Maoris, estimated as being 300–400 strong, made up the local population and they, too, showed signs of eating their enemies. A pole was set up with the Union flag on it and, omitting to seek the approval of these people, Cook took possession of the territory in the name of the King. Cook was now convinced that they were on a separate, more southerly, island but not all his officers shared his opinion. Clerke left no indication of which camp had his support but his admiration for Cook probably placed him in that of his commanding officer.

Disaster nearly struck again when *Endeavour* left the sound on 7th February; only the anchor prevented her being dashed against the rocks by the ebb tide. Cook sailed through the strait which now bears his name and when Cape Turnagain came into sight through the haze and cloud two days later the controversy as to whether or not they had been on a separate island was settled beyond doubt.

Cook turned his ship towards the south and began the circumnavigation of South Island. Meticulous as ever to ensure that the coast was charted exactly as it was, when Gore reported seeing land to the south-east Cook spent a whole day looking for it, although he was sure in his own mind that the sighting was nothing more than cloud. *Endeavour* rounded the southern point of South Island early in March 1770 and began her journey up the west coast. Towards nightfall on Wednesday the 14th an inviting bay which appeared to offer a good haven was sighted but a gale was blowing and, not wishing to risk the ship in the dark, Cook continued northward. He took careful note of the position of Dusky Bay and was delighted to make use of it during his second Pacific voyage, when he was in *Resolution*.

The west coast of South Island is very wild and beautiful but the visitors found it impossible to make a landing and by 26th March *Endeavour* was back in Queen Charlotte Sound. The first survey of the coastline of New Zealand was complete and had settled once and for all that the country was made up of two main separate islands. Cook had spent six and a half months charting the 2,400 mile long coast with an accuracy which was not surpassed for more than a century.

Charles Clerke played his part in this work. His immediate superior was the ship's Master, Robert Molyneux, a Lancastrian and younger than Clerke. He had been a Master's Mate with Wallis on *Dolphin* and had a reputation for intemperance. The Navy was full of heavy drinking men but Molyneux, like one of his Mates, Richard

Pickersgill, had what would now be called a drink problem. Knowing this—it would be impossible to conceal it in a small ship for a period of many months—the Captain did not completely trust him and Charles Clerke was probably having to take more responsibility.

The time had now come for Cook to decide on the homeward route and he called together his officers to discuss the options which were open to them. His orders left him free to return by the established route which went to the north of New Guinea but this held few attractions. The question of whether or not the Great Southern Continent existed had still not been settled and, thinking it might possibly lie in the area between New Zealand and South America, Cook was tempted to go by the Horn. This idea was discounted because it was now late in the season to go cruising in high latitudes and *Endeavour* was no longer in good enough condition to face the conditions to be expected there. The Cape of Good Hope lay the opposite way, but the geography of the area lying in that direction was already well known. To the north lay Australia and although the Dutch had mapped the west coast and some of the south, the east remained a total mystery. For a man of Cook's disposition the decision presented no problem.

Endeavour left New Zealand on the last day of March 1770 and made the first landfall by Europeans on the east coast of Australia on 19th April at a place somewhere between where Melbourne and Sydney now stand. The sailors made no attempt to get ashore and continued towards the north. At first there was no sign of human habitation but smoke was seen two days later and people the next. They could not find a suitable place to set foot on terra firma and it was a week before the first landing was made, on Sunday 29th April, at a place Banks named Botany Bay. The explorers had seen people standing by their huts who were unlike any they had seen before, entirely naked and with their faces and bodies painted in a white pigment. As they approached, all except two men ran away having stayed only long enough to throw darts at the strangers. As had happened in New Zealand, the first contact got off to a bad start when Cook found himself forced to fire small shot at them, hitting one. The Aborigines were not to know it but the uninterrupted existence which they had enjoyed for thousands of years had come to an end and it is hardly surprising that the next day Hicks was unable to persuade a group of about a dozen to come close. 'All they seem'd to want'—he wrote—'was for us to be gone'. This set the pattern for most subsequent meetings between the Europeans and the native Australian people who either ignored these weird creatures, threw stones at them, fled as fast as they could or, sometimes, just stood gazing.

In this environment of violence and mistrust it would not have been surprising if a war-like act had been the cause of the death of the next man to die but this was not the case. During Clerke's lifetime, tuberculosis was endemic in the Navy, there was no treatment for it and it killed Forby Sutherland, a 29 year old man from the Orkneys. He was the first European to die on the east coast of Australia, a distinction he would doubtless have been pleased to forego. His disease had progressed rapidly, the first signs had appeared as *Endeavour* came round South America.

Although Charles Clerke did not live long enough to know it, Botany Bay was destined to play an important part in the history of England and Australia. In the seventeen years following the first visit, by which time both he and Cook were long dead, no European went there until Captain Arthur Philip arrived on 26th January 1788 in *Sirius*, the escort to a fleet of ships carrying 736 convicts. Georgian England had been suffering from a crime wave. Hanging was the mandatory sentence for a whole host of crimes but some judges commuted it to one of deportation if they could find a reason to do so. There was thought to be a criminal class which society could well do without and there grew up a desire to clean the national nest. Deportation not only got these people out of sight, it also provided a pool of labour in parts of the world where it was in short supply. At first, thousands were sent to the settlements in North America and the West Indies but, when the thirteen colonies rebelled in 1776, this option was no longer available. The prisons could not then cope with the number of people being sentenced and they were soon bursting at the seams. It was thought that the rebellion in America was bound to fail and when that happened it would again be possible to send convicts across the Atlantic. In the meantime, the authorities resorted to a temporary expedient and prisoners were packed into the hulks of old ships anchored in the Thames.

In fact, the colonies gained their independence and it became necessary to find an alternative, preferably one as far away from England as it was possible to get. In 1779, the year Cook was killed and Clerke died, Joseph Banks went before a committee of the House of Commons and recommended Botany Bay as a suitable location for a penal settlement. The place is now full of the sound of aircraft taking off and landing, for it is where Sydney Airport has been built. After his arrival Captain Philip thought the Bay had too many disadvantages and he had himself rowed a little way towards the north. There he found a better site at a place now called The Rocks on Sydney waterfront, near the Ferry Terminal.

The convicts in the First Fleet were the advance guard of more than 150,000 people who were sent to Australia. Among those arriving in 1788 were several who had been sentenced in Chelmsford, at the assizes held in Charles Clerke's home county of Essex.

Anthony Rope was a twenty-six year old labourer from Rochford who was tried on the morning of 10th March 1785 and sentenced to seven years transportation for burglary. Twenty-five year old Thomas Tennant, whose home had been in Ardleigh, was brought from the hulks to be sentenced to seven years for theft. Henry Abrams, aged twenty-six years and from Wansted, had also spent time on the Thames before being sent to Australia for seven years on the night of 9th March 1785 for the crime of highway robbery. A thirty year old labourer from Shenfield, by the name of James Heading, was originally sentenced to be hanged for horse stealing before he was transported for life. Isaac Lemon was twenty-three years old, another labourer, this time from Coggeshall and, like Heading, had been involved in stealing horses when he was brought before the judges on the morning of 10th March to be told he was to be hanged. Eventually, his sentence was commuted to seven years deportation. James Mansfield had been tried two days earlier; he was only sixteen years old, was employed as a labourer, lived in Romford and stole a sow and seven pigs, a crime which earned him a penalty of seven years in Australia. He, too, had been to the Hulks. The only woman from Essex was Frances Davis who had stolen no less than £833-6s-6d. For taking this enormous sum of money she was originally sentenced to death but it was commuted to one of transportation for fourteen years, an example of the desire of some judges to avoid the supreme penalty if they could.

All this was in the future as *Endeavour* left Botany Bay at dawn on Sunday 6th May 1770 and sailed northward two to three miles offshore. Before leaving, Cook had one of his men carve into a tree the name of his ship and the date of her visit. *Endeavour* sailed past the entrance to Sydney Harbour (which Cook named Port Jackson) but did not enter because she was not in need of a haven. For the second time Cook failed to see one of the world's great natural harbours.

It was in May, as *Endeavour* sailed along in mostly good weather, that a curious event took place. Cook had a clerk by the name of Orton and one night he got very drunk and went, or was put, to bed.

For some reason or another Orton had made an enemy who went to his berth and cut off all the unconscious man's clothes. So far it was little more than a prank but then the assailant took the affair further and put it into the realms of a serious assault; he cut a piece from each of Orton's ears. Orton must have been very drunk indeed not to feel pain and it is difficult to believe the wounds did not bring him round in a very short time.

It was never established who committed the deed but Cook's suspicions centred on a midshipman called Magra. Cook had a poor opinion of Magra, calling him: ' . . . one of those gentlemen frequently found on board the King's ships, that can very well be spared, or to speake more planer good for nothing'. Magra was vulnerable because he had previously been heard to say that only the law had prevented him from murdering Orton. Cook was unable to establish Magra's guilt but he dismissed him from the quarter deck and suspended him from duty. If an injustice had been done it was at least partially mitigated in June when Magra was restored to his position. The incident must have been taken very seriously because, when *Endeavour* eventually reached Batavia, the officers offered a reward of fifteen guineas and fifteen gallons of arrack to anyone who could give any information, but there were no takers. It was then that one of the midshipmen deserted. Patrick Saunders had been in Clerke's party observing the Passage of Venus on Tahiti and he had later been suspected of being involved in some way with the Orton incident. No case was proved against him and he may have had other reasons, but pestilential Batavia was not the place most men would have chosen to leave a homeward bound ship.

The Great Barrier Reef is an outcrop made up of rock and coral rising abruptly from the sea bed. It is a vast structure running for several hundred miles from north to south off the north-eastern coast of Australia, most of it permanently submerged.

As night was drawing near on the evening of 11th June 1770 *Endeavour* was sailing easily under double reefed topsails, between ten and fourteen miles from land. Ever careful, Cook intended to keep well off shore during the hours of darkness and he had a man in the bows taking soundings as she went. The readings he called out gave no cause for concern for at 9.00 p.m. there were between fourteen and twenty fathoms of water under the keel. Suddenly, and without warning, the depth halved and all hands were called to stations to drop anchor. The leadsman called out that the water was again as deep as it had been before and all was thought to be well.

Just before 11.00 p.m., with seventeen fathoms apparently beneath her and without any warning, *Endeavour* struck. The sails were taken in and the boats were launched to enable soundings to be taken around the vessel. Although she was stuck fast, there was ample water not far off, both on the starboard side and astern. It could not have happened at a worse time, for it was high tide and as the water went down there was a distinct chance that the strains put on the ship's timbers would break her back.

So began the nightmare. There was no possible hope of help from a passing ship and no shipyard within thousands of miles, even if the vessel could be dragged clear of the reef.

At the time of the next high tide, 11.00 a.m. the following morning, an anchor was dropped into the clear water astern and the crew tried to pull her clear. Between forty and fifty tons of non-essential items were thrown over the side—iron and stone ballast, oil jars and even drinking water. The guns went, too, and one which was recovered in 1969 is now in the National Maritime Museum in Greenwich, not far from where it started its life. *Endeavour* would not budge, she began to take in water and the pumps were started. Everyone, Clerke, Banks, and even Cook took a hand in the work which was so strenuous that shifts of only a quarter of an hour were possible.

At 5.00 p.m., when the tide again began to flood, three of the four pumps were going (the fourth refused to work) but they were unable to prevent the water level rising in the hold. By the time 9.00 p.m. had come round concern was becoming acute because by then the water was gaining even more rapidly. Cook had to take a crucial decision, knowing full well that if he made a mistake and his gamble failed it was likely none of his crew would survive. He was well aware that the manoeuvre he must now carry out could tear the bottom out of his ship but near the time of high tide he ordered all hands who were not at the pumps to man the capstan. Every man in the ship strained with all his might at his appointed station, hoping desperately to hear the first click as the cable came in. Their united muscle power earned its reward when, at last, the ship began to move, terribly slowly at first, and finally came clear at 10.20 p.m.

Water was now flooding in at an alarming rate and Cook seriously began to consider running *Endeavour* ashore and building some sort of a vessel from her remains but one of his junior officers enabled him to avoid such a drastic move. Jonathan Monkhouse, one of the midshipmen, had seen a technique known as 'fothering' used on a merchantman which had begun to leak in mid-Atlantic during a voyage from Virginia to London. Neither Cook nor any of his more senior officers, including Clerke who had been in damaged ships during the Seven Years War, had any experience of the method but the situation was desperate enough, and Cook sensible and humble enough, to give Monkhouse his head. On June 13th an old sail laced with oakum was passed under the ship near the starboard fore-chains where the leak was thought to be worst. The outside pressure of the sea pushed the fabric into the wound and the intake of water immediately slowed down so that only one pump was needed to control the inflow. 'I must say that no men behaved better than they have done on this occasion'. wrote Cook.

The next problem was to find a place where *Endeavour* could be safely beached. The coast was quite unexplored and no suitable creek or inlet was visible from the masthead. The weather, which up till then had been mercifully calm, began to deteriorate but the plugging continued to hold. One of the Mates, it may well have been Clerke, was sent ahead in the pinnace and came back to report that a good harbour lay some six miles to leeward. *Endeavour* followed the boat as it closed the land but strong winds forced her to drop anchor about a mile off shore. Eventually, on Monday the 18th, she was warped in close to a steeply rising beach and the crew started to move as many stores as they could from the ship. This allowed them to get her even closer in shore and she finally came to rest with her bow driven into the river bank and her stern afloat. When the tide ebbed she was turned onto her side and the full extent of the damage became clear for all to see. It was even worse than expected and it was clear *Endeavour* had escaped destruction by the smallest of margins. A piece of coral had been snapped off by the impact on the reef and become stuck in the hole, thus forming a bung which reduced the inflow of water from catastrophic to manageable proportions.

Cook named the river after his ship and the land at its mouth he aptly called Cape Tribulation. Before long, Aborigines appeared and in the eyes of the sailors their behaviour was volatile and unpredictable; most of the time they showed every sign of friendliness but there were occasions when they were the opposite. One day the Europeans killed some turtles to supplement their supplies and took the meat on board the ship. The natives asked for them and when they were refused threw two of the creatures over the side, followed by anything moveable they could find. The Aborigines then went ashore and shortly afterwards, when a party of seamen from the ship landed on the beach, they set fire to a semicircle of grass around the sailors. The only injury was to an unfortunate small pig which was

10a. above and 10b. below.

Two views of Cape Tribulation where the Endeavour *was beached although a little further up the river (which Cook named Endeavour River) than where these photographs were taken.* [Author's (G.C.) photographs]

11a.

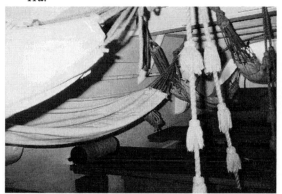

11b.

11c.

11a.-c. Three views of the interior of the replica Endeavour *taken during the* Endeavour's *British tour 1997. The relatively cramped conditions are evident.* [Author's photographs (G.C.)]

roasted before the natives were driven off by a volley of small shot.

A strange animal was seen by a shooting party, one which was: 'something less than a greyhound, it was of a mouse colour and slender made and swift of foot'. They had seen their first young kangaroo.

The ship's carpenters worked with none of the facilities available in Deptford. The only materials they had were those brought from England and whatever could be found nearby. Their work was spurred on by a will to survive, a motivation not often found in the Royal Dockyards. *Endeavour* was made seaworthy and after several unsuccessful attempts she was refloated on 6th July.

The next problem to be faced was how she could regain the open sea. The ship was inside the Barrier Reef and must somehow cross it again if she was to get home. Several times Cook and Banks climbed to the highest place they could find and spent hours looking through telescopes for an escape route, but all they could see were shoals. The Master was sent out in the ship's boats to find a way through and at his first attempt came back to report that he had been successful. Cook was ever mistrustful of Molyneux and sent him off again. This time he returned to say he had been over twenty miles out to sea and still there were shoals beyond his boat. Even the winds were contrary but at last they swung round and, on 5th August, *Endeavour* was warped out. Next day she was under sail and and making towards the north, blown along by a south-easterly breeze.

She cruised inside the reef for eight days always with one of her boats ahead until, on 14th August, the pinnace found a way through. It was still a dangerous place to be because two days later *Endeavour* was going along more than thirty miles off shore when there was almost a repetition of the episode on the Barrier Reef. The vessel was in water too deep to anchor in when the wind fell into a flat calm. All the ship's boats were launched and took her in tow but they could not prevent her drifting to within a hundred yards of where the sea was breaking on a wall of near vertical coral. Then, to the relief of everyone aboard, a small breeze came up and, together with the ebb tide, carried her through a small gap in the reef. Cook thought the danger was worse than it had been in June and that the life of every man on board had been in even greater jeopardy.

For the extra safety of future navigators, it was important that the position of the reef be accurately recorded so, while all this was going on, Charles Clerke was taking a lunar fix with the astronomer Charles Green.

The area was strewn with shoals so frequent as to make navigating the east coast of England seem like child's play and Cook named it the Labyrinth. They passed safely through it and reached the extreme northeast corner of Australia, which Cook named Cape York, on 21st August. Next day he went ashore, hoisted the Union flag and took possession of all the land of the east coast of Australia as far south as 38° S. and named it New South Wales.

Cook's views of the country and the people were probably typical of those of the whole crew. He thought the coast had a number of fine harbours but that, although the land was capable of growing grain and fruits, it did not produce anything that would entice Europeans to trade or found a settlement; Banks was yet to make his recommendation of what should be done with the convicts. Cook thought the native people not to be '. . . a warlike People . . . I think them a timorous inoffensive race, no ways inclined to cruelty . . . From what I have said of the Natives of New Holland they may appear to some to be the most wretched people upon Earth, but in reality they are far more happy than we Europeans'.

Cook thought there was a strait between Australia and New Guinea and having rounded Cape York he turned *Endeavour* towards the west and Batavia where the Dutch East India Company had established a settlement.

Cook passed Timor and continued towards the west until *Endeavour* came to the small island of Savu, which lay between there and Java. A Dutch flag had been seen, the first sign of European habitation that had been observed for many months, and on Tuesday 18th September Clerke's friend John Gore was sent off in a boat to investigate. He returned to report that provisions could be obtained but only with the approval of the Governor who proved to be a German. Johan Lange came on board the next day when he was entertained at an alcoholic lunch during the course of which he promised Solander and Sporing of Banks' party, both of whom could speak Dutch, that there would be no problem with supplies. With the exception of a few small bullocks, bought at a high price, the provisions failed to materialise and the sailors had to continue on their way with what they already had.

The Admiralty was determined to keep control over the publication of any information of where the ship had been and of what discoveries she had made. Now that *Endeavour* was nearing a port controlled by the Dutch, Cook collected all the journals which had been kept by the crew and put them under lock and key.

On Wednesday 3rd October 1770 the explorers met the first

European ship since leaving Rio. The captain of the Dutch vessel told them of troubles in America where the settlers were refusing to pay taxes, and of anti-royalist riots in the streets of London.

Eleven days later, at 4.00 pm on 14th October, _Endeavour_ dropped anchor in Batavia Roads. Already at anchor were thirteen Dutch ships, one from England and two from ports in English possession. _Endeavour_ had not a single sick man aboard and the crew laughed at the sickly appearance of the Dutch sailors they met. They were being a little premature because, although the town was the trading capital of the East, it was also one of the most unhealthy places on the face of the earth. It competed for the title with the West Indies which had such an awful reputation that it was not unknown for British regiments to mutiny when being told of their being posted there. Batavia's open sewers made a flourishing breeding ground for all manner of diseases, particularly dysentery, and clouds of mosquitoes covered every available stretch of water, making malaria commonplace.

Cook's methods, observed by Clerke and used by him in a later voyage, had resulted in only one man being lost to disease, a phenomenal achievement at that time and after such a long voyage. All that now changed and _Endeavour's_ crew was almost overwhelmed by illness. Cook, Banks, Clerke and every man except one was laid low with either malaria or dysentery. The only man not affected at this time was an elderly sailmaker, and he was drunk every day. On 7th November Dr. Monkhouse became the first to die and he was followed by seven others, even though a tented hospital was set up ashore. Not much could be done for those who fell sick and when a man noticed the first symptoms he considered himself to be beyond hope.

By the time _Endeavour_ left Batavia on Boxing Day 1770, only about a dozen men were fit enough to work her. Cook signed on nineteen English sailors in the port, all of them understandably anxious to get home, and this enabled the ship to leave. Cook was not impressed by Batavia and he wrote in his Journal:

> Batavia is a place that Europeans need not covert to go to, but if necessity oblige them they will do well to make their stay as short as possible otherwise they will soon feel the effects of the unwholesome air of Batavia which I firmly believe is the death of more Europeans than any other place upon the Globe of the same extent, such at least is my opinion of it which is founded on facts. We came in here with as healthy a ships company as need go to sea and after a stay of not quite 3 Months left it in the

condition of a Hospital Ship besides the loss of 7 Men and yet all the Dutch Captains I had an oppertunity to convers with said that we had been very lucky and wondered that we had not lost half our people in that time.

The ship, too, was in poor condition, worse than had been supposed, and the worm had got through the defences of the copper-covered bottom. Cook called a conference of all his officers and they decided what repairs were necessary to make *Endeavour* fit for the journey home. They were short of money but the Dutch Governor, Petrus van der Parra, would not allow the work to be done by the crew— they were probably too weak anyhow— and insisted that most of the repairs be done by local dockyard labour. The work they carried out was of a good standard and Cook thought that they used techniques which could usefully be adopted in England.

The Dutch ships anchored in Batavia harbour were gathering for the annual return of the fleet to Holland. They marked the appointment of the Commodore with a ceremony witnessed by *Endeavour's* crew but Cook, for one, was not impressed for he thought the ships were ill armed and badly manned.

The deaths continued even after *Endeavour* left Batavia. If anything, the dysentery was worse after she made the open sea on 17th January 1771. Marine corporal Jno Truslove died a week later and the deaths continued until the end of February. Alcohol had not given immunity to Jno Ravenhill, the drunken sailmaker, and he was one to die at this time and Charles Green, the astronomer who had taught Clerke the new technique of navigation, another. The second Monkhouse brother, the midshipman who had saved the ship by suggesting the use of the fothering technique after the accident on the Barrier Reef, also perished. Herman Sporing and Sidney Parkinson, the painter, both of Banks' party, did not recover from their illnesses. Robert Molyneux, the Master to whom Charles Clerke was Mate, was one of the last to die. Of him, Cook wrote '. . . a young man of good parts but had unfortunately given himself up to extravecancy and intemporance which brought on disorders that put a pirod to his life.'

Twenty-four men died between Batavia and the Cape— on one day alone four men perished— and by the time Cape Town was reached one third of *Endeavour's* crew was dead. She arrived off the coast of Africa on 5th March at about 32° S., just below where Durban now stands. She rounded Cape Agulhas, the southernmost tip of Africa, with a southeast wind to help her and next day, Thursday 14th March, she entered Table Bay to the salutes of the ships already there, Dutch, French, Danish and English.

There were still many sick men on board and they were taken ashore. The more healthy ones were given leave and ten extra hands were signed on. A month was spent in effecting repairs to both the ship and her crew before *Endeavour* set out on the last leg of her journey to England.

In mid-April she left the Cape and went to St Helena where, on 1st May, she found a homeward bound convoy awaiting a favourable wind. There were twelve Indiamen and two warships at anchor in the harbour and at first it was thought that the presence of the Navy vessels meant that war had broken out. This was not the case and three days later *Portland*, the commanding officer's ship, having hoisted the signal for the fleet to make sail, all the vessels sailed out of the harbour. *Endeavour* had been built for the East Coast trade, not for speed, and it soon became obvious that she was slower than her companions. She managed to stay in contact for three weeks but, before she was forced to part company with them on the 24th, Cook had a doctor come over from one of the ships to see if anything could be done for Lieutenant Hicks. He was found to be beyond hope and Cook entered in his record:

> . . . departed this life Lieut. Hicks and in the evening his body was committed to the Sea with the usual ceremonies; he died of a Consumption which he was not free from when we sailed from England so it it may be truly said that he hath been dieing ever sense tho he held out tollerably well until we got to Batavia.

The death of poor Hicks, who was 32 years old and a steady, reliable man, proved to be to Clerke's advantage although it is difficult to believe he would have wished his promotion to come in the way it did. Cook recorded on May 22nd:

> This day I gave Mr Charles Clerk an order to Act as Lieutenant in the Room of Mr. Hicks deceased, he being a young Man well quallified for that Station.

He was well qualified because he had passed the necessary examinations on 10th June 1766, a month after his return from the *Dolphin* voyage.[1]

The death of Hicks placed Cook in something of a personal quandary because his eldest son, also called James, had been entered in the ship's muster as officer's servant to Hicks in the rank of A.B. The boy was not aboard, being not yet nine years old, and had never left London. The entry was there so that if James decided on a Naval career he would be able to claim extra sea time and therefore be allowed to take his Lieutenant's exam earlier than he would otherwise have done. Strictly speaking, this was illegal but nevertheless it was common practice. On Hicks' demise the problem was solved by James Cook being entered in the muster as servant to Charles Clerke.

They were quite frequently meeting other ships now and picking up news from them. One, a whaler out of one of the New England ports, told them that there was peace in Europe and that the dispute with the American states had been patched up. A Liverpool ship must have given cause for wry comments because its crew told Cook's men that in London bets were being placed on their survival.

On 10th July Land's End came into view and *Endeavour* began the run up Channel. Two days later she picked up a pilot and one thousand and seventy-four days after leaving England, at 3.00 p.m. on Saturday, 13th July 1771, *Endeavour* dropped anchor in the Downs. One of the first things Cook did was to write to the Admiralty. Telling them of the death of Hicks he continued:

> . . . the vacancy made on this occasion I filled up by appointing
> Mr. Charles Clerke, a young Man well worthy of it, and as such
> must beg leave to recommend him to their Lordships. . . [2]

The return of the ship and her crew from the other, unknown, side of the world— an event equivalent in modern times to getting back from the Moon— might reasonably be expected to elicit some excited comment from the Press. Not a bit of it. On 2nd August 1771 the Chelmsford Chronicle celebrated the return of a ship in whose crew was a local man by reporting:

> H.M. ship *Endeavour* which is lately arrived in the river from the
> East Indies lost, by the unhealthiness of the climate, 70 of her
> hands, though they be picked hands and had been several times
> in the Indies. However, those that survive will have made their
> fortunes by traffic, having brought home some of the richest
> goods made in the East, which they are suffered to dispose of
> without the inspection of custom house officers. This, our
> correspondent says, is allowed them by government, as a reward
> for their hard and dangerous services, during a voyage of three
> years.

Neither was Cook being swamped with praise. He and his men took second place to the scientists, Banks in particular, and on 23rd August the Chronicle stated:

> Yesterday lieut Cook of the navy, who sailed round the globe
> with Dr Solander and Mr Banks, was introduced to his majesty
> at St. James . . .

CHAPTER FIVE

RESOLUTION

CLERKE RECOVERED FROM THE ILLNESS he had contracted in Batavia and on his return to England went home to Wethersfield where his father now had the Manor. Joseph was Charles' only surviving parent, his mother having died fifteen years earlier.

Cook was well satisfied with Clerke's performance and one of the first things he did when he returned in *Endeavour* was to write to the Admiralty: 'begging leave to recommend him to their Lordships'. The Admiralty agreed almost immediately and his appointment to 3rd Lieutenant on *Endeavour* was confirmed in a Minute on 31st July 1771.

Most people living in Wethersfield had never seen a ship, let alone been aboard one, and the homecoming of Charles from the other side of the world must have caused a sensation. He was a noted raconteur and his tales of near shipwreck and cannibals, which no doubt lost nothing in the telling, would find a ready audience at the dinner tables and hostelries of the village.

He was again asked to be a witness at a wedding. Thomas Whips and Mary Turner were married in the village church on 12th October 1771.[1] They were humble people for neither could write and each had to sign the certificate with a cross.

His fellow witness was his friend John Gore. He was a rare sight in Wethersfield, for not only was he a sailor, he was also an American, probably from Virginia. He was about eleven years older than Charles and had served as a Midshipman in *Windsor* during the Seven Years War before meeting Clerke on his transfer to *Bellona*. Gore had then circumnavigated the globe with both Byron and Wallis before sailing as Third Lieutenant, and then Second on the death of Hicks, in *Endeavour*.

A man with his background might be expected to spend his time ashore in places such as London, Plymouth or Portsmouth but Gore seems to have had a rather obscure connection with Braintree, a town about seven miles from Wethersfield. Four years later he wrote to Joseph Banks from *Resolution*, as she was about to sail from Plymouth, in terms which open up more questions than are answered:

> The Young one who you was so kind As to promise an attention
> To in Case of my Death, is under the Care of the Reverend Mr

73.

> Firebrass of Braintree in Essex . . . The Bearer of this [note, a
> Mrs Baker] is she who Petition'd To go the voyage with us, I
> wou'd have supported her in it did I not think it Wou'd prove
> inconvenient To her-self, she has Merit however appearances or
> her present Situation may be . . .

Gore obviously had some responsibility for the child but whether
they were assumed or the result of his being the father is obscure.
Who was Mrs Baker, who appears to have fallen on hard times? The
letter does not refer to her as the child's mother—was she its nanny
or guardian? In what capacity was she wishing to sail with them—
Gore must have been referring to the voyage to Iceland which he
undertook with Banks in 1772—and what would have been the
child's position if she had gone? Firebrass is an unusual name and it
smacks of being a pseudonym; there is no record of a clergyman of
that name in the Established Church serving in any part of Essex at
that time. The matter remains a mystery.

Clerke was to overtake Gore on the promotion ladder but the two
remained friends up to the time of Clerke's death. Gore sailed with
Charles on his last voyage and before his career was over he had
made the rank of Post Captain. He spent his last days as one of the
captains in charge of the Royal Naval Hospital at Greenwich before
dying at the age of about sixty.

Just outside Wethersfield, a mile along the road to Finchingfield, is
a house called Sculpins. In Clerke's time it was owned by Sir John
Marshall, a jolly soul who every Thursday kept open house to 'keep
alight the taper of old-fashioned hospitality'.[2] One of the pleasures he
provided was a large bowling green which, with its shades of Drake,
offered a fitting pastime for sailors. What else went on is perhaps
best left to the imagination for Coller writes that Sir John kept open
house for 'all comers to indulge the weekly carouse of licensed
revelry—with what effect upon the morals and habits of the
parishioners babbling history saith not'. It requires no great feat of
imagination to conjure up a picture of Clerke and Gore making their
way through the village and going up the winding road to Sculpins on
a weekly pilgrimage of Bacchanalian enjoyment.

For most people, two circumnavigations of the Earth would have
been enough but Charles Clerke was nothing if he was not a
professional seaman and he was now about to embark upon a third.
When the time came for him to sail again, on 13th July 1772, he had
been in England a year to the day. This was little enough time after
the long journeys he had already completed but he seized the
opportunity of going on what has been called 'perhaps the greatest

sailing ship voyage ever made'.[3]

Clerke's performance on the last voyage had impressed his captain and Cook now chose him to go on the next expedition. Sailing with the great navigator was coming to be regarded as an honour to be prized, a useful entry in the curriculum vitae of an ambitious young naval officer. Many who sailed with him prospered in years to come; Burney (the brother of Fanny, the novelist), Vancouver, Riou, and Bligh all reached positions of prominence before their lives were done. Cook had sufficient confidence in Clerke to appoint him Second Lieutenant on the coming expedition, having seen how his character was developing. He was now thirty-one years of age, a 'Brave and good officer, a general Favorite' wrote Elliott, and although he enjoyed the 'social' life, as he himself called it, there was another dimension to him. He was no longer the carefree youth of earlier years but a mature, highly experienced, competent seaman and if he remained genial and good company there was also a steadiness of purpose about him. He had built up good connections in a navy where patronage was important but the advancement of his career was based more upon his personal qualities than upon influence. On 28th October he: 'Rec'd a commission for His Majesty's Ship *Drake* which sloop I found in Dry Dock at Deptfotd'.[4]

His commission was noted in an Admiralty Minute dated 27th November 1771. 'Cook to command *Drake* and Lieuts Robert Palliser Cooper and Chas Clerke First and Second Lieutenants.'

The Admiralty was well aware of how close to disaster *Endeavour* had been on the Great Barrier Reef and of the desperately anxious hours her crew had spent before they saved her. To increase the margin of safety it was decided to revert to the former strategy and send two ships on the forthcoming expedition. *Endeavour* was not available for the voyage because she had been sent to the Falkland Islands but she had vindicated Cook's faith in Whitby-built Cats and had done everything demanded of her. The almost new ships purchased for the voyage had been constructed in the same town, were of the same type, and came from the Fishburn yard. They were bought from Captain Hammond of Hull and were called *Marquis of Granby* and *Marquis of Rockingham*. Although now forgotten, the men after whom they were named were then well known figures: Granby was John Manners, a soldier who had fought on the English side during the Jacobite rebellion and gone on to command the British army on the continent and won a victory at Minden; Rockingham was a Yorkshire landowner and a Whig who became First Minister in 1765 before being replaced by Pitt. Their names were not destined to go down in the history of exploration for the Navy rechristened them *Drake* and *Raleigh* but these names were dropped when it was realised that they would not endear them to the Spaniards who still had a presence in the Pacific. They were renamed *Resolution* and *Adventure*. *Resolution*, at 462 tons, was the larger with a crew of 112; *Adventure* displaced 340 tons and had eighty-one men.

The officer appointed to the command of *Adventure* was Tobias Furneaux, a thirty-seven year-old Devonian who, as Wallis' Lieutenant on *Dolphin*, had brought the ship home when his captain became ill. He was a well liked man but, as events were to prove, without the determination required of a successful explorer.

Even before *Endeavour's* return to England, Cook had been planning another expedition to settle once and for all whether or not there was a Great Southern Continent. He realised he had not covered all the possibilities of where it might be and, although he was no less sceptical than he had always been, he now proposed no less an enterprise than circling the South Pole in as high a latitude as he could. The vast distances which would have to be covered and the weather conditions which could be expected made it a huge task but he planned to tackle it, once he had arrived in the region, by always sailing towards the East, thus taking advantage of the prevailing westerly winds. The climate dictated that his intended sweeps towards the south must be made during the short Antarctic summer but Cook had no intention of wasting time when winter came and he was forced northward again. It was then that he would go cruising and make whatever discoveries came his way, once more using Queen Charlotte Sound and Tahiti as his bases.

As usual, the Admiralty had more than one purpose in mind. As in the *Endeavour* voyage, one of their main concerns was to do with navigation, such a vital subject for mariners. A ship's commander could be absolutely certain of his position only when he was in sight of a known landmark but as soon as he lost sight of the shore he had to rely on methods which were much less accurate. Sailors had long been able to set their latitude by using astrolabes, backstaffs, or cross-staffs, instruments which measured the height of the sun or a given star over the horizon, but the fixing of longitude presented greater problems. All that could be done was to use a system of dead reckoning, a method which judged the speed and drift of a ship and took into account the probable effect of known currents. It was more than an inspired guess, for a skilled captain was often fairly accurate, but it had obvious and serious defects. One method which had developed for getting to a place with an accurately known latitude but an uncertain longitude involved sailing down the line of latitude to about the supposed longitude and then to continue along that line, east or west as the case might be, until the destination was reached, hoping all the while not to collide with it.

These methods were far from ideal and in 1714 Parliament was so concerned to reduce the number of vessels lost by shipwreck that it passed an Act which set up a Board of Longitude. In these modern times a ship or an aircraft can set its position to within a few yards at the press of a button but the importance the Board attached to the matter in the eighteenth century may be judged by the size of the £20,000 prize it offered to the inventor of a system which could set longitude to an accuracy of half a degree.

The problem appeared to be quite simple because all that was required was to know the precise time in two different places: aboard a ship and at a place of known longitude, a location which eventually became Greenwich. One hours difference between the times is equal to fifteen degrees of longitude.

The two ways in which the problem could be overcome may be classified as the celestial and the mechanical.

One of the celestial methods took advantage of the moons of Jupiter. There were several hundred predictable eclipses of one or another of them each year and the time one was observed at a particular place on the earth could be compared with the time it was known it would occur at Greenwich. Another was the lunar method, particularly favoured and developed by the Astronomer Royal, the Rev. Nevil Maskelyne, which depended upon an accurate map of the stars and a prediction of when the moon would pass by any one of them. Hadley had developed the quadrant which enabled navigators to measure the angle between the moon and a given star; reference to a set of tables gave the time at which the same observation would be made in Greenwich. These techniques suffered from problems of parallax and the refraction of light, not to mention the difficulty of holding an instrument steady on a heaving deck. Not only that, the mathematical calculations which followed were very complicated, involved spherical trigonometry and took upwards of four hours to carry out. Maskelyne's technique was the one Charles Green, the astronomer, had taught Charles Clerke during the *Endeavour* voyage.

The theory of the mechanical method appeared to have the attraction of simplicity since all that was required were watches which were accurate and reliable enough to show the time at Greenwich and wherever the ship happened to be. The practical difficulties were immense because the swing of the pendulum of clocks then in use varied with the roll of the ship, barometric pressure, temperature, and the pull of the Earth's gravity. These problems were overcome by a Yorkshireman called John Harrison who had been born in 1693 and learned woodworking from his father after the family moved to Lincolnshire. His early clocks were made almost entirely from wood but in the later ones he used metal. When Harrison heard of the prize being offered by the Board of Longitude he set to work to build the first of his seagoing timepieces, machines which came to be called chronometers. His first, 'H-1', worked well but Harrison was nothing if not a perfectionist and it took him many years to make improved versions called 'H-2' and 'H-3'. Eventually, in 1759, he produced his masterpiece, 'H-4', a machine which was only five inches in diameter and weighed three pounds. Harrison wanted Cook to take 'H-4' with him on his second Pacific voyage but the Board decided it was too valuable and must stay at home. In 1770 Larcum Kendall had made a cheaper copy of Harrison's machine, costing £450, and this was the piece Cook took with him in 1772 and 1776; it stopped at about the time of Cook's death in 1779. Kendall built 'K-3' for £100 in 1774 and Charles Clerke took it with him in *Discovery* in 1776. John Arnold was another maker but Cook was not impressed with the first three machines he had made when he took them on the 1772-75 expedition because they were made inaccurate by the cold.

The machines were always kept low down in the ship and when a fix was due to be made a man was sent to set the time from the chronometer on a watch which was then taken to the quarter deck. These deck watches were eventually used for other purposes, such as timing the fall of shot. The Admiralty came to hold annual competitions to determine which manufacturers were making the most accurate pieces and for many years they bought the best ones for prices of up to £20 or £25.

Harrison and Maskelyne became enemies and it was only by appealing to George III that Harrison was able, after a delay of many years, to get most of the £20,000 prize from the Board of Longitude. Chronometers were much more expensive than the relatively simple instruments needed for the celestial methods and there was always the possibility of a breakdown, no matter how carefully the clocks were handled. Most mariners did not put their exclusive trust in either procedure and made use of both methods in a system of double checking.

In common with all other naval officers, Cook and Clerke took a keen interest in these new developments because when they were at sea the safety of the ships and crews for which they were responsible depended upon their ability accurately to fix a position.

In the meantime there were land based problems to be overcome. The most formidable one concerned Charles' friend from Lincolnshire.

Joseph Banks was a powerful man whose enormous income was matched by his ambitions and he decided to make a second voyage with Cook, again taking with him his botanical friend Dr. Solander. Banks, who had the ear of the King, was a friend of Lord Sandwich, the First Lord, and used his influence, together with an estimated £5000 of his own money, to advance his plans. It was not long before Banks came to regard the expedition as his own personal enterprise and in his mind the role of the Navy was relegated to that of providing the transport:

> Mr Banks seems thought to consider the ships as fitted out wholly for his use the whole undertaking to depend on him and his people and himself as the Director and Conductor of the whole; for which he is not qualified and if granted him would have been the greatest disgrace that could be put on His Majesty's Naval officers.[5]

Banks' retinue continued to grow and it was soon apparent that *Resolution* would not be able to accommodate all those he intended taking with him. The Navy Board had originally intended to slightly raise the upper works of the ship but Banks insisted that this would not provide his party with sufficient extra space. A more ambitious plan was adopted, against the advice of Cook but with the support of Sandwich, who was not a sailor, which involved the installation of a whole new deck. This was still not enough for Banks, a large man well over 6 ft tall, had not had sufficent personal space on *Endeavour* and he now insisted that Cook give up his cabin. The captain was to be moved into a structure built on the deck which became known as the 'Round House'. Cook knew full well that all these alterations would make the ship top-heavy and Hugh Palliser, who was now Controller of the Navy, was of the same mind. Clerke was an experienced seaman and he knew *Resolution* well because he had joined her on 23rd December 1771 and had spent four months helping to prepare her for sea. With his eye for a ship he, too, must have been disconcerted by the changes he had seen being made to *Resolution*.

She was taken on her sea trials on 15th May and at once succeeded in thoroughly alarming everyone on board. The sailors were relieved when they reached a safe haven and on his, perhaps fortunate, return to Sheerness Clerke wrote to his friend Banks:

> We weigh'd anchor at Graves-End this morning at about 10 O'Clock, with a fine Breeze from the Eastward, the wind from that quarter, laid us under the necessity of working down the Reaches which work, I'm sorry to tell you, we found the *Resolution* very unequal to; for whilst several light colliers were working down with their whole Topsails, Staysails etc one small Brig in particular with her Top Gallant Sails; these light vessels so upright, that a Marble wou'd hardly rowl from Windward to Leeward, the *Resolution* I give you my honour, under her reeft Topsails, Jibb and Main Top Mast Staysail, heel'd within three Streaks of her Gun Ports. She is so very bad, that the Pilot declares, he will not run the risk of his Character so far, as to to take charge of her, farther than the Nore without a fair wind, that he cannot with safety to himself attempt working her to the Downs. Hope you know me too well, to impute my giving this intelligence to any ridiculous apprehension for myself, by God I'll go to Sea in a Grog Tub if desir'd or in the *Resolution* as soon as you please; but must say, I do think her by far the most unsafe ship, I ever saw or heard of; however if you think proper to embark for the South Pole in a Ship, which a Pilot (who I think is, by no means a timorous man) will not undertake to carry down the River; all I can say, is, that you shall be most cheerfully attended to, so long as we can keep her above water.[6]

He wrote to his sister-in-law, Lady Lydia Clerke, at the same time and in similar terms:

> . . . I believe there never was such a ship before upon the Seas since Commodore Noah (who was the first Sea Officer of any kind that I ever heard of) to this present 19th of May 1772—The last time I had the pleasure to see my Dear Sis you know the *Resolution* was at Long Reach, we've left that place now 11 days, to be sure we've had rather a confusion of orders, and a little sailing backwards and forwards but it 'tould have saved our Lives, we cou'd not have got to the Downs, where we were order'd our first sailing, tho' make no doubt but some Vessels who sail'd at the same time with us may have got 300 leagues off to sea.[7]

Even allowing for Clerke's idiosyncratic punctuation and for the humour of his letters he was describing an alarming experience, a voyage which had been frightening even in the sheltered waters of the Thames Estuary. By now the Navy Board had had enough:

There is much concern at news of Raleigh proving so crank, as she has a very promising body and good dimensions and did well as a merchant ship. The trouble must be attributed to the accommodation for passengers and the quantity of heavy stowage. It is proposed she be ordered to Sheerness and alterations made in her . . . [8]

So to Sheerness she went and there a veritable army of carpenters and shipwrights descended on her and began to take out the recently installed structures for which Banks had paid good money and which were the cause of her instability. By June she was back to her previous, entirely satisfactory, condition and Clerke was able to record in his journal on Monday 22nd June:

. . . sailed out of the Harbour to the Nore . . . to try what effect the alterations had made upon Ship and soon found to our very great satisfaction that it had entirely remedied every ill quality she had—found her now a stiff ship—worked well and readily got every good way through the water.

To say that Banks was not pleased to see all the work for which he had paid being taken out would be something of an understatement. John Elliot, a Midshipman on *Resolution*, left an account of what then happened:

When this was done, Mr Banks was requested to go to Sheerness and take a view of the accommodations as they now stood, and try if he could go out in her, for in no other state could she go to sea, and go she must. Mr Banks came to Sheerness and when he saw the Ship, and the alterations that were made, He swore and stamped upon the Warfe, like a Mad Man, and instantly ordered his Servants and all his things out of the Ship.[9]

Whatever possessed Banks to think he knew more about the sailing qualities of ships than the experienced sailors with whom he had already been to the other side of the globe? How could he have defied the unanimous opinion of men like Palliser, Cook, and Clerke that *Resolution* in the form into which he had put her was top-heavy, unsafe and quite unsuitable for the waters of the Channel, let alone the stormy seas she would meet in the Antarctic? He wrote to Lord Sandwich on 30th May 1772:

. . . will the public be so ungenerous as to expect me to go out in a Ship, in which my people have not the Room necessary for performing the different Duties of their Professions, in a Ship apparently unhealthy and probably unsafe, merely in conformity to the official opinion of the Navy Board, who purchas'd her without even consulting me . . . [10]

This appears to be arrogance on the grand scale but he went on in the same letter to say that his personal requirements were modest, six square feet being adequate for his personal needs, and his real complaint centred on the lack of space in the Great Cabin in which his men would have to work. However, he was still undeterred and tried to persuade the Admiralty to provide him with a Ship of the Line. Not surprisingly, their Lordships refused him and eventually he hired a ship and took himself and Solander off on an expedition to Iceland. Banks invited Clerke and Gore to go with him but, although the latter accepted, Clerke thought he had committed himself so far he could not withdraw. Despite his friendship with Banks, his sense of loyalty to Cook and the Navy were greater; once he had given his word, there was no turning back.

Clerke wrote to Banks on the last day of May:

> *Resolution* at Sheerness
>
> I yesterday receiv'd your favour, and indeed am very sorry, I'm not to have the honour of attending you the other boat: Am exceedingly oblig'd to you, my good Sir, for your kind concern on my account: but have stood too far on this tack to think of putting about with any kind of credit, so must have recourse to my old Maxim: 'if I can't do as well as I wou'd, I'll do as well as I can ' and fear not, but I shall weather all . . . Captain Cook never explain'd his scheme of Stowage to any of us. We were all very desirous of knowing, for it must have been a new plan intirely: I know he kept whatever scheme he had quite a secret. Mr Cooper asked my opinion, and repeatedly declar'd he could form no idea how it was possible to bring it about. Mr Palliser was here yesterday, spent some time in looking about and examining her; the're going to stow the major part of the Cables in the Hold, to make room for the People even now; I ask'd Gilbert, if such was the present case, what the divil shou'd we have done, if we had all gone. Oh my God that was impossible, was his answer. . . . Wish you'd send me a Venture by me, of one of your small Cags of large Nails, for by what I hear, they are much better than any of my freight.

A great deal of provisions and equipment had been taken into *Resolution's* hold and stored in a way that had mystified Clerke and his fellow officers; there was so much the ship was riding too deep in the water and twenty tons of ballast had to be taken out.

Banks did not take umbrage at Clerke's refusal to go with him. On 17th June 1772 Clerke wrote a final letter to him from Sheerness before he sailed:

I receiv'd yours by your servant and am very much obliged for the Cag of Nails—think I am now set out compleatly freighted for the South Sea Marts, hope to make a good trading voyage of it, go matters how they will, and stow away in a curios Cabinet of Miti (*note—Tahitian for good*) curiosities at my return—flatter myself with the hopes of making an addition to the Burlington Street collection, will certainly make some increase, and I hope a good one; for shall be happy my actions shou'd bespeak my sense of your civilities and friendship—Must again express my unhappiness that I cannot have the pleasure of attending you, but can't help it, two or three years will blow all over, and replace me in Old London and its Purlieu, Captain of at least my own Carcass, to dispose of as I please; when, I assure you, you shall never want a Sailors attendance to run any where on this side of H- - - so long as remains above water.

Clerke wanted to trade because he knew that artefacts from the Pacific fetched a high price in England and on the last expedition the crew had been exempt from Customs. There was no chance of prize money for him on the voyage he was about to undertake and this was the only way open to him to supplement his pay. Gold was a generally accepted means of exchange in most parts of the world but it was too soft a metal to be made into objects with any practical use; the people of the Pacific had a good point in placing a high value on iron because it could be shaped into tools and weapons which were far superior to the stone ones they had always used. Wherever Clerke had been in the region it had quickly taken on the status of a currency. During the previous voyage the services of a woman could at first be had for the price of a nail but when inflation inevitably made its appearance the cost rose to three. Perhaps it is uncharitable to wonder if this may have had some bearing on Banks' final gift to Clerke.

Banks' decision to go to Iceland was not quite the end of the affair. When *Resolution* arrived at Funchal in Madeira on her way south, Cook was told by the British Consul of a young gentleman who had arrived at 'The Island' on an American ship. Mr. Burnet had been there for three months, waiting for Banks' arrival in *Resolution*, when a letter was received from the amorous botanist. This was a week before the ship's arrival and explained his change of plan. It was then discovered that Mr Burnett was a lady. Cook, and no doubt Clerke too, were greatly amused.

The man selected to replace Banks as the expedition's botanist proved to be an unfortunate choice. Johann Forster was a widely read and able German who had trained as a clergyman but he was also vain and rude and seemed to go out of his way to offend his companions. Forever complaining, he was soon thoroughly disliked by everyone. He was always either looking for insults where none existed or threatening to report Cook, or any other object of his disapproval, to the Admiralty. Clerke's relationship with him was at the opposite end of the spectrum to that which he had enjoyed with Banks; even his noted affability was stretched to its limit and before the voyage was over he was offering to have the disagreeable man arrested. Forster was no more popular on land than he was at sea for when he returned from the voyage he received from Lord Sandwich a reply to a letter he had sent him which sums up the reactions he was able to evoke:

> Sir / You are misinformed if you have been told that I have promised that one half of the plates shou'd be inserted in your part of the work with a general map: I have made no such promise, nor do I intend to make one for that purpose . . . [11]

Forster had attacked Cook's work and Sandwich went on to refute his allegations with a similarly dismissive choice of words. Fortunately, Forster's son Georg, who went with his father, was of a much more pleasant disposition.

At last all was ready and *Resolution* and *Adventure* moved from London River to Plymouth where the chronometers were taken ashore on Drakes Island and set to the correct time. Although it was considered a great thing to be able to say one had sailed with Cook, for many of the seamen the prospect of an absence of three years outweighed the anticipated delights of the Pacific. Desertion before a long voyage was commonplace but this time it was on an impressive scale. Of *Resolution*'s 118 men fifty-eight made off and *Adventure* lost thirty-seven of her complement of eighty-three. They were all replaced before the two ships finally left England's shores on 13th July 1772.

Since the two black spots on the previous voyage had been Rio and Batavia, it was decided to avoid both and the ships were directed to take an easterly route round the Cape. Off the coast of Spain there was a reminder that not all hazards were found on shore. The English ships came upon a small French vessel which had almost run out of fresh water and which the previous day had been refused so much as a drop by three passing Spanish warships. *Resolution* paused long enough to send over enough to see the Frenchmen home and then went on her way. Next day she was stopped by the same Spanish ships but when their commanding officer was told who they were he wished them a good voyage and the vessels went their separate ways.

At Madeira and the Cape Verde Islands they took on water and sailed on down the Atlantic. At 'The Island' Cook had the last say in the matter of *Resolution*'s refit when he wrote to William Hammond, the previous owner of the two ships:

> . . . have the pleasure of acqnt you that I find them in all respects as well as I could wish the *Resolution* so far from being Crank is most remarkably Stiff, her enemies must now be silent on that head.[12]

During the run south the officers saw the sailing capabilities of each ship and came to the conclusion that *Resolution* was slightly the better. A month out from England the first man was lost when Henry Smock, a carpenter on *Resolution*, fell overboard and was drowned before he could be picked up. He may have been one of the many men in the Navy who had never learned to swim, sharing a popular belief that it only prolonged a man's agony if he found himself in the water.

Resolution was the healthier ship because Cook enforced higher standards than did Furneux and *Adventure* lost two Midshipmen to disease soon after leaving the Cape Verde Islands. There was no sickness on *Resolution*.

They arrived at Cape Town early in the season, on 30th October, and found no other ships in the harbour. Clerke wrote in his Journal:

> Our people are all in perfect Health and spirits, owing I believe in great measure to the strict attention of Captain Cook to their cleanliness and every other article that respects their Welfare.

This was Clerke's second visit to Cape Town which was then only a small settlement. At the time of his visits the Cape was in the hands of the Dutch, although it had been discovered by the Portuguese. Bartolomeu Dias had been looking for a new route for the spice trade to the Indies when he arrived there in 1487; the previous one, which went by sea to Arabia and then across land to Constantinople, had been broken when the Muslims took the city in 1453. Dias went as far as Mossel Bay, on the east coast, and saw the Cape on his return—he had been too far out to sea to observe it as he went eastwards.

The Portuguese rarely stopped at the Cape and did not establish a permanent settlement there, preferring to set up bases north of the

Limpopo river. The Dutch were the first to settle at Cape Town when Jan van Riebeck built a fort there in 1652 and they kept control of it until 1795 when it passed to the British. The settlement was about half way to India and it became a base from which ships could obtain water, vegetables, cattle and, in the summer months, shelter. In the winter, gales from the northwest made it too dangerous an anchorage and False Bay, a little further to the south, was used as an alternative. *Resolution* and *Adventure* arrived at the end of winter and used Table Bay.

The ships were made ready for the next stage of the voyage with special thoroughness. Everything was put in good order— hull, rigging and supplies— because the conditions in the far south would strain all to the limit.

This was the last European administered town they would see for many months to come and the crews were given shore leave. It was during a run ashore that Clerke met a Dutchman who told him of a French explorer by the name of Kerguelen who had also been in search of the Southern continent. No doubt the tale was embellished in the telling, but the story as Clerke heard it was that the Frenchman, on coming across a group of islands at 48° S. had sent a ship's boat into a bay but was then driven out to sea again by the weather. Clerke thought inconceivable that part of the account which said that the boat's crew were left to fend for themselves.

When Cook pronounced himself satisfied that his ships were fit to go, they left Cape Town on 22nd November 1772 and began the first great sweep into the Southern Ocean. Cook had made clear his intentions: 'I now intend to steer until I meet with an interruption.' Richard Pickering was Third Lieutenant on *Resolution* and he was equally succinct: 'We began our first years misery.'

Although it was midsummer in the southern hemisphere it was not long before they were in ice. Very few of the men on board had seen such conditions during their previous voyages and all were amazed by the sheer size of the icebergs they met. Fearnought clothing was issued to the crew and this helped to keep out the cold. On Saturday 12th December Clerke wrote in his Journal: 'This afternoon passed an Ice Island. I believe as high as the Body of St Paul's Church'. Two days later the ships were brought to a halt for the first time by the ice. They made their way along the seaward side of the pack, always sailing towards the east and at the same time seeking to edge towards the south.

Christmas was celebrated at 58° S. in a jolly fashion. Cook took particular precautions with the safety of the ships because he knew the crews were sure to be the worse for drink and, perhaps trying to keep some control over the sobriety of at least some of his men, Clerke was included in a group of officers and Petty Officers the Captain entertained in the Great Cabin.

At the year's end penguins were plentiful which some took to mean that they were near land, but Clerke thought it more likely the birds were travelling on the floating ice. He took careful note of the animals, birds, and even the seaweed that he saw and tried to relate them to the presence of land or ice; penguins, he said, were often found miles from land.

Water for drinking and washing was always a problem on small vessels with large crews. *Resolution* had filled her casks at Cape Town and she had taken with her from England an apparatus for distilling fresh water from the sea. It was used only as an experiment, since it was obvious that its output of thirty five gallons a day fell far short of the needs of more than one hundred men. With supplies beginning to run low the men were put to work collecting loose ice from the sea, bringing it on board and melting it into potable water. Working the ship in the intense cold was bad enough, with ice-solid ropes cutting the men's hands and only the ship's galley to give heat down below, but this ice-harvesting was even worse. Fire was an ever present hazard in wooden sailing ships and the risk of loosing his ship from a stray spark or a smouldering ember was never far from a commander's mind. Cook was adamant that the utmost care be taken with the galley fire and he allowed it to be lighted at only certain times of the day. In the freezing conditions this was the only warmth which gave fleeting comfort to a few of the frozen men.

Pressing on through the pack ice, on 17th January 1773 *Resolution* and *Adventure* became the first ships ever to enter the Antarctic Circle. For more than a month they were in the ice looking in vain for the Southern Continent; Cook considered the ice islands to be as dangerous as rocks. At 67° 15' S. it became too thick, the barrier impenetrable, and they turned away to the east, sailing along the edge of the pack. Cook and his men had no means of knowing it but the Antarctic Continent was then only seventy-five miles away.

Clerke noted another example of the attention Cook paid to detail where the welfare of the crew was concerned:

> Captain Cook having Observ'd many of the People in rather a ragged condition, this forenoon he gave them some Needles thread and Buttons, that they may have no excuse for their tatter'd condition—they also have every Saturday to themselves to wash etc—that they may likewise have no excuse for a dirty,

or improper appearance.

Clerke had taken with him a sextant made by Ramsden, one of the greatest makers of scientific instruments in the eighteenth century, and he used it to make observations to set longitude by the lunar method, as the Admiralty had instructed.

It was a foggy morning on February 8th, 1773 when the two ships became separated and the contingency plan was put into operation. After waiting three days in the area without seeing any sign of *Adventure*, Cook knew that the rendezvous was now to be Queen Charlotte Sound.

Sailing on alone, *Resolution* was set on a south-easterly course. The thermometer dropped and kept on dropping and soon she was in ice again; Cook reckoned some of the gigantic icebergs they met were four times the size of his ship. Realising the conditions could only get worse and that the southern winter was coming on he turned towards New Zealand when the ship was at 61° 52' S. For months, ever since the arc into the high southern latitudes had begun, there had been no sign of anything but sea, sky and ice. It was understandable for Clerke to write: 'We now begin to long for a sight of the land'.

By the time *Resolution* reached New Zealand on 23rd March she had been at sea for seventeen weeks and three days.[13] Cook had intended going straight to Queen Charlotte Sound but out of consideration for his men, who were showing signs of wear and tear, he decided to cut short the journey and divert to Dusky Sound, an inlet near the south-west corner of South Island. This was the place he had seen, but not entered, on his previous voyage when he came upon it as night fell. Pickersgill was sent ahead in a boat to find a safe anchorage and *Resolution* followed him into a creek where the ship was moored in a place where tree branches arched over her deck. She stayed there for six weeks while her crew recovered and repairs were carried out. The men were in better condition than could have been expected after their ordeal and Clerke wrote:

> We've now arrived at a Port with a Ships Crew in the best Order that I believe ever was heard of after such a long Passage at Sea . . . particularly if we come to consult Climates; this happy state of Health was certainly owing to the Extraordinary indulgencies of Governt Crowt, Wheat, Malt etc together with the strickt attention paid by Capt Cook to the Peoples cleanliness.

Clerke and Cook had now been in one another's company for several years and they were on sufficiently close terms for them often to go ashore together either to survey or to go shooting for the pot.

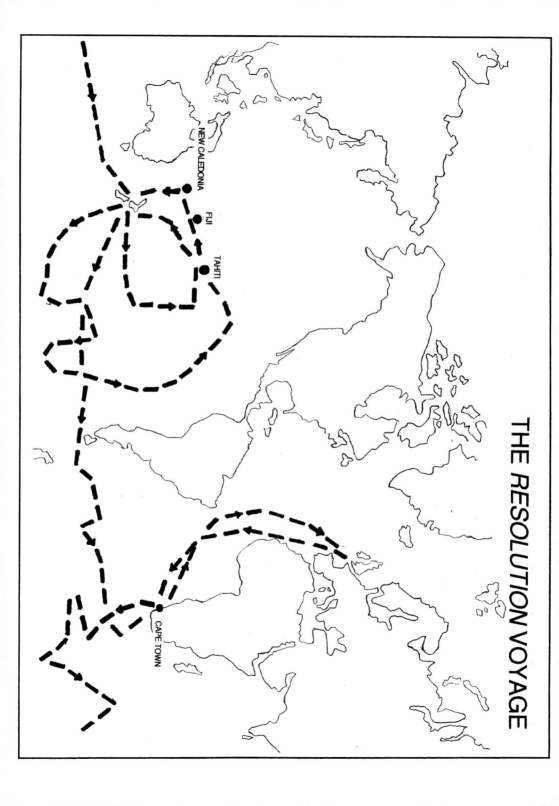

NEW CALEDONIA

FIJI

TAHITI

CAPE TOWN

THE RESOLUTION VOYAGE

13. *A view of Marlborough Sound in the north of South Island, New Zealand. This is adjacent to Queen Charlotte Sound which was a rendezvous for ships on these expeditions. Penetrating deep into the land these sounds provided deep water access well into the land much as do many Norwegian Fjiords although the surrounding New Zealand countryside is much less rugged and more temperate than the Norwegian countryside.*

Facing page 89.

Both men had their roots in the countryside and although New Zealand's South Island was very different from what either of them was used to in England it could still be appreciated for its beauty.

Contact was made with the Maoris living nearby. On Sunday 11th April the sailors had a visit from a local family:

> The Indian the Captain met with upon the Island came with all his family which consisted of two wives one jolly wench of a daughter about 18 or 20 and 3 small children with the cove in their Canoe and landed about 20 yds from the Ship.

Clerke had become a keen observer of native people and he noticed that these folk spoke a language similar to that in use in the North Island; what differences there were he put down to dialect.

A week later the same family came again and on Monday 18th

> The young lady his daughter returned to pay us a visit aboard the Ship. The gallantry of our people in general made them very anxious to pay some compliments to the young lady as twas the first Female we had seen for many months but the young lady did not seem at all inclined to repay them in the kind Indian women in general trade in and indeed the kind that most interested I believe by all men after so long an abstinence from the Sex

Charles Clerke enjoyed Dusky Bay and wrote:

> I do think that Dusky Bay, for a Set of Hungry fellows after a long passage at Sea is as good as any place I've ever yet met with.'

There was plenty of wood and good water was to be had from a nearby brook. Fish and ducks were easy to come by and 'the Gentry' judged the roast meat of the seals they shot to be better than beefsteaks.

When the repairs were complete and the crew had recovered, *Resolution* continued up the west coast and arrived in Queen Charlotte Sound on May 19th. Her crew were delighted when it was seen that *Adventure* was already there and greeting her approach with a two gun salute. Furneaux had followed his instructions after the ships had become separated and had been at the rendezvous for six weeks.

Adventure's men were not in good condition and Clerke was able to see the difference in the state of health in the crews of the two ships. Cook had instructed Furneaux to use his methods but he proved to be an unenthusiastic disciple and the inevitable consequences followed. Scurvy was the scourge of long-distance sailors (tuberculosis was the next most prevalent disease) and the understanding of its aetiology, a deficiency in Vitamin C, was still many years away. Cook did not follow the recommendation of James Lind, the naval physician, who had advocated the daily use of citrus juice, but although he did not know the exact cause of scurvy he realised that the condition had something to do with diet. His method of prophylaxis was always to issue a mixture of sauerkraut, malt, and meat soup, made into a cake, and fresh vegetables whenever they were available, prescriptions which he found to be effective. He was also meticulous about cleanliness, frequently ordering the fumigation of his vessel, and as a result his crews were always remarkably free from disease, by the standards of the time. In contrast with *Resolution*'s men, Furneaux's were still far from fit, although they had been in New Zealand for several weeks. Clerke recorded in his journal that about twenty had scurvy when *Resolution* arrived and one had died from it.

Clerke had learned to speak the Polynesian language on the previous voyage and he used it to converse with the various groups of natives he met. He spoke with several old acquaintances who told him they had recently been at war with some of the inhabitants of the North Island and that many had been killed in a great battle.

Furneaux and his men were to be disappointed in their expectations of a long winter rest in New Zealand for Cook was as anxious as ever to press on and he had no intention of wasting the winter months in idleness. His plan was to sail towards the east between 41° and 46° S. to between longitude 140° and 135° W. If no land was found, perhaps a peninsular of the Great Southern Continent, he would go to Tahiti before returning to New Zealand. He was doubtful of finding anything because the long swell again told him there was no great land mass to break up the movement of the sea.

Clerke was lucky not to be on *Adventure* because as the voyage went on the results of Furneaux's failure to follow Cook's health policies became ever more obvious. Despite the rest in New Zealand, more than one third of his crew went down with scurvy and by July he had to borrow men from *Resolution* to work his ship. Cook had been right, he did not come upon the Great Southern Continent, and when the ships arrived in Tahiti in August Furneux's crew were still in poor condition. This time they anchored in Vaitepiha Bay, at the opposite end of the island to their usual port at Matavai Bay, where *Adventure*'s sick were taken ashore. Those who were not so ill were nursed on board and the few who were fit enough were set the task of collecting water for the ship.

They were lucky to have got there because *Resolution* touched a reef off St. George's Island near the southern coast of Tahiti and nearly met the fate that *Endeavour* had so narrowly missed three years before. Clerke must have had a feeling of *déjà vu*, but his worries proved needless because when all boats from both ships were put to work they pulled *Resolution* clear without her suffering any damage.

Later, the two vessels were moved to the old anchorage in Matavai Bay where their arrival coincided with one of the periodic outbreaks of civil war which afflicted the island. Despite the conflict the people seemed pleased to see their visitors, gave them a warm welcome and immediately began thieving.

Cook had some idea of the impact these visits would have on the structure of the island's society and the health of its population, and he did his best to mitigate it, but he never knew how catastrophic the contact with Europeans was to be. Within the space of seventy-five years the combined efforts of missionaries, whalers, traders and beachcombers destroyed the Tahitian civilisation he had seen. Clerke was well disposed to the Polynesians— to the extent of learning to speak their language— and he would have shared Cook's opinion.

In many ways Cook was an enlightened man and he wrote of the island people:

> we debauch their morals . . . and introduce among them wants and perhaps diseases which they never before knew . . . If any one denies the truth of this assertion, let him tell me what the natives of the whole extent of America have gained by the commerce they have had with Europeans.

There was soon a disagreeable example of what could happen because, after so many months at sea, a degree of indiscipline had crept into life in the ships. Cook was furious when a marine and four sailors from *Adventure* went ashore without permission, got drunk and ended up quarrelling with the local people. The marine was judged to be most at fault and he was punished with eighteen lashes, the sailors had twelve each.

The Englishmen were told a garbled story about a French ship that had recently called and taken with it when it sailed four young Tahitian men. Cook took little notice of the story but a ship had been there in November and December the previous year— it was the Spanish frigate *Aguila* out of Lima— and the youths were to be instructed in Christianity.

Perhaps because of the war, supplies were not plentiful. Tahiti was fertile but at this time the island was unable to supply the amount of provisions, particularly fruit and vegetables, the visitors needed. On September 1st the two vessels went to the nearby island of Huahine where things were better and food more plentiful. Clerke was happy during the three weeks he stayed there and he was sorry when they left on September 18th:

> I must own 'tis with some reluctance I bid adieu to these isles where I've spent many happy days . . . both in the years 69/ and 73/ as in the first place (for we must give this consideration the preference after a long passage) you live upon, and abound in, the very best of Pork and the sweetest and most salutory of vegetables . . . in the next place the Women in general are very handsome and very kind . . . and the men civil and to the last degree benevolent in so that I'm sure when ever we get among them we may with very great safety say we've got into a very good Neighberhood and in short, in my opinion, they are as pleasant and happy spots as this world contains.

Living on Tahiti was a young man by the name of Omai who was thought to be a priest. He was curious about the world from which these strangers had come and he persuaded Furneaux to take him along with the expedition. Cook thoroughly disapproved of the idea of the Polynesian going to England and although Omai enjoyed his visit, made a great impression on London society (but only as something of a curiosity) and even met the King, his judgement was proved to be correct. The Tahitian was to be away from his home for four years and was never able to readapt himself to native life on his return, despite Cook's best endeavours.

Before heading once more for New Zealand the ships went westward in search of land reported by Tasman one hundred years before. They found Middelberg (Eua) and Amsterdam (Tongatapu), islands of the Tonga group. Cook named them the Friendly Isles in recognition of the welcome they were given. Clerke was enchanted by them both: 'the prospect is neither more nor less than one compleat Garden; which in reallity, it absolutely is, and I firmly believe one of the finest in the World.' Of the people he wrote: 'The Men are exceedingly Hospitable and Benevolent, but cannot withstand the temptation of European Toys if there motions are not well attended to – The Women are in general handsome . . . '

They sailed on 8th October 1773 and sighted New Zealand on the 21st. Next day they were caught in a gale near Cook Strait and on the 30th the ships lost contact. *Resolution* was eventually able to make Ship Cove in Queen Charlotte Sound but *Adventure* was blown far out to sea and when she eventually reached the rendezvous there was no sign of the other ship. Cook had waited for her for three anxious weeks but, knowing how short the Antarctic summer would be, he felt compelled to leave, accepting the risks of sailing with a single ship in dangerous waters.

It was during the wait in Queen Charlotte Sound that, on 24th November, Clerke saw with his own eyes the practice of cannibalism. Pickersgill, the Third Lieutenant, went ashore and came upon a Maori canoe. He lifted a covering lying in the bottom of the boat and saw the severed head of a man of about twenty years of age. For reasons best known to himself, he brought the gruesome relic to *Resolution* where it was placed on a capstan on the Quarter Deck. There it was seen by some natives who happened to be visiting the ship. They asked Clerke to give them the head and when he enquired what they wanted it for they told him they always ate their enemies. Two slices were cut from the cheeks, broiled on a gridiron and, to the horror of the onlookers, eaten with relish, one gourmet finishing his snack by enthusiastically licking his fingers.[14]

It is a pity Furneaux did not know of this incident, which took place while he was still at sea, as he might have taken extra precautions and spared some of his men the tragedy which was to befall them. When he eventually arrived in Ship Cove to find that *Resolution* had gone, he found the message which Cook had left for him in a bottle buried under a tree near to the spring from which the ships habitually replenished their water supplies and Furneaux promptly took it to mean that he need take no further part in the expedition. Cook's message had been vague, no rendezvous was specified and all he said was that he might go to Easter Island and Tahiti. The result of the failure of the two ships to meet was that *Resolution's* safety margin was reduced since she now had to cruise alone. Furneux set about making preparations for the voyage home and sent out a foraging party of eleven men. When they failed to return, James Burney was landed with an armed force with orders to search for them. He came back with the news that all were dead, the group had been attacked and all that remained of them were a few personal possessions and some parts of their bodies. Furneaux saw no point in prolonging his visit, made no more investigations and left New Zealand as quickly as possible. At first *Adventure* sailed towards the south-east but when she was almost level with the Horn, in 62°S., Furneaux had a change of mind and turned his ship towards Cape Town. He arrived safely in England a year before Cook and his men returned.

Cook had waited until 25th November 1773 before leaving Queen Charlotte Sound and heading south on the second great sweep towards the Pole. All hope had not been abandoned of making contact with *Adventure* and *Resolution* fired guns as she left harbour in case her consort was within earshot. The thought must have been in the minds of her sailors that when *Endeavour* had been so near to being lost on the Queensland coast, land was within reasonable reach and there was at least a chance that her crew would survive. Some kind of craft might have been built from the remains of the ship or the boats might have been able to crawl along the coast to Batavia. In either case food could have been obtained to feed the men. Not many years later, when Bligh was cast adrift from *Bounty*, he made his epic 3,600 mile small boat journey in seas not far from where *Endeavour* was nearly wrecked. *Resolution* was in different circumstances, heading for the cold, remote waters of the Polar region without hope of rescue if she ran into trouble.

In December the ship met the first ice and on the 20th she crossed into the Antarctic Circle for the second time. It was intensely cold and at times the sails and rigging were completely covered in ice. Cook was never very communicative and when the ship turned north on Christmas Eve at 67° 19' S. the crew jumped to the conclusion they were to head for the Horn. They should have known their commander better, for when the wind moved round into the northwest on 10th January 1774 he went about and sailed south once again. The last Saturday of February saw them at 71° 10' S. the furthest south man had ever been, at longitude 106° 54' W. There an impenetrable barrier of ice forced them to retreat.

Cook did not subscribe to the theory held by many people that ice could only come from fresh water and its presence indicated the existence of rivers, and therefore land. He was now sure that this was not the case.

There was still no sign of the Great Southern Continent although at one time it was thought land had been sighted. A disappointed Clerke wrote: 'our land was nothing more than a deception of the sight.'

Surrounded by vast ice fields and in intense cold Cook put in his journal:

> It was my opinion, as well as the opinion of most on board, that this ice extended quite to the Pole, or perhaps joins to some land to which it had been fixed from the creation.... I was not sorry at meeting with this interuption, as it in some measure relieved us, at least shortened the dangers and hardships inseparable with the navigation of the Southern Polar region. Since therefore we could not proceed one inch further, no other reason need be assigned for my tacking and standing back to the north.

He was now quite convinced that the Southern Continent did not exist but thought there could well be large islands awaiting discovery. He decided to spend the winter in search of them; all the officers agreed and Cook was grateful to them, and the crew, for their loyalty.

First, they stopped at Easter Island which Clerke described in his usual perceptive and humorous way. They anchored about a mile and a half off the west side of the island and obtained water from a well they found near a sandy beach. It proved to be very brackish but, as there was no alternative, they had to make the most of it. Of the people living on the island, who received them: 'with all the civilities they were masters of', he wrote:

> . . . The Men in general go naked except a little piece of Cloath about their Middle which is brought up between their Legs I imagine purely for Ornament for it secretes nothing from publick view—the Women wear a Mat about their middle etc etc and frequently a large piece of Cloath about their shoulders.

These lasses, he went on, were very complaisant and perfectly obliging to strangers. Their ears had been pierced to an extraordinary degree, making the present day's fashion (it is to be hoped a temporary one) of body piercing seem positively unadventurous. In the lobes of their ears was a large hole, big enough, he said, to get his fist through and in the case of the older women the disfigurement was such as to bring their ears down to shoulder level. To make themselves look even more attractive, 'when they dress and mean to look fine they clap in an elastic piece of Matter'.

He reserved his main comments for the extraordinary statues which he thought were to 'perpetuate the memory of the deceased', being 'too numerous to ascribe them all to Gentlemen that have sway'd the Sceptre'. He measured one that was 27 feet by 9 feet and saw another which he supposed was 30 feet high. They had crowns on their heads one of which, he thought, must weigh 12 or 14 tons. He could not understand how they had been made:

> . . . without any kind of Metal Tool . . . or the least knowledge of Mechanical Powers (or the means of using that knowledge supposing they had it, not having a bit of wood that woul'd make a Wedge in the whole Country) . . .

They left Easter Island on March 16th and sailed to the Marquesas which they reached three weeks later. Clerke described the four islands making up the group as being: 'More Hilly and Mountainous . . . than any I've ever yet met with in these Seas'. He was very taken with the inhabitants and judged them to be the most beautiful race he had ever seen. He particularly admired the tattoos of the men and the hair of the few women he saw. With some companions, he went on an expedition inland and found all the people to be very agreeable but suspected they were often at war. He saw what he took to be fortresses situated on the top of some of the hills and he was told that this was where they took refuge when their enemies came.

They stayed in the Marquesas for five days and managed to buy more supplies than they had been able to obtain at Easter Island, where food had been in short supply. *Resolution* sailed southwest to Tahiti, where she arrived on 22nd April 1774, having called in at the Tuamotu Islands on the way. Clerke had been there before, with Byron on the *Dolphin* voyage. He enjoyed Tahiti as much as ever. 'Nothing in Nature' he wrote, 'cou'd exceed the unbounded Civility and friendship with which they treated us.'

The centrepiece of the visit was the gathering at Pare of the Tahitian war fleet of more than 300 large canoes. Some of them were double hulled and up to seventy feet long with elaborately carved prows, and they met with Clerke's unqualified approval.

As *Resolution* was leaving Matavai Bay on 14th May, after a stay which had lasted three weeks, John Marra tried to desert. He was a thirty year old gunners mate from Cork and wished to settle in Tahiti. He was unlucky, for as he was swimming towards the shore he was pulled from the water, brought back on board and put under guard. He had often been in trouble before but this time he escaped any further punishment.

Huahine was again the next stop and it was there, early on the morning of 20th May, that while Clerke and two companions were out on a shooting expedition, they were set upon and had all their possessions, including their muskets, taken from them. Cook set all to rights by going ashore and detaining two chiefs until everything was returned.

On neighbouring Raiatea they were not a little sceptical when told of the recent arrival of two ships at Huahine. One, it was said, was commanded by Banks and the other by Furneaux. Clerke was sent to investigate but returned to report that the story was either a figment of the islanders' imagination or a practical joke.

In late June they had come to Nomuka, in the Tongan group of islands, and on Tuesday the 28th Clerke landed with the Master and about fifteen men to fill the ship's water barrels. A large crowd of natives gathered round and began to jostle the sailors, making it difficult for them to get the heavy casks into the boat. When Clerke had his gun snatched from his hand the thief made off at high speed and, in the general confusion which followed, the cooper's tools were taken for good measure. The sailors fired over the heads of the mob and Cook arrived with a party of Marines who promptly seized two large canoes which happened to be nearby. One man resisted, was fired at with small shot and was seen to be injured. His wounds were dressed by the ship's surgeon who, in the manner of the day, bled him. Despite this attention the patient recovered. Soon afterwards Clerke's musket was returned. Notwithstanding this episode, he liked the inhabitants of Nomuka and said of them:

> These People have only one bad particle in their whole composition, which is plac'd at their fingers ends, and is eternally itching to be at work upon some matters that's not their own . . . we made them return all that their great abilities and strict perseverance had procur'd them.

A man of Clerke's disposition could hardly fail to be amused by an episode which embarrassed his captain but delighted the crew. Cook was offered the services of a comely young woman, a proposition he refused by explaining that he was too poor. The islanders said he could have credit, which he politely declined, and an old lady berated him. Cook, saying he could resist the beauty of the young lady but not the abuse of the old woman, beat a hasty retreat to the ship.

The ship left Nomuka at the end of June and made west, leaving Fiji to the north of her track, and went to the islands of the New Hebrides group to spend the next six weeks in almost continual surveying. The Englishmen were now in Melanesia and found that the people were different, being smaller, with flat noses, thick lips and much darker skins. They were frightened of their visitors, wished them to be gone and often would allow them no further ashore than the beach. On Tana, for example, Clerke found their behaviour not to be the most friendly he had ever experienced: ' . . . they did not seem reconcil'd to the liberty we took in landing upon their Coasts'. On Malekula even Nature seemed determined to be unfriendly for when all the officers ate a meal of two large red fish they were poisoned and it took a week for them to recover. There were several unpleasant incidents and a number of the natives were either hurt or killed.

Before they left at the end of August Clerke was sent off in charge of a party with instructions to gather wood on the island of Eromanga. They could not get through the surf, but not wishing to come back empty handed, the men brought back with them a sea snake. His friend Banks might have given him an interest in zoology, but this was a foolhardy thing to do for some of the reptiles are among the most deadly creatures in Creation.

Resolution arrived off New Caledonia, one of the larger Pacific islands, on the 5th September and spent almost the entire month surveying the coast. The sailors made few excursions ashore but on one Clerke was given the task, together with Mr. Wales the astronomer, of making preparations to observe an eclipse of the Sun which was due to take place during the afternoon of Wednesday, the 7th September. Cook joined them and all three watched the moon's shadow pass over the Sun.

Clerke liked the people of New Caledonia who, he said, were well featured, woolly headed and of a dark mahogany colour. They were good natured, more than ready to help and less devoted to theft than usual. Their dress he found to be somewhat singular:

> Many of the natives came aboard and ran about the Ship with the happiest confidence immaginable . . . when we found them, they were totally naked to the Penis, which was wrapt up in leaves, and whatever you gave them, or they by any means obtained, was immediately apply'd there; nor wou'd they care one farthing for any article or trifle that could not in some form be made to contribute to the decorating of that favourable part . . . I gave one of them one day a stocking—he very deliberately pulled it on there—I then gave him a string of beads, with which he tied the stocking up—I then presented him with a medal which he immediately hung to it—in short let that noble part be well decorated and fine they be perfectly happy and totally indifferent about the state of all the rest of the Body.

His chuckle is almost audible, over two hundred years later.

Whenever they had the chance, *Resolution's* crew tried to supplement the monotonous ship's diet. Their Seine net frequently brought in a good harvest but one day it gave them what proved to be an unwelcome catch. A 'confounded ugly looking animal' was eaten by the Captain and his mess and once again all were made ill.

The southern summer was drawing closer and in the middle of September Cook turned *Resolution* towards New Zealand. One dark night at the end of the month she was almost wrecked on a reef near the southern tip of New Caledonia but by 10th October she had arrived at uninhabited Norfolk Island, about half way to New Zealand. The discovery of the island was of strategic importance to the Royal Navy. Huge pine trees grew there, some were 180 feet high and three feet in diameter and could be used to make the masts and spars which the Navy used in huge quantities. In Charles Clerke's time the only suitable timber came from the Baltic and any interruption to the flow, caused by the shifting alliances of European politics, made the

Navy vulnerable. This alternative source of supply was of great importance, particularly because good quality flax, from which sails were made, also grew on the island.

Resolution was back in Ship Cove in Queen Charlotte Sound by 18th. October. The message left for Furneaux was gone so Cook knew that *Adventure* had not been lost. Furneaux had departed in something of a hurry and had left no letter setting out his intentions but Cook, knowing his man, guessed that he had made for home.

Clerke was surprised to find that at first there were no Maoris at Ship Cove. Eventually a few appeared and, hesitantly at first, began to trade. Relations improved and by 8th November he was writing:

> The utmost sociability subsists between us and the Natives here . . . numbers of visits are paid and repaid.

Disturbing thoughts began to occur to Cook and his officers when some of their visitors began to speak about a shipwreck. The Maoris were evasive in what they had to say and as they talked all round the subject the sailors became more and more apprehensive. The tale they heard was very vague; anything that may have happened had nothing to do with the teller of the tale, always some other person was involved. Nevertheless, the crew were left with the impression that a tragedy had taken place but that it was unlikely to have been a shipwreck. There was no mention of a massacre.

As ever, the wear and tear on the ship had to be made good and when repairs were finished *Resolution* sailed out of Queen Charlotte Sound on 10th November 1774, homeward bound. Cook's intention was to follow an easterly track between 50° and 60° S. arriving at the Horn with time to explore the southern part of the Atlantic. It was summertime and *Resolution* sailed as she had never done before, bowling along in fine style. Clerke was delighted and on 27th November he wrote in his journal: 'We've had a fine steady Gale and following Sea these 24 Hours, and run the greatest distance we've ever reach'd in this Ship'.

Before *Resolution* left England more than two years previously, the main order the Admiralty had given Cook was to search for the Great Southern Continent as far to the south as he could go. Five weeks after leaving New Zealand *Resolution* completed her circumnavigation of the South Pole, having sailed in latitudes higher than any ship had done before, and Cook could report that he had seen no sign of that elusive land. He was convinced that it did not exist, unless it lay beyond the impenetrable ice barrier which had barred his way. The debate was over, the question answered. Cook's achievement had made a monumental contribution to the knowledge of the world's geography and he had shown that there was no continent which could be settled and no markets to be developed.

Clerke now turned his attention to another matter for, like Cook, he had been thinking about the Ice Theory. This postulated that sea water could not freeze and, if this was so, ice must come from fresh water which could only be found on land. Clerke had never seen any debris in the ice which would indicate that it had come from a river—pieces of wood from fallen trees or slicks of earth. He began to consider how the ice islands and giant icebergs which had so impressed him, floating many miles from land, were formed. He came to the conclusion that in high latitudes masses of snow fell, even in the summer, and where it was sheltered by bays it turned to ice which got thicker and thicker. Eventually, he reasoned, it broke away under its own weight and drifted out to sea

Resolution came to Tierra del Fuego on 20th December 1774. After breakfast next morning Cook ordered two boats to be launched and he took one, Clerke the other, to look for an anchorage. Cook found the better place and Clerke was sent back to bring the ship to it.

Two days later one of the Marines began his Christmas season early. William Wedgeborough, a man who had needlessly killed a native on Tana, went to the ship's head—the lavatory—which consisted of a few holes cut in a projecting piece of timber set either side of the bowsprit. He was very drunk and must have fallen overboard for he was never seen again.

They named their anchorage Christmas Sound. Cook never lost an opportunity to survey and he set off with Pickersgill and Clerke to explore, making observations as they went. Clerke found Tierra del Fuego to be a cluster of islands all looking much alike but they offered ships good shelter.

He enjoyed the Christmas he spent at the tip of South America:

> Wednesday 28th December 1774
>
> These have been 8 such days as I never had the least idea of spending at Tierra del Fuego—the weather fine—ship safe and abundance of good provisions—even the poor inhabitants (wretched as they seemingly are) contributed all they cou'd to our enjoyment by their compliance and sociability.

He had modified his opinion of the physical attributes of the people. They were no longer anything like those he had described to the Royal Society after his voyage with Byron when the nearby Patagonians had all attained the most extraordinary height. He now found:

> The appearance of the Inhabitants here immediately bespeaks
> your pity—a most diminutive race, walking exceeding ill, being
> almost crippled from the perpetual attitude of sitting upon their
> heels . . .

Resolution left Tierra del Fuego on 28th December 1774, and Cook
was again lucky when he made the passage between the Pacific and
the South Atlantic in good weather.

Dalrymple, Cook's old rival for the command of the *Endeavour*
expedition, had published a chart which purported to show a great
land mass to the southeast of the Horn. Cook went in search of it
but was not impressed when he found it to be no more than South
Georgia.

> I did flatter myself we had got hold of the Southern Continent,
> but alas these pleasing dreams are reduced to a small isle.

Cook was forever naming geographic features after people he
knew; some were important, some were not. Lord Sandwich, the First
Lord of the Admiralty, was in the former category and more than one
group of islands was named after him. Now it was Clerke's turn and
before the ship continued on to the south-east an outcrop of rocks
was given his name. It was now autumn in the southern hemisphere
and winter was not far behind. The ship was turned northwards
towards warmer waters and the ice and the cold were left behind.
Landfall was made at Cape Town on 21st March 1775.

Not long before she arrived *Resolution* came across two Dutch
vessels, the first European ships to be seen for many a long month.
A ship's boat was sent over and it was learned for the first time that
Adventure had called at the Cape a year earlier and that it was
believed her boat's crew had been eaten at Queen Charlotte Sound.
Two days later they passed the *True Britton* whose captain confirmed
the story.

At first sight the name of this ship seems innocuous enough but to
Charles Clerke it would have conveyed another meaning, reflecting as
it did an aspect of the turbulent politics in England at that time. The
choice of the name by a ship owner shows the widespread prevalence
of anti monarchist feeling in the country for it was also the title of a
publication owned by a firebrand politician called John Wilkes who
had probably selected it to emphasise the difference between his own
origins and those of his Hannoverian sovereign.

Wilkes was one of a long line of radicals which continues right up
to the present day. Although his character was not without
blemishes he held strong opinions, one of the foremost of which was

a disbelief in 'The Divine Right of Kings'. Seeing no reason for Parliament to be merely the instrument of the ruler of the day, he was much involved in the opposition to George III's attempts to dominate the assembly through his placemen and 'Wilkes and Liberty' became a popular slogan. More than once, Wilkes was imprisoned and prevented from taking his Parliamentary seat, despite having won elections by large majorities. As a consequence, there were civil disturbances and when troops opened fire on rioters outside the gaol in St. George's Fields when he was incarcerated there a number of people were killed.

During the three years he had been away Charles had had no opportunity to observe contemporary politics but when he caught sight of the *True Briton* he must have been reminded of the situation in England and that Wilkes had become a symbol of opposition to the policies of the King.

After being so long at sea it is hardly to be wondered at that *Resolution's* men took some license when leave was given at the Cape. Elliot wrote in his diary:

> . . . it was no uncommon thing, in our rides in the Country, to see three sailors on a Horse, in full sail, and well fed with grog. At other times I have seen them laying asleep by the roadside, and the Horse standing over them.
>
> No men could behave better under worse circumstances than they did. The same must be said of the officers and I would add that I believe there never was a Ship where for so long a period, under such circumstances, more happiness, order and discipline was enjoyed.

They stayed at Cape Town for a month before departing on 27th April 1775. Their leaving was a colourful affair with *Resolution* sailing from Table Bay in company with two frigates, one Dutch, the other Danish, and an East Indiaman. The air was made merry by music from the band of the Danish ship and the merchantman saluted as they left for home.

Their route took them by way of St Helena and the Azores and *Resolution* arrived at Spithead on 30th July, 1775, three years and eighteen days after leaving England. Early that morning Clerke took up his pen, wrote to his friend Banks and sent the letter to London with the civilians who were hurrying there:

> We're now past Portland with a fine fresh N.W. Gale and a young flood Tide, so that in a very few Hours we shall anchor at Spithead from our Continent hunting expedition . . . send me one Line just to tell me you're alive and well, if that is the case,

for I'm as great a stranger to all matters in England as tho' I had
been these three Years underground—so if I receive no
intelligence from you I shall draw bad conclusions and clap on
my suit of black; but you know I never despair, but always look
for the best . . . Excuse the paper, is gilt I assure you, but the
Cockroaches have piss'd upon it

For the second time, Clerke had had an opportunity of seeing how
effective Cook's health measures had been for not one man had been
lost to disease.

It had been a long, hard voyage and Charles had had plenty of
time to consider the things he had seen.   He had come to a firm
conclusion:

I'm of the opinion this Ship's voyage has clearly witt'd there can
be no Continent or Isle at all worthy the attention of any People
under the Sun.

CHAPTER SIX

THE KING'S BENCH

WHEN CHARLES CLERKE ARRIVED IN ENGLAND during the summer of 1775 he found a country which was nominally at peace but anticipating war. There was already fighting going on in North America where the thirteen colonies were in turmoil and drifting towards open rebellion; in more extreme circles on the other side of the Atlantic there was increasing talk of a complete break with the Crown. France could be expected to take advantage of any embarrassment which this might bring about and England was beginning to pay more attention to her defences.

Clerke left Portsmouth and made his way to London where he took rooms in the house of Mr Henry Wyate, a hosier, whose property was in Panton Street, just off the Haymarket. Charles had chosen a convenient place because his lodgings were near both the Admiralty and the houses of his friends, including Banks who lived in Burlington Street. Panton Street was only a short walk from the Thames where boats provided the easiest way of getting across the city and it was a simple matter for Charles to make his way to the Navy's dockyard at Deptford.

The weeks which followed his return were a mixture of satisfaction and worry and there must have been times when he wished he was back in the relative tranquillity of the Pacific.

Firstly, he could celebrate his survival. His last voyage had been a particularly dangerous one with his ship sailing alone for much of the time, often in ice, and nearer to the Pole than any vessel had ever been before. In the next century the entire Franklin expedition was lost while looking for the North-West Passage in conditions not dissimilar to those his ship had faced. On the other hand, *Resolution* had been a healthy ship and had experienced none of the disease with which *Endeavour* had been afflicted as the result of her stay in Batavia. When he reached home Clerke seemed to be in robust health.

Secondly, he was promoted to Commander and given his first command on 26th August 1775. *Favourite* was a ship of 360 tons, had a crew of 125 men, and had arrived at the Nore from the West Indies ten days earlier. William Simpson, her captain, had died during the voyage and the ship's log, which now has several folios missing, was kept by his widow Elizabeth from the time the ship was passing Portland on 12th July. Mrs Simpson signed it 'Elizabeth Simpson, Widow and Admx of Willm Simpson'. The Admiralty acted swiftly on learning of the death of *Favourite*'s captain and ordered her Master, Greary Gardener, to take charge of the vessel. On the day Clerke was appointed to her command, Gardener brought her to Five Mile Channel off the Isle of Sheppy. She off loaded her powder at Galleons Reach in mid-October and then went on to Deptford where her crew were paid off on the last day of the month. There is a gap in her log from the end of October 1775 (two months after Clerke was given command) to exactly one year later but in none of the surviving folios is there any mention of Clerke's going on board and hoisting his pennant. It had been rumoured in London society that he was to return the Tahitian, Omai, to his homeland in *Resolution* and Solander wrote to Banks on 7th September 1775: 'Clerke has been made commander of *Favourite* but is promised *Resolution.*'

Charles Clerke never took *Favourite* to sea and it is doubtful if he ever set foot in her. He had probably been appointed her captain to enable him to draw the pay of a Commander; it was at a time when he needed it.

Charles' homecoming was marred by news of the death of one of his brothers. Thomas Clerke had gone to Surat, on the west coast of India, to be the chaplain of the English Factory, or settlement, there and had succumbed to disease.

At some time during the five months between August 1775 and the end of the year the great tragedy of Charles' life occurred when he was arrested and sent to the King's Bench Prison in St. George's Fields, Southwalk. The day the officers of the court took him into custody must have been the blackest of Clerke's life because his arrest might have meant the end of the career to which he was dedicated. Ever since he had left Wethersfield his whole existence had been devoted to the sea and on this day all his hopes were in danger of disappearing, leaving him with little to which he could look forward.

His imprisonment has long been something of a mystery. Beaglehole, Cook's admirable biographer, wrote: '. . . the affair is obscure in its details and dates'[1] and Hough speculated that he may have obtained his release by bribery or by climbing over the wall.[2] Even Cook was being deliberately vague when the time came to sail again and he had to give an explanation for Clerke's absence. The younger man, he said, had been detained in London on business. There was more to it than that and recent research now allows some light to be shed on this important and tragic part of Charles Clerke's life.

Charles was innocent of any intended crime but he had certainly been unwise, for he had stood guarantor for the debts of his eldest brother and fellow sailor, Sir John Clerke, who had gone off to the East Indies without satisfying his creditors. Charles was not in a position to settle John's liabilities so he was arrested and held in his place.

Sir John had gone off owing the huge sum of £4,000. On 28th January 1780 the *Chelmsford Chronicle* reported that news had been received of the death of Captain Cook and continued:

> Captain Clerke, who succeeds captain Cook, is the son of a country gentleman at Wethersfield in Essex; he did not purpose going out, but having been bail for a friend to the amount of 4000 L who fled from his bond, he was obliged to it by circumstances. He is a very good seaman, and much loved by his men.[3]

What Sir John had done with the money, whether he had indulged in high living which had outstripped his resources, gambled it away or made some unwise investments remains a mystery but by one means or another he had got through a large sum. It is very difficult to judge how much £4,000 would be worth at today's values because so many changes have taken place during the past two hundred and twenty years and there is no absolute yardstick against which it may be judged. This was the age before the Industrial Revolution, an upheaval which changed the old order for ever, a time when new skills developed and there was a consequential rearranging of the relative positions of people within society. Nevertheless, some idea of how much Sir John had borrowed may be gained from quoting two examples. Firstly, the average wage of a farm worker in the mid-eighteenth century was seven shillings a week and has now risen by a factor of five hundred: secondly, the Admiralty bought Clerke's ship, *Discovery*, for £1865. The sum owed by the eldest Clerke brother would have bought two such vessels. It would not be unreasonable to suppose that in today's money he sailed away owing between one and two million pounds.

John Clerke's financial difficulties were of long standing when Charles was arrested, for he seems to have been in trouble as early as 1768. He was then living in the Hotel de Londre in Rue du Colombian, Fauxbourg St. Germain, in Paris (perhaps trying to evade his creditors) when he wrote to his wife, Lydia, telling her that soon all would be well:

> Your letter, my very dear Girl, has filled my Heart with every tender sentiments that humanity can feel, and I this moment

love and honor you, if possible, more than the first day you bestowed your self on perhaps a very wrong headed, but not a bad hearted Husband—Be of comfort my worthy, my dear, my noble girl, This long separation will have its advantages and I doubt not but there is still Happiness in store for us. My peregrinations have been long and painful, My schemes manifold and hereto unsuccessful—I have never forgot you, and if I have seemed to neglect you, it has been because I have no good tidings to give you . . . The spring carries me most undoubtedly to England . . . With regard to a voyage I shall be glad of one on many accounts . . . Lord Rochforts continuance in the Ministry may be of service, his Lordship and I am extremely well together. You know my dear Friend the repugnance I have to obligations to a certain party . . . On the subject of money, I have drawn on our worthy friend Ekins for a hundred Guineas which you will remit to him forthwith and I hope it will be the last I shall have occasion for before my return—Therefore employ your savings in whatsoever manner you please . . . I have still hopes of something clearer during the winter . . . [4]

One of the schemes to which he was referring appears to have been dealing in wine because, four years later, on 19th May 1772, Charles wrote to his sister-in-law from *Resolution*. One passage concerns his brother:

. . . Pepper return'd the wine to the Merchant at Calais again so that thank God there's no great loss there, tho' the Poor fellow was amidst numbers of perils and dangers with it . . . Jack Wood has undertaken to get him to India - Poor fellow he is to be sure a most unfortunate Dog but he was fortunate almost to a miracle in saving the wine but that was our Dear Johnny's fortune.[5]

John Clerke was obviously an improvident man and it is ironical that at one time he had been in command of a ship called *H.M.S. Prudent*. The name tempts the conclusion that the person who allocated the vessel to him was not without a sense of humour.

The money John had borrowed was owed to at least four persons, as will be seen, and they were, presumably, bankers. There are several reasons for knowing they were Jewish: one is a letter from Charles Clerke to Banks in which he wrote: 'the Israelites cannot now have any ill effects upon our intended attack on the North Pole' and another contains the phrase ' . . . if I can outsail the Israelites, get to sea and make every return in my power'.

Charles was either enormously generous or incredibly naive to take responsibility for such a sum. He did not have a firm financial base, he certainly did not possess the assets to cover a loan of this size and it was unlikely he would ever be able to put together enough money to repay it. Being the fourth of Joseph's sons meant, on the face of it, that he would have but little chance of inheriting his father's property—he was not to know of the premature death which came to each of the Clerke boys. His naval career had been based mainly on exploration and, other than during his early years at sea in *Dorsetshire* and *Bellona*, there had been no opportunities for prize money. In any event, riches did not often come this way for, while some officers picked up huge sums of money, others made little or none at all. The vague expectation of prize money made a very insecure foundation for any guarantee and was certainly inadequate for one of this magnitude.

While it was an amazingly generous thing for Charles to do, it was done in the full awareness of what the consequences to him would be if John defaulted. It was common knowledge (and there were lawyers in the family to make sure the point was taken) that imprisonment or flight was the lot of those who did not pay or those who had gone surety for them. Loyalty was one of the hallmarks of Charles' character and nowhere is it better demonstrated than in the way he put his trust in his brother.

Somehow Sir John persuaded Charles to act as he did. It is tempting to believe he did so by passing the matter off as one which would be resolved when some anticipated deal paid off—perhaps while Charles was away on Cook's second voyage. More likely, in view of Charles' affection for both his elder brother and his family, John simply took advantage of his good nature. Charles was certainly very fond of his brother and in a letter he wrote in 1772 to his sister-in-law Lydia he said:

> . . . Heaven grant good health may ever attend the Dear Dear fellow. I woul'd only wish no more than his good, benevolent heart Desires. Dear Sis, we shall all certainly enjoy Days in Hill Street I enjoy it in prospect . . . no other man on earth gives me exquisite feelings, such grateful joys, Oh the Dear fellow how I do love him . . . [6]

The die was cast either by an exchange of letters or in a meeting which took place during 1772, the last occasion when both were in England. John left for the East Indies in that year to take command of a small squadron. Charles was expecting to sail with Captain Cook in the summer and his act of generosity may have been intended to allow his brother to get to India. It was one which was to lead to the cause of his death.

Life in an English debtors' prison in the eighteenth century was not a joyous experience although things had improved a little after about 1750. A debtor confined there under the usual rules lost more than his liberty; he entered a vicious circle in which he also lost his ability to earn money to pay off his creditors, which in turn meant that he could not be released. This extraordinary system had begun in the time of Henry VII and continued for nearly four hundred years before being abolished in 1869.

The prisons were stark, miserable, unhealthy places where debtors had to provide their own bedding, food and drink. Ordinary felons were better off because they were provided with bread and a rudimentary diet which was at least capable of sustaining life. Most debtors had to rely for their survival on any remaining resources they might have, supplemented by help from friends or family. If all else failed, only simple charity was left— if they could get it. In these conditions, disease was rife and tuberculosis and typhus were commonplace. On the other hand, prisoners with sufficient means could buy a degree of comfort, perhaps even a room, and were able to live in some style.

The system was coming under attack for not everyone was prepared to put up with it. A reform movement was just beginning, because this was the time when John Howard was visiting gaols and gathering material for what would become his life's work.

The King's Bench was a branch of the High Court and dealt mainly with civil cases, although it had a criminal element to its work. Its prison, in which Charles was incarcerated, was one of six gaols in the borough of Southwalk. Many of the London prisons were in this area just south of the Thames for it was also the site of the Marshalsea, the County, the House of Correction, the Borough Compter, and the one whose name has become the synonym for all prisons, the Clink. Ironically, the last was situated in the grounds of the London palace of the Bishop of Winchester.

As eighteenth century gaols went, the King's Bench Prison was one of the better ones. The building was relatively new, having been completed in 1758 on a two acre site in St. George's Fields, an open area of marshy land off Borough High Street near London Bridge. It had cost £7,800 to build and it replaced a nearby gaol which was so bad it had been condemned as being 'unsafe for the custody and dangerous to the health of the prisoners'. The mind struggles to imagine what it must have been like.

The main building in the new, 1758, prison was a structure 360 feet long. In front of it was a parade of flag pavings about three yards wide which gave on to a courtyard. In this open space stood three water pumps around which were benches. In better weather prisoners sat there and whiled away the hours telling fellow inmates of their tribulations. On one side of this recreational area were courts where games of rackets and fives could be played, as well as one called Bumble Puppy which involved rolling marbles.

The entire ground floor was taken up by shops which belonged to the prisoners. Here they tried to make a little money by trading with fellow debtors and, for those with the necessary skills, by offering services such as tailoring. Virtually anything could be bought there with the exception of spirits which were, officially, proscribed. As in most cases of prohibition, a ban creates a market and there was a thriving business in liquor smuggled in by visitors.

The main problem was overcrowding. The rooms to accommodate the prisoners were on the upper floors and none was more than nine feet square and had only a single bed. Some debtors took their families to gaol with them (many dependants had nowhere else to go) and this small space had to suffice for them all. Charles Clerke may well have added John Howard to the list of influential people he had met because the great reformer visited the King's Bench Prison in the summer of 1776. He found 1399 people living there; 395 prisoners, 279 wives and 725 children. There were just not enough rooms to take them all and many had to sleep in the chapel while others had to share beds. The place had no infirmary and there were no facilities for taking a bath.

The prison was described as being: 'situated in fine air, but all prospect of fields, even from uppermost windows, is excluded by the height of the walls with which it is surrounded'.

Prisoners could temporarily escape from this stifling environment by giving their parole and making a small payment. They were then allowed to go into a nearby area known by the confusing name the 'Rules of the King's Bench Prison'. Part of it was in open ground in St. George's Fields with the eastern boundary abutting on to Borough High Street where many taverns were to be found. The law prohibited debtors from using the bars but landlords overcame this restriction by setting aside rooms in which only prisoners could go. The poorer debtors, if they could scrape together the fee, could not afford to indulge themselves in this way but they could take advantage of their temporary and limited freedom to go begging.

To some people, life in prison did not seem to be too bad. William Smith wrote a report in in 1776 entitled *The State of the Gaols in London* in which he said that:

> Many prisoners, whose actions are supersedable (sic) . . .
> occupy rooms, keep shops, enjoy places of profit or live on the
> rent of their rooms a life of idleness; and being indulged with the
> use of the key, go out when they please and thereby convert a
> prison into an alms house for their support.

Smith said that he had been told that: '120 gallons of gin (the law
on spirits not withstanding) and eight butts of beer were drunk each
week'. A butt was 108 gallons.

Despite all this, the inhabitants of the King's Bench Prison seem to
have gained some sympathy from Londoners because the building
was set on fire and the prisoners freed by a mob during riots which
took place in 1780.

The whole area is now unrecognisable from the place which
Charles Clerke knew in 1776. Borough High Street still follows the
same course but there have been several London bridges built since
his time and St George's Fields and the site the prison once occupied
have long since disappeared under bricks and concrete.

With these conditions prevailing, it is not surprising that there
were many fugitives from the courts. Debtors anticipating arrest
would often gather together whatever assets they could and decamp
abroad, seeking to get themselves beyond the grasp of their pursuers
and outside the jurisdiction of the Bench. As a rule they went only as
far as the other side of the Channel— to places such as Calais,
Dunkirk or Holland. Sometimes they sought sanctuary in more
distant lands and Bengal, Jamaica, Virginia, Constantinople, and
Philadelphia all appear on the lists put before the courts as places to
which fugitives had taken flight. One enterprising escapee even made
his way to Greenland.

An intriguing entry appears in one list of people living abroad,
beyond the grasp of the King's Bench. The Surrey Insolvent Debtors
Book for 1775 records that, on Tuesday 11th July, in the Midsummer
Session held at Guildford, a James Clark was said to be in Madras.
The plaque to Joseph Clerke in Wethersfield Church tells us that his
eldest son, Sir John Clerke, died in Madras in September 1776. In
each case the initial letter of the Christian name is 'J' and, if the
scribe made a mistake and 'John' became 'James', the absconder was
not in court to correct it. It is interesting to speculate on the
possibility that it was Sir John since there cannot have been many
bankrupt J. Clarks in Madras at that time.[7]

It is puzzling that his father did not do something to help Charles.
He had cause to be proud of his two naval sons since one had a
knighthood and had done well in the Navy and the other was putting

together a reputation as one of the famous Captain Cook's senior officers. Joseph had become a Justice of the Peace and, knowing about the living conditions in prisons could not, surely, have wished them upon his innocent younger son. Nor can he have been ignorant of Charles' plight. Even in the unlikely event of Charles' not having told him directly, the news would soon have spread from London, which was less than a day's journey away from Wethersfield, and found its way to the circles in which the Clerke family moved. Sir John in far away Madras knew what was happening, so did Banks, and Solander had been told of it by another party.

Joseph was not a rich man in the way the owners of the great estates were wealthy but he was certainly a man of means. David Samwell was a Surgeon's Mate in *Discovery* when Charles Clerke was in command of her and an entry in his journal, written in August 1779, shortly after Charles' death, tells us that Joseph had an income of £500 a year. In view of his land holdings in Wethersfield and nearby villages, this may well be an underestimate. In terms of capital, the properties and land which Joseph had inherited from his father in 1768 were sufficiently substantial for Charles' grandfather to have commissioned a survey of them. This had been carried out seventeen years earlier when a large scale coloured map was made which recorded their holdings.

The creditors' point of view is easier to understand. They had lent Sir John an enormous sum of money, obviously not on very good security, and then seen him sail away. Here now was his guarantor preparing to go on another long voyage to the other side of the world. What certainty was there that either would come back? As it happened, their apprehensions were well founded since neither lived to return to England.

Finding himself in prison, a large part of Charles Clerke's energy was directed to securing his release. Much of his time was spent with lawyers but the roots of the way in which he was able to gain his freedom, and thus resume a career which had seemed to be facing destruction, lay in a series of events which took place thousands of miles away from London on the other side of the Atlantic. They, in their turn, had their origins in the Seven Years War.

While the French had lost heavily in that contest and been humiliated by their defeat the British had not escaped unscathed. For them the financial cost had been high and funding the war had resulted in a huge increase in the National Debt. Much of the money had been spent in North America, to the profit of the inhabitants, and the thought grew in the minds of the King and his ministers that the thirteen colonies should bear part of the costs. They reasoned that the war had freed the Americans, most of whom were Protestants, of any threat of interference from France and the possibility that Roman Catholicism might be imposed upon them. The Westminster Parliament passed a series of Acts designed to raise money in North America which included ones meant to tax sugar and prevent smuggling, both of which were associated with the lucrative liquor trade. Another measure was a Stamp Act which applied to all legal documents. The people living in the colonies did not see things in the same way as did the politicians in faraway London; to them the authorities there gave the impression of wishing to impose restrictions on their trade for the benefit of merchants in the home country and plantation owners in the West Indies.

By now, pliable Lord North had become the King's first minister and was at the head of a weak administration. Neither he nor George III, a stubborn man, could comprehend the American case and considered the existing arrangements to be about as near perfect as any reasonable man could wish them to be. Nevertheless, North repealed the Stamp Act, together with several other tariffs to which the Americans had taken particular exception, but kept the tax on tea. It was decided that from then on the East India Company could ship tea directly to America without it having first to travel to England and pay duties there. This resulted in American merchants losing their profits (and was taken as another example of preference being given to traders based in England) but a halving in the price of the product to the consumer, even after the colonial tax had been paid.

This would seem fair enough but the government in London had managed to alienate several groups of influential men who lost no time in producing propaganda which sought to stoke up indignation in the general population. They were so successful that on December 16th 1773 a party of Boston citizens, disguised as Mohawk Indians, threw into the harbour a consignment of tea, valued at many thousands of pounds, from British vessels lying there. It was not the most serious of events but the British responded by closing the port to all trade, a devastating blow to the townspeople.

In September of the following year, 1774, all the colonies except Georgia sent delegates to the first Congress which was held in Philadelphia. Despite mutual antipathy between the delegations, fiercely expressed, there was sufficient support for them to decide on a ban on the importation of all goods from Britain.

In the middle of 1775, while Charles Clerke was sailing homeward bound up the Atlantic, Lieutenant General Gage, the Commander-in-Chief in North America, was told by loyalists of a cache of arms at Concord, a village lying to the west of Boston. He sent off a 700 strong force to seize the weapons but after engagements at Lexington and Concord between his men and the local militia the redcoats had to struggle to regain the safety of Boston. This was the beginning of what was, essentially, a Civil War between Britain and the $2^1/_2$ million people of the American colonies.

By the middle of the summer Boston was under siege from irregular forces raised mainly in the New England states of Massachusetts, Connecticut, Rhode Island and New Hampshire which stopped all access except by sea. In June, the Second Congress appointed a new C-in-C, a certain George Washington, the man who had been on the British side in Braddock's ill-fated expedition during the Seven Years War.

In the same month the British decided the time had come to clear the rebels from around Boston and the battle of Bunker Hill was fought (it was actually on Breed's Hill, Bunker Hill was the Americans' fallback position). The King's forces won the day but at high cost—almost half their number became casualties, killed or wounded.

Up to this time opinion was divided on both sides of the Atlantic as to the merits of the insurrection. In America, many took the line that they were loyal subjects of the King and were seeking to bring genuine grievances to his attention, perhaps in an extreme way, but that he was getting bad advice from his ministers. Calls for independence were few but some were beginning to speak more and more openly about complete separation from the mother country. It has been estimated that, even at the height of the troubles, the population of the colonies was evenly divided between those in favour of the rebels, the supporters of the King, and those who just wished to be left alone. In England, not everyone was against the rebels and in Parliament Pitt and Edmund Burke were among those who spoke in support of their cause.

All this changed in June 1775, at about the time Clerke returned to England, so he would be able to pick up the threads of what had been happening, when Congress decided to invade Canada. Attitudes on both sides of the dispute became more polarised, the position of those in England who had some sympathy with the rebels became untenable and that of George III, who had already decided that the rebellion must be put down, was reinforced.

From the British point of view, the situation was obviously

deteriorating and the authorities in London came to realise that if the rebellion was to be put down a major effort would be needed. Their problem was that after the Seven Years War the forces had been run down to the point that the Army now numbered a mere 45,000 men and the Navy was in little better condition. Britain was the only major power not to use universal conscription but the Government, realising that it was likely that France would try to take advantage of the situation (she joined in during 1778), introduced the Press in June 1775. Recruitment to the Services was not easy partly because serving in the Forces, the Army in particular, was regarded as a refuge of last resort and partly because while fighting the French was popular, fighting distant cousins in America was not. To fill the gap, resort was made to a technique often used in the past and 30,000 mercenaries, mostly Hessian, were engaged.

The British strategists identified New England as the centre of the revolution and decided that the main effort in 1776 was to be in New York. Sir William Howe had succeeded Gage as C.-in-C. and in March he ordered the evacuation of Boston. His forces boarded the ships gathered in Boston Roads and waited there for ten days before sailing away, leaving Washington to puzzle over their destination. It was New York.

The main build up of the British forces began in February 1776 at about the time Charles Clerke was putting his name on the list of Navy and Army officers seeking release, as will be seen. In that month a fleet of nine warships and thirty transports, carrying 2,500 infantry under the command of Lord Cornwallis, left Cork in Ireland and sailed to Charlestown in North Carolina where they arrived on 1st June.

This was only the beginning of a vast armada which crossed the Atlantic that year because William Howe was not the only one heading for New York. He arrived there on 25th June with three ships but was soon joined by forty-five more and then by a further eighty-two. In the second week of July he was joined by his brother, Sir Richard Howe, who was the Commander-in-Chief of the Royal Navy on the North American station, who brought with him 150 ships, fresh from England. Cornwallis' expedition to Charleston had not been a success and his force, too, made for New York where the whole force was augmented by the arrival of Commodore Hotham with thirty-four ships. Altogether, 32,000 soldiers had been transported by 10,000 sailors.

Bringing together this number of ships and men placed a strain the Navy but this was not the only burden it had to bear. The rebels sought to do as much damage as they could to British merchant shipping and used a fleet of privateers to do it. Before the conflict was over several hundred American ships, mainly converted merchantmen, were deployed in this way and the Royal Navy had to give whatever protection it could. And all the while it was looking over its shoulder at France, where the real enemy lay.

Huge as the concentration of British forces on the other side of the Atlantic was, the strategists in London regarded the American theatre of war as of only secondary importance. Anticipating that France was likely to join in the war, their main attention was directed towards the old enemy and on the need to maintain control of the Channel so as to protect England from invasion. It was obvious that many more trained men would have to be found.

It was in this environment that the government became aware that a number of officers, both commissioned and warrant, were unavailable for service because they were in debt and, as a consequence, either in prison or self-imposed exile. It was decided the time was opportune to remedy the situation.

Parliament passed a measure called: 'An Act for the Relief of Insolved Debtors; and for the Relief of Bankrupts in Certain Cases'.[8] Here may lie a clue to explain Joseph Clerke's inactivity. As a Justice of the Peace, he had legal connections and one of his sons was a lawyer. Between them they would know that Charles would soon be released under the terms of the Act, the passage of which was imminent, and that it would not be necessary to hazard the family fortune.

The main provisions of the Statute required gaolers to prepare lists of prisoners in their custody on 21st January 1776; debtors living abroad must surrender themselves before 26th June to take advantage of the legislation. Schedules of each prisoner's assets and liabilities were to be drawn up and then sworn, and three notices were to be placed in the *London Chronicle* to allow objections to be heard. At the next Quarter Sessions, or the one following, the judges were to order the transfer of the debtor's money and property to the Clerk of the Peace, who was to receive two shillings from each applicant for his trouble. These assets were then to be made over to Assignees named by the court whose task it was to get in the estates, sell them within two months and make a dividend within three. Justices for the County of Surrey, the county in which was situated the King's Bench prison, were empowered to assemble at the Town Hall in Southwalk. When the procedure was complete prisoners meeting the requirements of the Act were to be freed.

What it amounted to was that the creditors had to take whatever was going.

John Clerke in faraway India knew what was going on and by one means or another he managed to put together some money which he sent home. Solander wrote to Banks on 22nd August:

> Several of the *Resolution* men have called at your house to offer you their curiosities—Tyrel was here this morning.
>
> Poor Clerke, as I hear, has been in a sad scrape. Upon going out, he gave a joint bond with his Brother, for paying Sir John Clerke's debts. I've wondered much why I had not seen Mr Clerke since the Ship came up to Deptford, but I this day learnt, that he has been obliged to live among Lawyers etc 'till he could quiet the Creditors, which I hope he has now done, at least I was told so. Sir John Clerke has sent some money home from India but not enough—and now I have been told Ch Clark (sic) is to pay them £100 immediately and part of his pay quarterly. However I don't know if it is so.

Charles Clerke put himself in debt in his own right to raise the cash needed to augment the money his brother had sent to England. Again, it seems there was no contribution forthcoming from his father. In fact, Charles had raised even more than Dr Solander had heard about—he borrowed £150 from two friends.

Charles Clerke left two wills—the first made on the day of his release, 29th July 1776, and the second on 17th August 1779, only five days before he died.[9] In the first he left £100 to 'my good Friend Sir Robert Ainslie at present his Majesty's Ambassador at Constantinople' and £50 to 'my good friend Dr Maty of the British Museum'. In the second will there is a significant amplification because the money going to Ainslie now becomes: 'one hundred pounds with the interest due to the same thereof', and that to 'Doctor Maty or his sons, 'the Sum of fifty pounds with the lawful interest due to the date hereof'.

These were not mere legacies, they were the repayment of debts he had expected to settle on his return to England.

It is not known how Clerke came to know Ainslie, but they may have met at Banks' house and must have become close friends for Ainslie to lend such a large sum. Their acquaintance is another example of the important circles in which Clerke was moving, because Ainslie was a long serving diplomat, becoming an ambassador in the year the loan was made and staying in the post for seventeen years.

The involvement of Dr. Paul Henry Maty is easier to explain—he was Charles' brother-in-law. Maty's father, Matthew, had been a physician and the principal librarian of the British Museum as well as the foreign secretary of the Royal Society in 1762. It was to him that Clerke had written in 1766 about the extraordinary Patagonians. The elder Maty was a man of substance and when he died in 1776, the year Charles was in so much trouble, he probably left a legacy to his son. Paul lived in Bloomsbury, was three years younger than Charles and had married Hannah Clerke in St. Mary's Church, Wethersfield, on 18th September 1775, not long after Charles' return from the South Seas. The younger Maty was making his way in the world and was now Assistant Librarian at the British Museum having been Secretary of the Royal Society. It is not clear which Maty advanced the money, but the words used in the will and the timing of it suggest it was Paul. Whichever it was, it makes Joseph's apparent inactivity seem even more extraordinary.

Paul Maty and his wife made an odd couple, at least in the opinion of Anne Clerke who wrote in September 1779 to her brother John's wife, Lydia, who was in Gosport. Her letter is interesting for a number of reasons: her knowledge of what was happening on the Continent although she was living deep in the English countryside, her opinion of her sister and brother-in-law and, not least, because she was fed up to the back teeth with some of her family:

> Where shall I find you my Dear Sister in this time of great alarm . . . I cannot help being anxious about the French and Spanish fleets when I read it in the papers that it is supposed they will make an attempt upon Portsmouth and that all the inhabitants of Gosport are preparing to abandon their habitations . . . Sir Charles Hardy being at Spithead will secure your part of the Kingdom whatever depredations may be made by the enemy elsewhere but I will hope that the Almighty who blew with his wind and scattered the invincible Spanish Armada will again find means to deliver us from the invasion of these perfidious Gauls . . .

> Mrs Maty is still with us her health is I think much mended since she came to us but it is a great misfortune to both her and her Husband that they can have the advice of Physicians for nothing. I'm satisfied they would have both better health if they would listen less to ? and use plain reason and common sense in the preservation of their health. I expect they will stay with us till the latter end of this month and by that time we shall all be very glad to part for indeed if it was not for the amusement the Dear innocent Child affords me I'm afraid my patience would scarcely be sufficient for the occasions Mrs Maty gives me to exert it for she is indeed the same woman at seven and forty that

she was at seventeen as one can possibly imagine a woman to be. I don't mean as a person but mind of manners. Harry is a very honest fellow but a great oddity and my father not less so, that I am often at a loss how to act between them.[10]

Paul and Hannah Maty may not have been to Anne's taste but her father must have been on good terms with them because, in his will, he left them Bright's Farm in Gosfield, a village close to Wethersfield.

When Charles sailed away he left owing smaller sums to people other than Ainslie and Maty. In his last will he made provision for these debts by leaving £1-16-0 to 'John Ramsden, Optician of Piccadilly' and £7-11-8 to Henry Wyate of Panton Street, London. Ramsden was the well-known manufacturer of navigation instruments who had made the sextant Charles used on previous voyages and the money owing to him would have been for either the purchase or the repair of a piece of equipment. Wyate was Charles' landlord in London. The most likely explanation for the inclusion of his name in the will is that it was rent that Clerke had left unpaid when he made his hurried departure from London.

The Admiralty was planning an expedition to go in search of the North-West Passage and had detailed two ships, *Resolution* and *Discovery*, to undertake the voyage. On 10th February 1776 Charles Clerke was given the command of *Discovery* and he was becoming desperate to break free of the clutches of the King's Bench and to sail away in her. He had applied for release under the terms of the Act and in June had appeared before the court. The Justices could not agree, adjourned his case for a fortnight and, to his disgust, wrote to him expressing the hope this would not prove too inconvenient. On the 28th he wrote to Banks: ' . . . I am fairly cast away— the damnation Bench of Justices fell out among themselves, upset and fairly frustrated the friendly intentions of Sir Fletcher Norton etc.' Norton was the Speaker of the House of Commons and, having an interest in science, (he was a Fellow of the Royal Society) was another who had probably met Clerke in Banks' house in Burlington Street which was the centre of the scientific community in London.

Clerke was under increasing pressure from the First Lord of the Admiralty, Lord Sandwich, to settle his affairs because time was going by and the last date by which *Discovery* could depart for the southern summer was rapidly approaching. Several times Sandwich went aboard his ship at Deptford when the matter must have been discussed.

It was only natural for Charles to wish to regain his complete freedom and to get to sea once more, but there was an added incentive. Andrew Kippis was one of the earliest of Cook's biographers and in his book, first published in 1788, he writes that the Government had agreed to give a £20,000 reward to anyone who discovered a North-West Passage between the Pacific and Atlantic. The offer was contained in an Act which was passed in 1776 and differed from a previous one in that it applied to anyone who made the discovery and not only to men who were not directly employed in the King's service. This meant that if Charles was part of Cook's forthcoming expedition and the Passage was found, his share of the reward would go a long way towards relieving his financial difficulties.

Clerke tried to buy time and he wrote to the Admiralty Secretary on 13th June, saying he was detained in London by:

> . . . some of my own private affairs of the utmost importance to me requiring my attention to them in Town. I wou'd be highly oblig'd to their Lordships if I cou'd be indulg'd in attending them and sending the ship round, under the Command of Lieut. Burney.[11]

Sandwich went along with this as well as he could but he wrote to Clerke on 5th July and Charles sent a letter to his friend Banks, telling him what the First Lord had said:

> I this day receiv'd a letter from Lord Sandwich acquainting me he shall certainly order the *Discovery* to Sea very soon, in short giving me to understand that if I cannot leave Town by the 10th or 11th inst I must give all up . . . I shall certainly be cleared the 16th or 18th inst and shall then be happy.

Sandwich thought the expedition was very important and wanted it to be on its way, although he had plenty of other things demanding his attention. For some time, one of the most important had been the condition of the fleet. From the time of the first rumblings of discontent in America he had realised that the French would exploit any English embarrassment on the other side of the Atlantic, and that the Spanish might also join in. Many of the ships built during the rapid expansion of the Navy which took place during the Seven Years War had been constructed from inferior materials and many were falling apart. Much of Sandwich's time was taken up in trying to rectify the deficiencies of the Royal Dockyards and in ensuring for them an adequate and continuing supply of properly seasoned timber. Despite these pre-occupations he still found time for Clerke and his problems.

Nevertheless, Charles' sensible sister Anne was not impressed by his important friends. Although the letter she wrote from Ely, where she was presumably staying, to Lydia was dated June it gives no year but the contents suggest it was 1776: ' . . . I am guilty of a very great error if the connections Charles has found in Town among the great (some few excepted) will ever be of any real advantage to him'. She gave no indication of whether or not she thought Sandwich might be an exception.

By the end of June, Charles was acutely aware that time was rapidly running out, that his career was rushing towards a precipice and that unless he could quickly secure his release all would be lost. He knew that the responsibility for his predicament had been caused by his good nature and he was determined to do whatever he could to pay his brother's creditors but, such was the despair of this habitually cheerful man, that he began to consider making a run for it. He confided his thoughts in a letter to Banks on June 28th:

> . . . however tho' we cannot help misfortunes we can help deserving them . . . therefore I'm resolv'd to decamp without beat of drum, and if I can outsail the Israelites get to Sea and make every return in my power.

He eventually decided against absconding and relied upon the process of law to secure his release in a legitimate manner. Charles had placed his name on the gaoler's list and arranged for the required notices to be placed in the *London Chronicle* but he did not fully comply with the terms of the Act. This called for entries to be made on three separate occasions but he put in only two, the first on 18th June 1776 and the second four days later. Perhaps the law was turning a blind eye or was smitten by a sudden attack of amnesia. This is surprising because Charles was convinced his brother's creditors were pressing for the law to be administered to the very letter and were carefully watching him in the hope of finding him in breach.

A court consisting of Sir John Mawby, Sir Richard Totham and nine gentlemen gathered in St Margaret's Hall in Southwalk Town Hall on 29th July 1776. Clerke was the first applicant to be brought before it and to his relief he obtained his release.[12] This was no mere formality for not all his fellow applicants were successful. Thirty-one prisoners were sent back to St George's Fields that day for a variety of reasons; some had obtained the money they owed by false pretences or by embezzlement and this prevented their qualifying, others owed more than £1,000 to any one person and thereby put themselves outside the scope of the Act.

This part of the Act which limited the amount which could be owed to one individual shows that when Sir John departed for the East Indies with debts of £4,000 the money he owed had been advanced by at least four people.

Desperate and uncomfortable as Charles' position had been, there is evidence to show that he had not been confined for twenty-four hours a day in the Kings Bench Prison. Firstly, his entry for 10th February 1776:

> This day I was commissioned by their Lordships to the Command of his Majesty's Sloop *Discovery* which Sloop I found in the Dry Dock at Deptford; many carpenters aboard her. At 11 hoisted the Pendant [*sic*]. The shipwrights and various artificers of the yard so wholly engrossed the vessel that we could not act in the least towards her equipment for sea until the 10th of March; when we haul out of the dry into the wet.

Then on Sunday 9th June he was writing:

> At 1/2 past 1 Lord Sandwich went on board the *Resolution*— manned ship and saluted with 17 guns. At 3 His Lordship came on board and enquired if our equipment was just as I would wish; I affirmed him that whatever might be the event of our Endeavours, our equipment was every way adequate to the voyage; at which his Lordship was pleased to express his Satisfaction: Soon afterwards wishing us success he took his leave, when we Saluted with 17 guns.

Most explicitly, in his 5th July letter to Banks he says:

> . . . now what completes the wretchedness of my situation I find the Jews are exasperated and determin'd to spare no pains to arrest me if they cou'd once catch me out of the Rules of the Bench—this you know wou'd be striking the finishing stroke.

These entries were written between 21st January 1776, when the gaolers prepared the lists of those in custody who might be eligible for release, and 29th July when he secured his freedom. Clerke writes in the first person singular and describes events of which he was an eye witness so he cannot have been permanently confined in prison. This is explained by the existence of a second system, in addition to the 'Rules of the Bench' by which a prisoner could gain temporary freedom. He could be allowed out under 'Day Rules', a privilege granted expressly by the Court which allowed a debtor, on giving his parole, to leave the prison during the day to transact his affairs, providing he was back by 9.00 p.m. A fee was payable; in 1820 it was 4/2d a day, or 21 pence in modern currency. Today this seems a tiny amount but in Clerke's time it was the equivalent of a day's pay for a Lieutenant. Charles' taking advantage of this concession would account for his being able to prepare *Discovery* for sea and being able to report in person to the First Lord of the Admiralty that her equipment was satisfactory.

Even though he may not have been held in close custody, Ann was worried about him. She enquired of Lydia whether she had seen him and said she did not know how he had been able to support himself in London. 'I have some fears for him that nothing will effectively remove but the certainty of his being sailed.' She was concerned, too, about his health and went on:

> . . . Another thing I'm inclined to fear is that he takes no sort of care of his health for I was told the other Day by a Gentleman who saw him in Town about a month since that he thought the gay life he had for some time past led in Town is injurious to his constitution as a South Sea voyage could be if he might judge by the appearance he then made.[13]

After his release on the morning of Monday, 29th July 1776 Charles Clerke paused only long enough to put his signature to his first will, left Southwalk and set off posthaste for Plymouth where *Discovery* awaited him.

Charles was never to know that his brother predeceased him in Madras, Southern India, in September 1776 where he had command of a small squadron. Charles was *en route* to the Cape when John died and news of the death had not reached Table Bay before he sailed from there for the Pacific.

It is a testimony to his character and the generosity of his spirit that despite all the troubles brought upon him by the actions of his brother, the apparent failure of his father to mitigate a manifest wrong and the loss of his hopes of a distinguished career, he retained his affection for his family to the very end. In his last will, made as he lay dying in the Great Cabin of *Resolution* and knowing his life had only days to run, he wrote of: 'My dear and honoured father', his 'Dear brother and friend Sir John Clerke', and of 'my dearest friend Lady Clerke wife of my brother'. There is no bitterness, no recrimination, he seemed unaware that he had been badly treated.

Charles had secured his release but he had paid a heavy penalty. He had contracted tuberculosis.

CHAPTER SEVEN

DISCOVERY

CHARLES CLERKE WASTED NO TIME in making his way to Plymouth, where *Discovery* awaited him having been brought from London by Lieutenant Burney. By the following morning, Thursday, Clerke was writing to the Admiralty Secretary, telling him he had arrived at the port on the night of the previous Tuesday and was proposing immediately to get his ship under weigh. He was as good as his word for he went aboard *Discovery* at midday and sailed within the hour.

He was now a very different man from the impetuous youth who had sailed in *Bellona*. Clerke was now thirty-five years old and one of the most experienced explorers in the Navy and, indeed, in the world. There were few men, not even Cook himself, who could claim to have sailed round the globe three times. His loyalty and reliability were beyond doubt, he was still good humoured and popular with ratings and fellow officers but his experiences had matured him. He now had the authority befitting a captain and an ability to exercise firmness when it was required although, by the standards of the day, he never descended to harshness.

His courage was undiminished, as he was to show when facing his lingering death, fully aware of what the inevitable outcome of his illness would be but choosing to do his duty to the end. With maturity had come judgement as he was to show, for example, after Cook's death when he refused to rush into precipitate, unconsidered action merely to satisfy the wishes of his men. He carefully weighed up the situation and then took a cool, considered decision.

The ostensible reason for the voyage that Clerke was about to undertake was to return to his home Omai, the Tahitian. It had originally been suggested that *Favourite* be used but the idea was abandoned and the Admiralty, as usual mindful of the public purse, was trying to kill two birds with one stone. Omai had been brought to England at his own request by Furneaux when *Adventure* made her early return from the search for the Great Southern Continent and he had enjoyed a wonderful time in Europe. He had been an object of great curiosity in London society, learned to ride a horse, to wear western clothes and had stayed as Lord Sandwich's guest at Hinchinbrook. When he met George III, to general delight he had called the monarch 'King Tosh'.

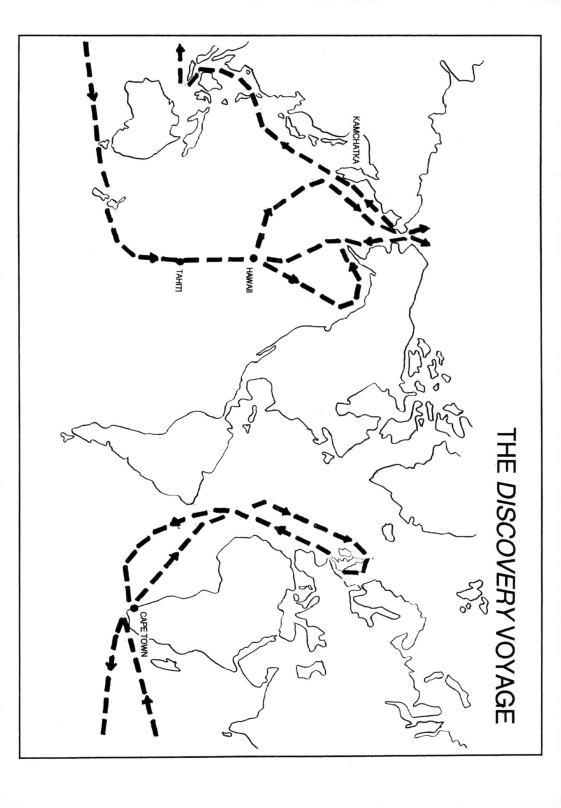

THE DISCOVERY VOYAGE

KAMCHATKA

TAHITI

HAWAII

CAPE TOWN

His return to Tahiti was little more than a cover story, for the Admiralty's real purpose was to mount another search for the North-West Passage. When Clerke had sailed with Byron in 1762 this had been one of the main tasks set the expedition but Byron had been in such a hurry he failed even to begin to look for it. Cook and Clerke were now to rectify his omission. There had been numerous attempts to find the 'Passage' by approaching it from the east but the new voyage would be the first serious attempt to find a way into the Atlantic from the Pacific side. They were seeking a route over the top of the world and, if it existed, it was calculated that 6,000 miles would be cut from the journey between Europe and the Far East and China. If a short way could be found between the Pacific and the Atlantic, or even the North Sea, it would bring increased trade, political influence and perhaps even opportunities for settlement to the nation which discovered it. These magnets were powerful attractions, strong enough to persuade the authorities in London to finance the endeavour. Its discovery would also mean that ships would no longer have to sail the long route round the Cape, or the even more dangerous one round the Horn, to gain access to the Pacific. There was another reason for Britain's interest for it was realised that the country's geographic position would give her a measure of control over a northern gateway to the other side of the world. The importance given to the discovery of the Passage may be judged by the size of the reward which, Kippis wrote, was offered in an Act of Parliament passed in 1776. No less than £20,000 would go to *any* of George III's subjects who found a route, whether it was from the Atlantic to the Pacific or vice versa. It replaced a previous Act, passed thirty-one years previously, which limited the payment of the reward to men who were not serving in the Royal Navy and who found a passage westward from Hudson's Bay. The 1776 Act provided for the prize to be divided between 'the commander, officers, and seamen of a ship belonging to his majesty' and if Charles Clerke was part of a successful expedition his share of the money would go some way towards relieving his financial worries.

There was a symmetry to the thinking about the existence of the Passage for, in the same way it had been believed there had to be a Great Southern Continent to counterbalance the northern land masses, perhaps there might be a connection in the northern hemisphere between the Atlantic and the Pacific mirroring that through the Magellan Strait or round Cape Horn. Byron's annexation of the Falklands had given Britain a means of exercising a degree of control over the southern access to the Pacific and to be able also to dominate the northern route would place her in a very strong position.

Underlying all this reasoning was the fear that the French, defeated in the Seven Years War which had ended more than ten years earlier and still smarting from the loss of Canada but retaining a presence in North America, might yet break through to the west coast.

Despite its preoccupations, the Admiralty had not lost sight of the long term strategic requirements and Palliser and Lord Sandwich showed the importance they attached to the expedition by allocating money, men and ships for it at a time when so many other demands were being made upon them. They were frequent visitors to the ships during their fitting out, making sure that everything needed was provided. In June 1776 the entire Board of the Admiralty accompanied them on one of their visits to *Resolution* and *Discovery* at Deptford.

Given his qualifications and the wealth of experience he had of the Pacific, it is not surprising that when the Admiralty had come to examine the matter of who should lead the forthcoming expedition Clerke's name had been prominent in the list of candidates. He had been in the Admiralty's mind for some time and two months after he returned from Cook's second voyage, Solander wrote to Banks on September 5th 1775:

> Clerke has been made commander of the *Favourite* but is promised the *Resolution*.[1]

His old shipmate Pickersgill had been one of those considered for the appointment but his defects of character told against him. Furneaux had not distinguished himself on his voyage with Cook and his candidature was unsuccessful.

Cook was now only two years short of his fiftieth birthday and the unremitting toil and the weight of responsibility he had shouldered for so long were beginning to show. He had hardly been at home since the time of his marriage in December 1762 and it would be only reasonable for his wife not to wish him to go to sea again for some time. Cook was in need of a rest and a sinecure was found for him in the position of one of the four Captains in charge of the Royal Hospital at Greenwich. Captain Clement had died and Cook was appointed in his place at the handsome salary of £230 a year plus a ration allowance.

On the evening of the day Clerke received his commission to command *Discovery*, 10th February 1776, a dinner was held at the London house of Lord Sandwich. It was a gathering of important men for in addition to His Lordship it was attended by Sir Hugh Palliser, Philip Stephens, the influential Secretary to the Navy, and Cook himself. At some time during the meal they came to the main purpose of the evening, the subject that was in the minds of them all—who was to command the North-West Passage expedition? The qualities and the flaws of each of the candidates were thoroughly considered and opinion seemed to be favouring Clerke. It was true that he was living under the jurisdiction of the King's Bench but the men gathered round the table knew of his hopes of an early release under the terms of the Insolvent Debtors Act.

Cook had never really settled to his sedentary life ashore, comfortable as it might be. He had been restless ever since his return and he told his friend John Walker, his old employer in Whitby, of his mood in a letter written on 19th August 1775:

> A few months ago the whole Southern Hemisphere was hardly big enough for me and now I am going to be confined within the limits of Greenwich Hospital which are too small for an active mind like mine. I must confess it is a fine retreat and a pretty income, but whether I can bring myself to like ease and retirement time will show.[2]

Perhaps it had always been his intention, but suddenly Cook stood up and said he would take charge of the expedition provided that he could return to his position in Greenwich Hospital on the completion of the voyage. It was by such a narrow margin that Clerke was denied the fame which went with the senior position for he was made second in command, a position which in any enterprise is seldom given much public recognition.

Cook's announcement was greeted with relief by the other men in the room. They were glad to have had the offer, which was accepted at once because, as Dr Kippis put it, they could hardly have *asked* him to go on a long, third expedition.

Cook was no longer the man he had been. Some of the decisiveness had left him and during the voyage to come he was subject to bouts of irrational behaviour and temper, defects which had not been there before. Since his return in *Resolution* he had spent much of his time overseeing the preparation of his Journal for publication and this was partly the reason for his supervision of the fitting out of the ships at Deptford being deficient. The Royal Dockyard got away with things which a younger Cook would never have tolerated.

Palliser, Sandwich, and Stephens may have been pleased with the outcome of the evening but Beaglehole gives a different judgement: '. .

. the dinner party was a great success, a triumph of organisation. It was a disaster'.[3]

The Admiralty was not overly given to sentiment and Clerke's appointment as second in command was not a consolation prize. Cook had great confidence in him and was determined to have him as his deputy, his current difficulties notwithstanding. It was to prove a good choice.

For centuries the possibility of the existence of a North-West Passage had excited the minds, and often the imaginations, of European sailors, cartographers and politicians. They had been stimulated in their debates by Spain and Portugal claiming a monopoly of the Pacific and attempting to exclude all competitors.

Cook and Clerke were to follow in the wake of other English explorers who had sought the elusive passage. Their names were to join a list of distinguished men which already included Davis, Frobisher, Hudson and Drake.

Francis Drake had been one of the earliest. In his great voyage between 1577 and 1580 in the *Golden Hind* he entered the Pacific through the Straits of Magellan and then plundered his way up the west coast of South and Central America. Having filled his ship with an enormous amount of loot taken from the Spaniards he then had to find a way home. Drake had every reason to think that his enemies would seek to block his route to the south but he was not to know that the ships they allocated would not appear until after he had left the Pacific.

Drake decided to try to find the shortest way back to England, through the Straits of Arian, as the North-West Passage was then known. He sailed up the western coast of North America until he reached 48° 0' N., just south of where the Canadian border now lies, before abandoning the attempt through a mixture of lack of success and cold. He called his discovery New Albion because the high cliffs he found reminded him of England.

Golden Hind was a tiny ship of no more than 160 tons and she had already come a long way. Drake knew she still had a huge distance to travel and, if his vessel was to have a chance of getting home safely, she must be put into the best possible condition before going on. He took her into the bay where San Francisco now stands and made her ready; there are still arguments about exactly where the place was.

Realising that two of the three possible options open to him were closed, he accepted the remaining one without too much reluctance and sailed westward, thus committing himself to a circumnavigation of the globe. He became the first Englishman to circle the Earth and came home to a triumphal welcome via the Philippines, the Indian Ocean and the west coast of Africa.

It had always been recognised that there was a possibility of finding the Passage from the Atlantic side—the approach route for European explorers had the advantage of being much shorter—and all the previous attempts made by Englishmen had been from east to west, with the exceptions of the less than wholehearted efforts of Drake and Byron.

At the same time as Cook and Clerke were getting ready to search for it from the Pacific side, their old shipmate Richard Pickersgill was preparing a ship for an Admiralty expedition through Baffin Bay and the Davis Strait. The *London Chronicle* of 6th June reported his vessel lying at Plymouth:

> . . . also the *Lion,* Pickersgill Commander, bound on discoveries
> to the North-West Passage.

Several attempts had been made before Pickersgill was given the task and in his mind must have been the experience of his immediate predecessor. Captain Constantine Phipps had set out three years previously but had managed to get only as far as Spitzbergen before being trapped in ice and escaping with difficulty.

Everything was to go wrong for Pickersgill. His ship was an armed brig and neither it, the equipment, nor the crew was suitable for the task. One must suspect that Pickersgill was not either. His background was similar to that of Clerke and their careers had overlapped. He had been a 'captain's servant' on *Tartar* before sailing with Wallis in *Dolphin* and then with Cook in *Resolution* but, at a time when the consumption of alcohol in the Navy was very high, he was a noted drinker. He sailed from Deptford in mid-May 1776 and crossed the Atlantic to the place where he was supposed to protect a whaling fleet, only to find that it had gone home. He went as far as 68° 26' N. and met ice and bergs before going on to the coast of Labrador. By now Pickersgill's crew were suffering from scurvy, despite the knowledge their commander had gained in his voyage with Cook. He abandoned the attempt and was back in Deptford five and a half months after his departure.

Pickersgill's performance had not impressed those in authority and on his return he was court marshalled for drunkenness and put on half pay. Eventually, with his fortunes at a low ebb, he took command of a privateer and his life ended when he was drowned in the Thames after slipping on some steps.

The lessons of *Endeavour* on the Great Barrier Reef, and of *Resolution* spending much of her last voyage cruising alone after contact had been lost with *Adventure*, had not been lost on the Admiralty and it was again decided to send two ships to widen the safety margin. Clerke was to prove himself made of sterner stuff than Furneaux for at no time were *Resolution* and *Discovery* separated for long.

Resolution was judged to be fit enough to go again and was given a crew of 112 men. She underwent a refit at Deptford but the work left her in worse condition than for her previous voyage and she leaked all the way to the Cape. It was a faulty mast which caused her return to Hawaii and led to Cook's death.

Charles Clerke's *Discovery*, a 298 ton ship, was the smallest of all those used by Cook. She was only eighteen months old when the Navy bought her and had been built in the yard of G and N Langborn in Whitby. She was 91ft. 5in. long with a beam of 27ft. 5in. and her shallow draught of 11ft. 5in. made her ideal for the inshore work she would be called upon to do. Like all Cats she was full built and roomy. *Discovery* came rigged as a brig but was altered to ship rig at Deptford, her two masts being replaced by three; some were of the opinion this made her over-masted.[4]

The Admiralty bought her from a Mr Herbert for £1865 and spent £550 on various alterations. Her armament was made up of eight four-pounders, eight swivel guns and eight musquetoons. The crew to sail her consisted of five officers, sixty-one men and one servant, a total of sixty-seven men. Clerke's accommodation was in the Great Cabin, very different from the tiny cupboard-like space with its 4ft. 7ins. headroom which had been his in *Endeavour*.

All in all, *Discovery* was a thoroughly good ship and, although small, well suited to the long journey she was to face. Cook, always an excellent judge of ships as well as of men, rated her as being faster than *Resolution* and better able to claw off a lee shore.

When work on the refitting was well advanced it was time to bring on board the provisions, sufficient to last far into the voyage. As usual, nearly everything was either stored in casks or on the hoof. This time Cook in *Resolution* had to take an extra cargo. George III had developed an interest in farming and the thought came to him that what better way could there be for him to show his regard for his fellow monarchs in the South Seas than to send them an animal or two? He could have had but little idea of the lack of space on board ships because one morning there appeared on the quayside an 'agricultural show' of sheep, pigs, horses and rabbits which had to be packed in somewhere, reducing the amount of room available to the humans.

'Farmer George' did not stop there for his generosity extended to his sending an assortment of seeds which, he thought, might help to supplement the diet of the people of the Pacific islands.

Clerke was a popular officer and several men asked to be transferred to his ship including two men from Pickersgill's *Lyon*.

When all was ready on 12th May 1776 the two ships moved down to Galleon's Reach to take on powder. They went on to the Nore where Cook came aboard, having left his wife for the last time at their home in the Mile End Road. *Resolution* and *Discovery* sailed to Plymouth where they arrived on Wednesday June 26th and anchored close together near Drake's Island. They each gave Admiral Amhurst a thirteen-gun salute, as befitted his rank. Charles Clerke was, of course, detained elsewhere and *Discovery* was brought round by James Burney, the First Lieutenant.

Early in June, Omai took leave of 'King Tosh' and went to join *Resolution*.[5] During his stay in England he had learned to read and write:

> Omiah who is now on board the *Resolution* in order to return to Otaheite, has made such good use of his time while in England that he was able to write his Sentiments in our language. The following is a copy of the card he sent to several of his friends. 'Omiah to take leave of good friend. He never forget England. He go on Sunday. God bless King George. He tell his people how kind English to him'.[6]

On Tuesday July 9th a full complement of marines arrived and were squeezed into the ships wherever space could be found. There were twelve of them, a sergeant, a corporal, nine privates and a drummer and some were to play a part in Cook's last moments.

As usual, not everyone was convinced that the voyage was an event not to be missed. It was common for there to be desertions before a ship sailed on a long cruise— and this was scheduled to be a very long one. *Discovery*'s forthcoming departure was no exception. Marine Moses Smith made off but was quickly retaken. Burney ordered that he be given twelve lashes for staying ashore without leave and selling his clothes, this always being taken as a sure sign that the man was preparing to desert. This was the standard punishment for the offence and was not regarded as being excessive. A seaman by the name of Jerimiah Holloway was in trouble, too, in his case for striking an officer, and he paid the same penalty as

Moses Smith. A contributory cause of the trouble was that the crew had received all the wages due to them to date plus two months in advance. This was normal practice before a long voyage and no doubt it encouraged some over-indulgence and consequential bravado among men who knew they would be away from home for several years.

On his arrival on board *Discovery*, Clerke had found that not everyone was fit. He reported to the Admiralty Secretary:

> . . . was busied yesterday in getting two men in lieu of two I've sent to the Hospital, one with Small Pox which was rather an unfortunate precedent, but I've exchang'd the only two marines that have not had this distemper for others that have, and among the seamen there are only two who have not had it . . . I shall immediately get under weigh and proceed according to their Lordships instructions and hope in the course of the Voyage to act in such a manner as to render myself not wholly unworthy that distinguish'd indulgence their Lordships have been so good as to favor me with.

The apparent prevalence of small pox is very surprising if Clerke's words are taken at face value. When he writes of the men who had had the disease he cannot have been referring to vaccination because Edward Jenner did not begin to use the technique, using cow pox, until 1796. Taken literally, his report means that virtually every man aboard had, at some time or another, suffered from the disease.

Cook's imminent departure had been noted in the London press which took a great interest in naval affairs. The newspapers were always full of reports of arriving and departing ships, of convoys gathering and, sadly, of vessels which had been lost. On 13th June 1776 the *London Chronicle* wrote:

> Capt. Cook, of his Majesty's Ship *Resolution* who is going out for the third time on further discoveries to the South Seas, took leave of his Majesty, he being in a few days to sail in company with the *Discovery*, Capt. Clerke now at Gravesend, on the said voyage.

It is interesting that six weeks before he was released from St. George's Fields, Clerke was named in the press as commander of *Discovery*.

Cook knew that if he was to make best use of the southern summer he must soon leave England. He was aware that Clerke expected to secure his freedom in the near future but he did not know exactly when that would be. Early in July, Cook was instructed by the Admiralty to get to sea as soon as he could and not to wait too long for Clerke at the Cape.

In his turn, Cook left instructions for his second in command. Clerke was to follow him to the Cape of Good Hope without a moments loss of time and if Cook was not already there, and did not arrive within thirty days, he was to conclude that some accident had happened to him and he was to carry out the expedition alone according to the Admiralty's orders. Cook took *Resolution* out of Plymouth Sound on 12th July 1776 and set off for Cape Town and the Pacific.

As had happened before, the Admiralty had issued Cook with a second, secret set of orders which had been sent by the Admiralty Secretary to Plymouth in a sealed package. There was a copy for Clerke, with instructions for them to be opened only if the two ships failed to meet. The vessels were to make their way to the Cape via Madeira, and go on by either the Cape Verde Islands or the Canaries. They were to be away from Southern Africa by the end of October and then sail eastward. On his last voyage, Cook had met a French explorer named Crozet, then in command of an East Indiaman, who had told him that he had discovered, four years before, a group of islands lying in the Indian Ocean to the south-east of the Cape. The Admiralty ordered Cook to make an accurate fix of these islands as he went eastwards and of another group, not far away, called the Kerguelan Islands, where the French sailors had allegedly been abandoned. The ships were to go to Queen Charlotte Sound and thence to the old base in Tahiti where Omai was to be resettled and any necessary repairs to the ships carried out. They must leave there by February 1777, at the latest, and sail to make landfall on the north-west coast of North America, Drake's New Albion, at about 45° 0' N. in the region of present day Portland, Oregon. They were then to follow the coast to the north in search of any waterway which might lead towards the north-east, going as far as 65° 0' N. The winter was to be spent in the Russian port of Petropavlovsk on the Kamchatka Peninsular. When spring came again, and conditions had improved sufficiently, the search was to be resumed.

Spain still had a considerable presence in the Americas and the British Government had troubles enough without adding any more; the last thing that was wanted was for the Spaniards to give help to the American revolutionaries— although they eventually did so. Cook and Clerke were under strict orders that they were to keep well away from any territory claimed by Spain and any unavoidable contact was to be kept to a minimum.

Finally, the orders said that if the expedition was not successful in finding a direct way into the Atlantic the ships were to make their way home by any route the commanders thought best.

Charles Clerke left England for the last time in the early afternoon of Thursday 1st August 1776. A firm breeze from the south-west helped *Discovery* on her way as she cleared Plymouth Sound, passing the homeward bound *Richmond* and *Camilla* the next day. He was in high spirits, as well he might be, and wrote to his friend Banks:

> . . . Cook sail'd tomorrow it will be 3 Weeks a damn'd long stretch but we must see it out—I shall get hold of him I fear not . . . Huzza my Boys heave away—away we go—adieu my best friend . . .

He was, of course, anxious to catch up with Cook who was now well on his way to Cape Town and *Discovery* was passing Cape Finisterre, on the north-west corner of Spain, by the 7th. Such was his hurry he did not follow the usual practice of stopping at Madeira for water; *Discovery* went no nearer 'The Island' than five leagues— about seventeen miles. Inevitably there was a water shortage and it had to be rationed to two quarts a man per day. Clerke had taken with him a machine which distilled salt water and, although it worked well, it did so painfully slowly. After operating for three and a half hours it had produced only six gallons; not much when divided between sixty-seven men.

Early in the voyage he began to put into practice the health and hygiene techniques he had seen used by Cook. Cleanliness and order were top of the list. When a sailor went to sea he put all his possessions in a sea chest which he stored wherever space could be found. *Discovery* was a small ship and she was overcrowded so, three weeks after leaving Plymouth, in order to make a little more room, Clerke ordered most of the chests to be thrown over the side and replaced by the canvas bags he had issued. Cook was a great believer in fumigation so on 27th August Clerke had fireballs lighted to smoke the ship. Their therapeutic effect was probably minimal but if it demonstrated to the crew a commitment to hygiene it was no bad thing.

From all his previous experience, and particularly having seen what it had done to Furneaux's crew, Clerke was well aware of what havoc could be wreaked by scurvy. After a few weeks at sea without a proper diet the gums began to bleed and the teeth loosened, then there was haemorrhaging into the joints, making them excruciatingly tender, and then came increasing weakness followed by death.

Resolution had been entirely free of the curse and Clerke had seen how this was achieved. There was no sign of scurvy on *Discovery* but he was taking no chances and he had the doctor issue wort, one of the remedies by which Cook set great store, to all the men thought to be most at risk.

Disease was not the only cause of death on board ships and the first man to be lost was the victim of an accident. George Harrison was the Marine corporal and he fell into the sea from the bowsprit on 24th September. A boat was launched but all that could be found after a thorough search was his cap. Following the Naval custom, his personal effects were auctioned six days later.

Clerke was not known as a harsh disciplinarian but he accepted corporal punishment as an essential part of the Navy's way of maintaining order. He soon had to exert his authority. At different times he ordered that Harmet Thompson, William Passmore, and Fulke Lowe each be given twelve lashes for committing one of a variety of the usual offences which included neglect of duty, drunkenness, and showing contempt for a superior officer.

Discovery justified Cook's opinion of her being a faster ship than *Resolution*, although she was no ocean racer, and Clerke pushed her hard. He took her along a track which was well out towards the Brazilian coast to pick up the favourable winds he knew were to be found there and during the morning of Sunday 10th October the men on *Resolution*, anchored under Table Mountain, saw *Discovery* come out of the mist and sail into the bay. She was three and a half weeks behind Cook's ship, having been delayed off the Cape by a south-easterly gale which had blown her out to sea again. *Resolution* was the only ship in Table Bay which had not dragged her anchor and it had taken *Discovery* ten days to cover the last few miles. Clerke thought the wind had been violent enough to knock over Table Mountain. *Resolution* had arrived rather later than she might have done because, as Clerke had anticipated, Cook had experienced difficulties with George III's floating farm and had been forced to stop at Tenerife to pick up food for the animals.

Clerke's crew was in a healthy state although, he said, the men had a 'little of the Small and an abundance of the French Pox among us at our sailing'.

The Navy was never short of men of initiative and one of Cook's crew had shown himself to be a man of some enterprise during the voyage south. William Hunt was an armourer and he had whiled away a few hours making counterfeit coins. While his technique may have been impeccable, the authorities did not appreciate the results and his efforts were rewarded with a return passage to England on board the *Hampshire* which was about to sail when Clerke arrived. Forgery was a serious crime and Mr Hunt may well have ended his days hanging from a rope.

He was not the only malefactor. William Brown of *Discovery*, having been in Cape Town a fortnight, found the attractions of shore life greater than the appeal of a three year voyage and deserted on 26th November.

Discovery had been leaking ever since leaving Plymouth. By the time of her arrival at the Cape, *Resolution's* maintenance was complete so the crews of both ships were set to the task of re-caulking the new arrival. Before Cook left England, Clerke had arranged with him that when *Resolution* arrived in Cape Town her cooks would save time by baking bread— ships biscuits— for *Discovery's* use. Other provisions had been bought from the traders of Cape Town and these were loaded aboard, ready for the next stage of the journey.

Charles Clerke and the officers and men of the two vessels made the most of their last chance for a run ashore in a European-style port. One of his shipmates was David Nelson, a gardener from Kew, who followed pursuits which were different from those which interested most sailors. He had been engaged by Banks to collect plants and Nelson went ashore to gather specimens for the great botanist from the abundant flora of the Cape. Nelson was involved in a similar task a few years later when he went with Bligh in *Bounty* to collect bread fruit plants in Tahiti. He survived the long voyage in an open boat after the mutiny only to die in Timor in June 1789. Clerke's friend Gore, who was always the hunter, went on a shooting expedition in the countryside, albeit not a very successful one.

Cape Town was a place which was gaining in importance as a staging post to the Far East and, although the town was still small, everything that the crews wanted was there in abundance. For the duration of the stay the men from both ships lived on the fat of the land.

Clerke was raring to go and full of optimism when he wrote from Cape Town to Banks:

> Here I am hard and fast moor'd alongside my Old Friend
> Capt. Cook so that our battles with the Israelites cannot now
> have any ill effects upon our intended attack on the North Pole.

On December 1st, when leave was over and preparations were as complete as they could possibly be, *Resolution* and *Discovery* left Table Bay and sailed in company towards the supposed position of the Crozet Islands. As Clerke told Banks, he was now returning to his old trade of exploring.

Before they left, Cook gave written instructions of what he must do if the ships became separated. He was to spend one day looking in the immediate area and, if contact had not been re-established after twenty-four hours he was then to go on to Queen Charlotte Sound. If the ships had parted before reaching Mauritius there was a variation to the plan because Clerke was then to spend seven to ten days looking for islands reported by the French to lie at 48° to $48\frac{1}{2}$° S. by 60° E. Only then was he to continue to Queen Charlotte Sound before going on to Tahiti. If Cook had not arrived in Polynesia within six weeks he was to carry out their Lordships' instructions, sailing on alone.

Strong winds did cause them to loose contact but they soon rejoined, made a precise fix of the islands and continued on the way east. They lost one another again in thick fog in spite of *Resolution* firing a gun every hour and Cook was alone when he found Kerguelen Island on Christmas Eve 1776. *Discovery* was not far behind.

All was not well with Clerke. The tuberculosis he had contracted in England, probably during his sojourn in the King's Bench Prison, was now beginning to make its presence felt. He was feeling unwell and would have been suffering from the night sweats associated with this stage of the disease. Charles was convinced he had caught it in prison but consumption was a very common condition in the Navy where many of the men, when they were ashore, lived in the poorest parts of the towns in unhealthy conditions. Tuberculosis flourished in these places and it could spread quickly in an overcrowded ship if brought on board by a man suffering from the active phase of the disease. The condition sometimes takes some time to manifest itself and it is at least possible that Clerke had contracted it on his previous voyage.

Before they left Kerguelen on 30th December, the ships took on water. They had no tanks to store it in and it was always hard work collecting it in barrels, rolling them to the beach and then manhandling them into the ships' boats before hoisting the casks aboard. On this voyage it was more exhausting than usual for extra provision had to be made for King George's version of Noah's Ark. The animals also needed fodder, and mountains of grass were cut and brought aboard in the form of haystacks.

Clerke thought Kerguelen Island was a desolate and wretched place. Seals and penguins were caught to augment the diet and he found them:

> . . . tolerably palatable and very nutritive, but our Voyage at
> present is too young; we have not yet eat Salt Beef enough to
> give a zest to these good things, which sometime hence we shall
> have a much better relish for.

Clerke had heard the story of the alleged abandonment of the
French sailors on Kerguelan and a member of one of his working
parties found evidence which confirmed that *Resolution* and *Discovery*
were not the first ships to visit the place. In the true tradition of
desert islands, one of his men, while walking along the shore line,
came across a bottle with a message in it, written by a fellow sailor
three years earlier.

In the New Year they continued on the way eastward across the
Southern Ocean and arrived at Van Diemen's Land, the island we
now call Tasmania. When the sailors waded ashore on 26th January
1777 they were the first people to visit the race since Tasman came in
1642 and Furneaux in 1773.

Time was so short that there was no opportunity for exploration,
so neither Cook nor Clerke were ever to know that Tasmania is
surrounded by sea and is not the southern tip of Australia.

Next day they saw the first people. The crews of the ships were
engaged in cutting wood at the time when they appeared and the
Tasmanians were amazed by technology so much in advance of their
own. To them, there was something almost magical in the way
European tools could cut through timber; so much so, they came
again the following day to marvel and Clerke was pleased to see them:

> We again had the pleasure of their company, it really was a
> pleasure as they were perfectly innocent.

He was a keen observer of all the indigenous people he met and
these Tasmanians were no exception. After an acquaintance of three
days he wrote:

> The inhabitants seem to have made the least progress
> towards any kind of improvement since Dame Nature put them
> out of hand of any people I have met; when they came to us they
> were perfectly naked, excepting 2 or 3 of the women who had
> infants with them. They each had a Bag made of the Skins of
> the Kangaroo in which the child was hung at their backs. They
> had no kind of Arms and seemed to have no Idea of doing or
> receiving any Mischief; there was a harmless Cheerfulness about
> them which appeared to me the effects of this happy
> unsuspicous temper.

Their standards of hygiene were another matter, and these he
found less impressive, for he went on:

They had little idea of anything we deem decent, that they absolutely let their water run about them as they went along, with a perfect Indifference as the filthiest animal we have among us could possibly do.

The sailors never seemed to learn and Clerke had to deal with indiscipline in his crew; most cases were caused by over indulgence in alcohol. A typical example that occurred during the stay in Van Diemen's Land was when four of *Discovery's* marines stole some liquor and were found dead drunk in the bottom of one of the ship's boats. This he could not tolerate and each was punished with twelve lashes.

The ships' stay in Van Diemen's Land was short, for Cook was anxious to go about the main purpose of the voyage, and they sailed on the penultimate day of January 1777. An incident took place soon after the two ships left for New Zealand, this time with a tragic outcome. George Hood fell overboard on 4th February and, try as they might, his shipmates could not find him. *Discovery* and *Resolution* were not far apart at the time and Clerke sailed closer until the distance was narrow enough for him to be able to shout the news to Cook across the water.

The Maoris of Queen Charlotte Sound were very apprehensive when the Englishmen returned on 12th February 1777. Four years before, Furneaux had sent ashore a grass cutting party from *Adventure* after she had become separated from *Resolution*; every last man had been killed and some had undoubtedly been cannibalised. The Maoris were right in thinking the incident had not been forgotten.

Cook and Clerke wanted to know what had happened and on the Sunday morning of 16th February 1777 they went to Grass Cove where the massacre had taken place. After landing from their boat, they met Maoris whom they recognised from the previous voyage and began to question them. They received a variety of answers. The first was that the Englishmen had wandered a little way from their boat and sat down to eat lunch, a native tried to snatch some bread and fish, there was a quarrel in which punches were exchanged and two Maoris were shot dead. The boat's crew were then seized, knocked on the head and killed.

A second account told of a native stealing a coat from the ship's boat, being struck by Ferneaux's black servant and the men then being set upon.

A chief called Kahourah was a visitor to the ship and Omai pointed him out as the man who was said to have led the attack on Furneaux's people. When nothing was done about it, Omai queried the English sense of justice, wanting to know why, if the death penalty was applied for killing one man, Kahourah was not killed for having slaughtered ten. Cook thought getting at the truth was more important than retribution and went out of his way to reassure the chief that he was in no danger. This gave Kahourah enough confidence to offer yet another account of what had happened. It all began, he said, when a Maori offered for sale a stone hatchet and, when a sailor took it but would not pay, this was the time when the bread and fish were taken in lieu of trade goods. To show goodwill, before he left Cook gave presents; two goats and a kid and two pigs were given to the Maoris.

Clerke, too, could see no useful purpose being served by punishing Kahourah although he was doubtful of the truth of the stories being told. He summed up his feelings in this way:

> There are few Indians in whom I wou'd wish to put a perfect confidence, but of all I ever met with these shou'd be the last, for I firmly believe them very capable of the most perfidious and cruel treachery . . .

There was no advantage to be gained from prolonging the stay and the ships remained only long enough for Cook and Clerke to obtain the provisions they needed—water, vegetables and more grass for the animals—before leaving on the 25th of the month. The winds were not favourable but there was now no sense of urgency because the commanders had come to realise that it was now too late in the season to get into high latitudes that year.

Both food and water were beginning to be in short supply early in April 1777 and, while still at sea, Cook sent Clerke written instructions which dealt with the new situation in which they found themselves. Because the contrary winds made it impossible to get to Tahiti and then begin the search for the route into the Atlantic via the North Pole, the ships were to set course for the Friendly Islands. The usual arrangements were made if they became separated and there were orders about where and how long each should wait for the other. In essence, Clerke was told that if Cook had not made contact by the end of October, he was to carry on alone and execute the Admiralty's orders. He had been given a copy of them at the Cape and was now at liberty to open the packet.

Shortly after their arrival at Anamooka (to which earlier explorers had given the European name of Rotterdam) on 2nd May a local dignitary appeared and presented himself as King Feenbow. He had with him his Prime Minister and this worthy recited at length the names of the islands over which his master held domain. Clerke counted up to a hundred of them before he gave up: 'those were Isles enough in conscience for any one Man'. Charles felt far from well but he was still observant enough to take note of Feenbow's ladies: '. . . half a dozen very fine young Lasses composed his Majesties Seraglio.' Each side entertained the other; the marines exercised, Cook gave a fireworks display and Feenbow ordered about one hundred men to dance and sing to the beat of drums. Clerke thought the movements of the dancers were more uniform than those of the marines. The women followed and played their part in the performance by the light of torches made from the burning leaves of Palm trees soaked in oil:

> The ladies were peculiarly attired for their Exhibitions in various coloured robes in which they looked very graceful and beautiful; they performed to Music of Drums and singing, were perfectly regular in their motions, which however were to us altogether novel . . . everything was conducted with the utmost good humour and cordiality.

At the end of May, Clerke and Cook had reason to doubt Feenbow's claims to sovereignty and began to wonder how important he really was, for another King had appeared on the scene. Clerke describe Powlahow, for such was his name, as an 'indolent, fat, greasy rogue whose sole delight was laughing, drinking, and the diversions of the Seraglio' but it was noticeable that when Feenbow returned from a journey he was quick to defer to the newcomer. Powlahow provided another form of entertainment, far removed from the innocence of the dancing and almost reminiscent of the Roman Games; it was then that the sailors saw a more violent side of the life of the islands. A circle was made of upwards of 3,000 people and within the arena so formed there were wrestling and boxing matches followed by men who:

> Fought with clubs . . . they banged each other about the head most heartily . . . but though they were thus set on to knock each other about for the amusement of their superiors. They put up with The very disagreeable sensation with the same complacency they would have shown in the most innocent and pleasing amusements . . . but such was their great good Nature and happy disposition, that I never saw anything like a passion or the least heat of temper.

Clerke took a traditional view of the activities in which women could take part and was horrified when:

> The women are introduced into these boxing Matches and do lay one another about the face and eyes most intolerably; this however we put aside in some measure during our stay, for to us

who are accustomed to pay such attention to the Ladies it appeared a most unnatural and barbarous amusement.

The two captains were then told of the existence of an even greater potentate, who, they were assured, it was of the utmost importance they cultivate. He would have come to the ships in person, Powlahow told them, but he had heard that people would walk on the deck over his head, and this was quite unacceptable. Clerke and Cook asked to be taken to this great man. When they were told that anyone admitted to the presence had to be naked from the waist up they replied in no uncertain terms that when they met King George— who was a much more powerful monarch— all they did was to take off their hats and they had no intention of doing anything else for this king.

Powlahow agreed to take them next day to meet King Mallawogga and they set off on a six mile row, taking with them appropriate presents. When they arrived at his village an interminable wait began— one can only imagine what was said by the visitors— and Clerke 'began to be inquisitive to know when his Majesty wou'd be enough at leisure to give us a few minutes Audience'. A variety of excuses was offered— he was either ill, at his religious offices or, least likely of all, at the ships. The officers' patience passed breaking point and they went back to where the vessels were moored.

The denouement came the next day when they were told that Mallawogga was on the beach close by. They promptly went ashore and found a very old man, plainly in his second childhood, sitting under a tree surrounded by a great rabble. The conclusion they came to was that the whole situation had been set up to extract more gifts, and, indeed, the plot worked because Cook gave a present of a bull and a cow, a horse and a mare and some sheep and goats.

Another of the ugly sides of life in the Friendly Isles was seen when William Ellis, a surgeon's mate on *Discovery*, was asked by a local chief if the muskets he had seen in the hands of the Europeans were capable of killing a man. An islander happened to be passing in a canoe and, when Ellis confirmed that they were, he was asked to give a practical demonstration: 'He is only a slave', said the chief. He had to take the guns' powers on trust for he was not obliged with a demonstration.

Wherever they went there were few problems with the exception of the constant thieving, which was as much a cause of friction between the Europeans and the native population as it had been on previous voyages. For example, on 22nd May Thomas Stretcher had been

142.

posted as a sentry 'purposely to prevent the committing of any thefts'. Unfortunately for him his attention was distracted for a moment and while his back was turned a thief swooped. Poor Stretcher had six lashes for 'suffering the Indians to steal his boathook'. Two months later another sailor had cause to resent the habits of the natives when Christopher Kervin had twelve lashes for having his ramrod 'stolen by the Indians'. Cook had become increasingly intolerant. He resorted to flogging islanders who were caught stealing and even, on a few occasions, to cutting off their ears. Today, this seems a barbaric thing to do but his action should be judged by the standards of a society which accepted as normal punishments which would today be regarded as being cruel in the extreme. *The Chelmsford Chronicle*, in common with most provincial newspapers, quoted the London press in giving accounts of public executions. It gave detailed reports of how men and women were taken to the gallows, printed verbatim accounts of their last speeches, related if they were defiant or repentant and told of the reactions of the onlooking crowd—the members of which usually seemed to have had a thoroughly enjoyable day out. If a particularly notorious criminal was to be executed, high prices were paid for windows overlooking the scaffold and were booked days in advance. One 1780 edition of the *Chronicle* even carried a report of a man being branded. For their time, the corporal punishment inflicted by both Cook and Clerke was relatively modest and they rarely went beyond the twelve strokes allowed a captain. There were a few occasions when they went as far as forty, but they were very rare.

Although Clerke ordered floggings he sometimes used more subtle methods in less serious cases. He believed in the power of ridicule and one of his techniques was to shave off half the hair and half the beard of some native offenders and then have them thrown overboard. An added advantage was that persistent thieves could easily be spotted in a crowd.

Clerke was on good terms with Powlahow and when he complained to him that yet more things had been stolen the King said he would execute the next thief to be caught. Clerke did not take him up on the offer and when the next villain was apprehended he confined himself to having him flogged and pitched into the sea. There the man stayed for the next fifteen minutes, quite ignored by his fellow islanders, until a passing canoe stopped and picked him up.

During the first few days of July, Powlahow issued a special invitation to Cook and Clerke to join the gentry of Tonga at a ceremony to mark the coming of age of his son. One of the customs of the island dictated that two great people could not eat or drink in sight of one another; the forthcoming ritual would remove the ban and the son would then be allowed to dine with his father.

Men armed with clubs cleared the streets of people, knocking on the head anyone who was out of his house during the hours when the ceremony was taking place. Although the King had given the officers a personal invitation, when they arrived at the grassy knoll upon which the sovereign sat under a canopy, they were told it would not be possible for them to see what went on. It came as something of a surprise when they were placed behind a bamboo screen but it was no great challenge for them to separate a few strands and look through the resultant gap. What they saw before them was a crowd of about six hundred of the island's noblemen who were offering their allegiance to the Heir Apparent by giving presents. In between times, priests were conducting religious ceremonies. This went on all day and when the proceedings started again twenty-four hours later Cook and Clerke were there again, once more in position to see what was going on. They were observing only the preliminaries to an even more important event and Clerke was told that in a repeat performance, which would take place in two months time, ten men would be sacrificed before the young prince. David Samwell, surgeon's mate on *Resolution*, was given an even higher estimate and was told that as many as fifty people would die. Samwell heard that to honour Powlahow each chief would have to offer sacrifices, the number to be determined by his rank. Feenbow's quota was six and the lesser chiefs between one and four, with each chief personally carrying out the execution by knocking the victim on the head with a club. Samwell asked if the poor men knew they were to be killed and was told they did not, for if they did they would run away.

Clerke saw another example of the crueller side of island life when one day, while he was walking through the market place, he saw a male adulterer being given a severe beating. The woman was left untouched and Charles was surprised to see that a few minutes later everyone was going about their usual business and the incident had been forgotten.

A short time later his cats were stolen from on board *Discovery*, although he noticed that the rats had been left untouched. Clerke was fond of his animals and tried as hard as he could to get them back but apparently the islanders' affection for them was deep for they refused to part company with them.

Despite some of their habits, he liked and admired the people of the Tongan islands.

> The people in their persons surpass in beauty every Nation I
> ever yet met with, excepting the natives of the Marquesas . . .
> Chastity is by no means the reigning virtue of these Isles, the
> Good Lasses readily contributed their share to our
> Entertainment and rendered our Bill of Fare compleat, but I am
> very sorry to have Occasion to observe that at our arrival this
> time, we found them cursed with Venereal Taints.

Clerke was intrigued by the structure of the society he saw which was far removed from the ideals ascribed to it by the philosophers of the Age of Enlightenment. The word of Powlahow, Feenbow and Mallawogga was absolute, and there was no appeal against any judgement they might make. Priests could do as they liked, and men who were higher up the social scale could help themselves to the goods of those who were inferior to them. One day Charles saw a priest beat a man who had not got out of his way quickly enough. The attack was so severe the victim had a discharge of blood from his ears and mouth and he went into convulsions. Another time he saw four or five men armed with clubs launch an attack on a man which was so vicious his skull was injured and a thigh was smashed. The Englishmen tried to stop them but it was too late because his injuries were so serious he died soon afterwards. His crime, they were told, had been to be on over-friendly terms with the wife of a priest. Clerke was again amazed that the bystanders were quite indifferent to what was going on and were behaving perfectly normally five minutes later.

The Tongans went in for self-mutilation, for it was their custom to mark the death of a parent by cutting off the tip of the little finger; left for the mother, right for the father, and beating their faces until the blood ran. Mallawogga's wife died during their visit and one girl that Clerke knew well carried the practice so far, as a mark of respect, that he was unable to recognise her.

These incidents represented the unpleasant side of life in Tonga but, for the sailors, they were far outweighed by the warmth of the welcome given them. The Friendly Isles lived up to their name and everywhere they went they were met by smiling faces; it was this that left the lasting impression. Well into the next century, old men must have sat in taverns and beer houses in England, telling tales of their experiences in Tonga when they were young.

By now Clerke had acquired a fair measure of fluency in the Polynesian language and in conversation he was told of an island five days away by fast sailing canoe, which he judged to be at a distance of about 200 leagues, or 650 miles. The inhabitants of Fiji were held in great awe, with the men being described as being good to have as friends but veritable devils as enemies. It seemed that Fiji, like Tonga and Tahiti, was not a classless society:

> They tell us the Fidgi gentry frequently eat their Prisoners and deem a jolly good Carcass of a man the most delicious Fare in the World, so much so, that the Feast is wholly devoted to the Gentry, the lower Class not being suffer'd to taste.

During his stay in Tonga a canoe came in from Fiji. Clerke was ill but he had not lost his powers of observation and saw that one man had had the gristle of his ears cut out and that the fleshy part of the ear hung down to his shoulder.

Resolution and *Discovery* left Tonga and went to Tahiti, reaching the old anchorage in Matavai Bay on the morning of 13th August. When he landed, Clerke was surprised to see a native coming towards him dressed in richly embroidered clothes, quite unlike anything he had seen on his previous visits. He asked the man how he had come by them and was told they had been given him by the captain of a Spanish ship which had been there the previous evening. Clerke thought this was an unlikely tale but Cook had to be told so he went over to *Resolution* to pass on the news. The native went with him and gave a convincing performance in the Great Cabin by reciting the names of the officers on the Spanish vessel.

The two English captains were still not convinced but, to be on the safe side, they ordered away a boat to neighbouring O'Tahiti Bay 'to see whether Signior was or was not there'. In the meantime Clerke was rowed back to *Discovery* and cleared the ship for action: 'in case the Gentry should prove troublesome'.

It took the boat two days to get back to report that no sign had been found of the mysterious ship. Clerke wrote in his Journal his conclusion that the episode was 'nothing more than another Proof of the fertility of the Genius of our good Friends here, in puffing these kinds of Stories'. He recognised that Englishmen did not have a monopoly on a sense of humour.

He was being a little harsh because what had really happened was eventually uncovered. At the end of 1774 two Spanish ships from Lima had called at Tahiti and stayed for two or three months during which time the captain died and the crews erected an inscribed cross. When the vessels departed, taking with them two Tahitians, three or four Catholic priests were left behind and were picked up when the ships came back ten months later. The Spanish officers were not unduly modest and told the Tahitians that they were very great men indeed and their sovereign was King of the Universe. The Tahitians asked about England and Clerke's record of the ensuing conversation may owe a little to his imagination:

> England says Signior, England . . . I recollect the place you mean; there was a damned little dirty piratical State called England . . . but our omnipotent King, who immediately sent a few of his Ships and Troops, destroy'd the Country, and ras'd the rascally breed from the Face of the Earth, so that that State is now no more and the very name nearly forgot.

Clerke talked with one of the men who had made the journey to Peru and was told that in his opinion Lima was a poor place because it had none of the red feathers so prized by the Tahitians. The Spaniards left more useful presents because they made the islanders a gift of various animals including a bull which Clerke eventually came upon in Opare:

> . . . the bull we found at Opare, and a fine fellow he is, but poor Devil, he was the only Being I'll answer for it, throughout the Isle, that could not now and then Solace himself with a little Amorous dalliance; however this defect was supplied by Capt. Cook, who gave them some Cows.

A war between the islands was brewing and the rulers came to the conclusion that what was needed to gain a head's start over the opposition was a little Divine Intercession. One of the parties decided to send a messenger to the Gods to make sure their superior case had a proper hearing so their King sent out men to:

> . . . find the most worthless, unconnected rascal in the whole district (who at this time had not the least idea of the Honourable business he is going upon) and privately gives order for 4 or 5 of his people to go and knock him on the head, which they take care to do . . . the poor fellow having not the least Notion of the Business till these Executioners begin to work upon him . . .

Two or three days later a great congregation gathered and the victim's body became the centre of a ceremony conducted by a group of six to eight priests. Various rites were performed and prayers were offered to the unfortunate intermediary (who may well have felt disinclined to oblige) to:

> . . . intreat of him as a very particular Favour that he will make use of all his Interest with the Omnipotent Being and beg him to further their Arms with Success, and assist them to destroy the Enemy they are now going to fight against.

Although Clerke's sense of humour had not failed him his health was notably worse and he was now considering a drastic course of action. He was not the only man on *Discovery* to be suffering from tuberculosis; Anderson, the ship's surgeon, had also contracted the disease. Burney, the First Lieutenant, left an account of what happened on Tahiti in August 1777, as he was told it by Anderson about a month before the doctor's death.

Anderson had a professional knowledge of a condition he must have seen many times during his service in the Navy and it was in the light of this that the two sick men discussed their situation. The doctor thought the cold weather for which they were bound was sure to be the death of them both but that a warmer climate might just give them some small chance of recovery. The two men agreed they should ask permission of Cook to stay in the Society Islands but Clerke could never quite bring himself to make the final request. At Huahine, Ulietea and Bolabola he found his books were not in order and his excuse in the Sandwich Islands was that the natives were less civilised. All the evidence suggests that it is doubtful if he ever seriously intended being left behind. His sense of duty pulled more strongly than concern for his own health and he merely toyed with the idea, all the while meaning to see the matter through to the end.

On the days when he was well enough, Clerke sometimes went riding with Cook along the beach of Matavai Bay, on the horses sent by King George. The Tahitians had never before seen such animals and they could hardly believe their eyes when they made their first appearance. The islanders quickly came to the conclusion that what they were witnessing was nothing less than man-carrying pigs.

Attention was now turned to one of the main purposes of the voyage, the resettlement of Omai in his homeland. His fellow countrymen were less than overwhelmed by his reappearance and at first chose to ignore him, but he eventually managed to engage the attention of some of them by displaying part of the wealth he had accrued in Europe. They were suitably impressed when he produced a cache of red feathers, much prized in Tahiti. Cook decided that Omai had a better chance of being accepted on Huahine so he was taken there. When the ships arrived at that island the carpenters were put to work building a stout house on the outside of which was copied the inscription:

Georgius Tertius Rex, 2 Novembris 1777
Naves { **Resolution, Jac. Cook, Pr.**
Discovery, Car. Clerke Pr.

Other men from the crews laid out a garden. Cook was still worried about what would happen to Omai when the Europeans finally left so a code was devised which he could use to communicate with the ships while they were still in the area. If Omai sent two white beads it meant that all was well, two brown signified that they were indifferent and two blue ones would tell Cook that things were going badly. It was not long before the indifference the people of Huahine had shown to Omai turned to animosity. One man in particular was incensed by Omai's flaunting of his wealth and by his association with the visitors, which he sometimes emphasised in an attempt to impress his peers by riding with Clerke and Cook. There may have been other reasons for his hatred, perhaps the resurrection of an old feud but, whatever the reason may have been, his inability to control his anger was to cost him dear.

Omai's enemy went on board _Discovery_ on Wednesday, 22nd October and stole a sextant. To the thief, whose name is now lost, it was probably only another piece of metal but to Clerke it was an essential instrument of navigation. The sextant was soon recovered and the malefactor was 'deprived of his ears and turned on shore'. It is no surprise that he was determined to get his revenge and he set about his task with determination.

The new garden had been finished and the vengeance-seeker saw a means of settling the score. He broke in and did as much damage as he could, including taking up the newly planted seeds. His big mistake was to brag about the exploit; the news spread to Cook and, before he knew where he was, the man had been arrested and clapped in irons on board _Resolution_.

He may have had determination but he was sadly lacking in judgement. He showed resourcefulness five days later when he escaped, swam ashore but then promptly made another major error. He asked the first person he met to help him to set fire to Omai's house and the furniture inside it. Of all the people on the island he could have chosen, he picked on one of his enemy's few friends. The alarm was given, which was just as well because Omai had stored inside his house some gunpowder that Cook had given him. The arsonist beat a hasty retreat and disappeared into the community. His actions met with public approval and he was either a popular man or one who had evoked general sympathy because, despite the high value placed by the people of the island on all things made of metal, the offer of a reward of twenty axes never found a taker.

When the time drew near for his friends and protectors to depart, Omai gave a farewell banquet, perhaps seeking to extract a final morsel of credit with his neighbours from his close association with these powerful allies. Clerke's health was so poor he was now only rarely able to go ashore and he was too unwell to attend the festivities.

The bead code was used in November 1777 when Cook had gone on to Ulietea and Omai sent a message that all was well but that a goat had died. Cook sent him two kids by return.

Losing men through desertion was a constant problem for commanders in the South Seas and this voyage was no exception. This is hardly surprising because to lower deck sailors, who usually came from the most squalid parts of the English ports, the allure of what appeared to be the easy living of the Pacific islands must have been well nigh irresistible.

A marine who deserted from *Resolution* on 16th November was soon retaken but this was only a prelude to a more serious episode which took place a few days later, on the 24th, on the island of Raiatea.

It was the custom to muster the ship's companies each day at sunrise and sunset to deter desertion but that morning it was found that two of Clerke's crew had made off during the night. The men who had gone were Alexander Mouant, a sixteen year old Midshipman, and Thomas Shaw, a twenty-three year old gunner's mate from London. Mouant's desertion was particularly unfortunate because he was the son of Captain Mouant who had served with Cook at Quebec in 1759 and had then been in command of *Tamar* when she sailed with Byron. The young man had a girl friend and had asked permission to stay with her on the island but Cook had refused.

Clerke went off in pursuit in two boats, taking his marines with him, and when he returned empty handed he sent off Burney in the cutter with instructions to go round the island. When he, too, had no success Cook himself took up the chase and returned with the news that the men were on the nearby island of Bola-Bola.

Clerke now turned to subterfuge. It was the custom of three well connected Tahitians, the son, daughter-in-law and a son-in-law of Orea, the local chief, to make frequent visits to the ships. They were popular with the crews and Clerke wrote of them that 'he had a really strong partiality for them'. This did not prevent his enticing them aboard *Discovery* on the pretext of giving them presents of hatchets, beads and knives and then preventing them from leaving. At some time during the afternoon Clerke and Gore were rowed ashore and at about six o'clock that evening men on *Discovery* shouted across to

Cook, on the other ship, that the officers had been seized by the Chief's supporters. At almost the same moment, canoes were seen leaving *Discovery* and rushing towards the beach. Cook immediately sent a strong party in pursuit with orders to rescue the two officers but the excursion proved to be unnecessary. All that had happened was that a group of men armed with clubs had threatened them but had made off on Clerke's walking towards them while flourishing a pistol, which he discharged, and on hearing the sound of muskets firing at the retreating canoes. When Clerke felt well enough, he and Cook would sometimes take a swim together in a freshwater stream. The local people, of course, knew this and the two captains came to the conclusion that they had probably been intending to abduct them, mistaking Gore for Cook.

Within an hour of the three young people being detained in *Discovery*, a large party of women had gathered under her stern and began to give out a piercing wail. They kept up their performance for three hours, with the hostages joining in, and when it did not produce the desired result they further demonstrated their distress by cutting their heads with sharks' teeth.

The three being held eventually realised that things were not as bad as they seemed to be and they spent a pleasant time with the ship's officers in the Great Cabin of *Discovery*. Clerke, too, seems to have enjoyed his evening:

> When we got rid of the Tragedians we set down to dinner very cheerfully . . . My friends and companions in the Cabin are very happy, we now and then have a little serenade from a dozen old Women under the Stern, which interrupts their wonted cheerfulness a little, but they are now of short duration and we soon recover ourselves.

The islanders had realised that the game of hostage-taking was one which could be played by more than one side; they had not abandoned their kinsmen and a rescue operation was mounted. An armed party was sent to *Discovery* with the intention of seizing Clerke and holding him against the release of their own people but its effort ended in failure when a vigilant sailor, realising what was happening, shouted out an alarm. The crew rushed on deck armed with whatever came quickly to hand and repulsed the attack before harm could come to the Captain.

The King was naturally anxious to secure the return of his relatives and he sent men to Bola-Bola with strict instructions that Mouant and Shaw must immediately be brought back. The 'stray sheep', as Clerke called them, were retaken and punished; the gunners mate with twenty-four lashes and Capt. Mouant's son by being sentenced to serve before the mast for the remainder of the voyage.

The Tahitian hostages were returned to their families on 1st December and their deliverance was celebrated in style:

> In the evening they desired to be conveyed to the shore where they were received with as much ceremony and festivity as tho' they had narrowly escaped destruction.

Clerke seems to be forgetting that, while he knew that he was bluffing and that no harm would come to the people he was holding, they and their families were not privy to this happy information. The youngsters quickly recovered from the experience and before the ships left had made several further visits.

Despite his disgrace, things worked well for Mouant for in the fullness of time, in 1790, he made the rank of Commander. In the light of the success of his future career, two questions may be asked: did Mouant appreciate Cook's action in not allowing him to stay in Tahiti and did his experience make him more lenient with lovelorn deserters?

Resolution and *Discovery* left Tahiti for the last time and stopped at the nearby island of Bola-Bola where it was known that Bougainville had lost an anchor during his stay. The effort involved in retrieving it was worth while because of the high value placed on iron all over Polynesia. After the anchor was dredged up the armourers made it into objects such as axes, ready for trading.

Eighteenth century medicine had no treatment to offer Clerke and his illness followed its inexorable course. By this time he was losing weight, always feeling unwell and without energy, the lassitude being brought on by the underlying anaemia. The tuberculosis affecting Anderson had reached a more advanced stage and the two men again discussed what they should do. They resisted the temptation of staying in Tahiti, although they knew they would not live to see the completion of the voyage, and made the decision to stay with the expedition.

As they went on their way, Cook and Clerke used a system that they had developed which made it practicable for them to explore as much as possible of the area through which they were passing. The two ships spent the night cruising near to one another, but each morning *Discovery*, being the faster ship, hoisted as much sail as she could and set off on a slightly different course until the evening, when she hauled to and allowed *Resolution* to catch up with her.

There was always the possibility of their becoming separated as they sailed towards the west coast of America and when they were at Uliete Cook gave Clerke his updated instructions as to what he should do if this happened. They were complicated, for if contact had not been made within five days of the ships losing sight of one another, Clerke was to set course for New Albion to make landfall at about 45° N. and then cruise there for ten days. He was to go into the best and nearest harbour he could find, take in wood and water and, if he had not met up with Cook by 1st April 1778, he was to go to 56° N. and cruise until 10th May. Then he was to search alone for the North-West Passage and, if unsuccessful, spend the winter in the Russian port of St. Peter and St. Paul in Kamchatka, ready to resume the quest the following year.

On Christmas Day 1777 they came to a low, barren, sixteen miles long island which was destined to be the site of atomic bomb tests nearly two hundred years later. Two boats went ahead and found a channel into a lagoon filled with sharks. Next day Clerke sent ashore a hunting party which stayed overnight and returned the next day with forty or fifty turtles whose meat was used to supplement the diet of the crews.

Sailors are sometimes said to be less adept at finding their way on land than they are at sea but, as Christmas Island is only three miles wide, getting lost on it would seem to present something of a problem. Although Thomas Tretcher was a Londoner, and could presumably find his way round the streets and alleys of his home town, he and Bartholomew Lowman managed it. As they wandered along, without any idea of where they were, they could find no water and became more and more thirsty. Things were becoming desperate when they came across a turtle and cut the throat of the unfortunate animal. One of the men was in such a state he forced himself to drink its blood but the other could not bring himself to follow his example. They became separated and one of the exhausted sailors was found after twenty-four hours, the other after two days.

On the penultimate day of the year there was an eclipse of the sun and Cook, Bailey, and King went ashore to observe it and take measurements. Clerke was feeling very unwell; his health was at such a low ebb that he was unable to go with them.

The voyage continued and when landfall was made at Kauai on 20th January 1778 the sailors became the first Europeans to reach the Hawaiian Islands. It was the most northerly of five islands identified by Cook in a group he again named after the First Lord of the Admiralty, Lord Sandwich. The Hawaiians were fascinated and overcome with curiosity to see these vessels and men from another world. There was great excitement and in no time at all dozens of canoes were coming out from the shore. One of them tried to pass under the bows of *Discovery*, misjudged her speed and was accidentally rammed and sank; the occupants were soon fished out of the water and Clerke tried to make amends by giving them a few presents. Quite mollified, they returned the compliment by giving him a bowl which they had conveniently to hand. It was not only Hawaiians who finished in the sea because a week later Clerke's Marine sergeant, James Kich, fell overboard and was lucky to be rescued.

When Cook went ashore he was astonished by an act he had never before seen during his Pacific voyages. A large crowd of several hundred people was waiting for him and as he approached they all fell flat on their faces as a mark of respect because, to them, he was a demi-god landing from a gigantic canoe, as legend predicted would one day happen. Nevertheless, in at least one respect, deities were treated no differently from anyone else and thieving was soon all the vogue. Metal was as irresistible in Hawaii as it was everywhere else in the Pacific and soon any article made from it became an attraction which could not be denied; one enterprising man made off with the butcher's cleaver. That day, the 20th January 1778, Clerke's cabin was full of Hawaiians but it was not long before he had to clear them out because:

> . . . my Guests were exceedingly curious and very desirous of handling and examining whatever came in their way, especially if composed of the favourite Metal, Iron. The Cabin Windows were open and suspended by Iron Hooks; one of them in examining one of these Hooks, withdrew its Support from the window, which immediately shut down like a trap Door; something of the Kind I believe my poor friends took it for, for they directly made their way out at the other Windows (some of which by their crouding they broke in their way) with as much confusion and fright as tho' a battery had been opened upon them; we were going upwards of 4 knots at the time, however their canoes soon picked them up.

At Kauai a chief came out in a double canoe—Clerke was impressed by the Hawaiians' craft and the way they handled them—but, try as he would, he could entice him to go no further than the gangway. A group of attendants clasped hands and made a protective ring around the chief but when Clerke, in an attempt to show friendship took him by the hand, he was asked not to touch him because he was sacred. The two groups parted on good terms having exchanged gifts— a piece of beige cloth for a cava bowl.

Clerke thought the Hawaiians were attractive people, although he preferred the Tahitians. The houses in which they lived must have reminded him of his home village, for they were thatched and looked just like barns, reminiscent of those in Essex. Like the Tahitians, the Hawaiians mutilated themselves upon the death of a chief or a husband, in their case it was by the removal of the front teeth. Their dentitions were very good but, such was the frequency of one tragedy or another, it was unusual not to see gaps.

The visitors were well treated on Hawaii and obtained all the supplies that they needed for the coming voyage to the far north. Cook and Clerke had plenty of experience of their men spreading sexually transmitted diseases and, ever mindful of the need to reduce as much as possible the impact of new arrivals from Europe, they took preventive measures. Women were not permitted on the vessels, sailors were prohibited from spending the night ashore and any men known to be suffering from venereal disease were not allowed to leave the ships under any circumstances. No doubt a sailor's natural ingenuity gave some the chance to avoid the regulations, tempted as they were by the knowledge of what was in store for them during the coming months.

The stage of the voyage had been reached when the search for the North-West Passage was about to begin. The north-west coast of North America was still virtually unknown and the plan was to explore and chart it as the ships went towards the north. It was again necessary to consider in detail what must be done if the ships were to become separated and the resultant instructions which Cook gave to Clerke were much as they had been before. When they sailed in early February 1778 it had been decided that if contact was lost for any reason *Discovery* would stay five days in the immediate area. At the end of that time, if neither ship found the other, Clerke was to make his way to the coast of Drake's New Albion at about latitude 45° N. and wait a further ten days. If there was still no contact he was to follow the coastline northward to about 46° N. and cruise there until 10th May. If there was no sign of *Resolution* he was to continue the search alone and if he did not succeed in finding the Passage he was to take *Discovery* to winter in St. Peter and St. Paul, known to the Russians as Petropavlovsk. Clerke was a more determined man than Furneaux and it was not necessary to invoke these elaborate plans because, after leaving the Sandwich Islands on 2nd February, he kept in contact with Cook during the passage across the Pacific.

As they went norhwards, Clerke began to feel the cold, perhaps the more so because of his illness, and in February he wrote:

> We have been so long Inhabitants in the Torrid Zone, that we are all shaking with cold here with the Thermometer at 60°. I depend upon the assistance of a few good North Westers to give us a hearty rattling and bring us to our natural feelings a little, or the Lord knows how we shall make ourselves acquainted with the frozen secrets of the Arctic.

They reached the coast of North America on 6th March 1778, close to their intended landfall on the 45° N. parallel, near the present day site of Eugene, Oregon. Cook and Clerke were in need of a harbour because both vessels were leaking badly after the long passage. The weather was bad, gales prevented their finding a haven and they were forced to stay at sea longer than they would have wished. It was not until Sunday 29th March that a suitable port was found at Nootka Sound, on the west coast of Vancouver Island. As soon as the vessels dropped anchor, about forty canoes left the shore and came out to view the strange men in them.

Clerke again used the lessons he had learned from Banks and took a keen interest in these people. He had already recorded his thoughts on the inhabitants of the Pacific islands, New Zealand, and Patagonia and now it was the turn of the first people he met on the west coast of North America to be the object of his uninhibited judgement:

> The natives here are exceedingly ill made, having large knees, contracted Calves and protuberant Ancles.

The deformities had been brought about, in his opinion, by their habit of sitting on their legs. Clerke always noted the appearance of the women but this time he was unimpressed because he thought they were exceedingly dirty and very ugly. The men of Nootka offered the services of their ladies but few of the sailors felt inclined to accept their generosity:

> They are the dirtiest set of people I ever yet met with; they are continually rubbing their faces and Bodies with one kind of filth or another by way of beautifying themselves, and by this frequent Repetition they have so ingrain'd the dirt into the Skin, that it is absolutely hard to tell what colour our good Mother Nature originally gave them. . . . Their hair in general is black and thick and they wear it mostly long; and, it may be of a piece with the rest of the body, very full of dirt and Lice; the pulling

these Lice out and eating them passes away (seemingly very agreeably) many a leisure Hour.

Despite these unattractive habits, the people were fashion conscious for they sought to improve their appearance by making holes in the cartilage of the nose and ears and placing pieces of copper there. If no metal was available, in went an old tooth but 'ornamented they must be or they are unhappy'.

One thing Clerke did find in their favour—they were good at catching whales with harpoons and he bought from them one hundred gallons of oil to burn in the ship's lamps.

It was clear to all who saw him that his health was deteriorating, although he remained unfailingly cheerful. The persistent cough from which he now suffered was probably due to secondary infection. This did not diminish his determination and, although he was so ill, he summoned up from somewhere the energy to go ashore several times with Cook to visit native villages. He found the people, who were clad in garments made from animal skins, to be quite friendly but he could not bring himself to approve of their thieving habits, cleanliness, or diet. His calls were returned and on April 22nd he wryly observed:

> I cannot say much for the honesty of these good People when aboard, for if they did not steal at any time when they came to the Ship, it was because they cou'd not find the Opportunity; for I believe they were too industrious ever to neglect any.

Clerke thought, but was not entirely convinced, that they might be cannibals and there was some evidence to support his suspicions. On one occasion his visitors brought with them some human skulls and a few dried hands but he must surely have been mistaken, or there was a breakdown of communication, when a little girl of four or five years was brought on board and offered for sale for the price of a small hatchet. He understood the vendor to be insisting she would make good eating.

Resolution was found to have developed several defects, mainly as the result of poor work done at Deptford, and trees had to be felled to make new spars for her. Nootka Sound was left on 26th April and the two ships cruised towards the north, enjoying calm weather until coming to Alaska in May. *Resolution* had seen hard use and had sprung another leak, and once more she needed the attention of her carpenters. She was taken into a bay, beached and heeled over so that the damaged area was exposed. While this was being done, one of the sailors contrived to catch his legs in an anchor rope, the outflow of the hawser carried him to the sea bed and it was little short of a miracle that he survived, although he had two broken limbs.

Early one morning at about this time a party of the local people, armed with knives, crept up to *Discovery* in the half light and attacked the deck watch. They had no intention of trying to take the ship and their purpose was no more sinister than to steal anything portable which they could lay hands on. They were unable to work in complete silence and the noise they made aroused the sleeping crew who, grabbing cutlasses and whatever other weapons that came to hand, rushed on deck and threw the thieves off the ship.

The days lengthened as May ran its course and the land they passed became more and more barren but, despite a few hopes which were soon dashed, not a sign did they find of a channel running towards either Baffin or Hudson's Bay.

In June they had come to the Alaskan Peninsular and, as usual, were met by a fleet of canoes. Clerke fired three guns as a signal for *Resolution* to stop. A man in one of the boats who looked different from his companions took off his hat, bowed and tied a small wooden case to a rope he had been thrown. When the box was hauled on deck it was found to contain a message, written in Russian and dated 1776, which no one on board was able to translate. Clerke at first thought it might be from shipwrecked sailors but on further reflection came to believe that it was more likely to be from a Russian trader whose messenger had mistaken them for a ship belonging to one of his fellow countrymen.

The vessels followed the southern side of the peninsular, passing country which Clerke considered to be a 'damn'd unhappy part of the world'. He was no more enamoured with the sea because the numerous shoals made it scarcely navigable. They found a passage into the Bering Sea round Unalaska, one of the Aleutians Islands which are an extension of the Alaskan Peninsular, and came to Samgoonoodha, or English Bay, as they called it.

Two days after their arrival another unusual man was seen, this time of European appearance. He was sitting in a native canoe and, noticing that he had been seen, he took a Cross from around his neck, kissed it and went on his way without making any other contact. After another two days a non-European presented them with two salmon pies, which was thought to be strange, and Cook sent off his corporal of Marines, armed with presents of rum and wine, to make contact with the Europeans he was now convinced were in the vicinity. The Marine returned with three Russian fur traders who had a house and a thirty ton sloop which were out of sight but not far away. Their particular interest was in the pelts of the sea beaver. The Russians issued a cordial invitation, which was quickly accepted, for Cook and Clerke to visit them.

Clerke met a whole series of extraordinary people in the course of his life but few showed more individuality than this Marine corporal, whose name was Lediard. He came from Connecticut, and on his return to England the thought came to him that it would be a good idea if he were to walk across America, going by way of Siberia and seeking whatever passage he could find over the Bering Strait. The journey to meet the Russian traders had made an impression on him because his purpose in embarking on this expedition was to try to establish trade in north-west America. Joseph Banks raised a subscription for him which raised £50. and he set off in 1786, travelling via Hamburg, Copenhagen, and St. Petersburg. He eventually reached Irkutsk in Siberia but after various wanderings he was arrested and deported to Poland where the Empress of Russia ordered that never again was he to enter her empire without her personal permission. Kippis told the story in 1788 and the latest news that he then had from Lediard, who often wrote to Banks giving details of his wanderings, was that the American was in Königsburg and that he was proposing to return to England.

In fact, Lediard survived his journey and then set out on an African expedition, but died in Cairo in 1788, aged thirty-seven years.

Clerke was given two more tasks. Cook was becoming worried that the supply of trade goods was running low and, realising it was important that the price of the remaining stocks be kept high, Clerke was given the responsibility of being the only officer who could authorise anyone to trade. Cook was again trying to control the spread of disease and, although the temptation to transgress was less than it had been further south, Clerke had to ensure that no women were to come on board. In addition, if a seaman known to be suffering from V.D. went ashore (a list was kept on the Quarter Deck) and had relations with a woman, he was to be severely punished.

For months Clerke had known that he had no hope of recovery but his destiny was staring him in the face when Anderson died between three and four o'clock in the afternoon of August 3rd. The doctor's illness had run a parallel course with his own and the effect this must have had on Clerke can only be imagined. It was two days before he learned of the death of his friend when Cook sent him a letter bearing the news. It is tempting to think that Cook was in a quandary as to how he should tell him what had happened. In the circumstances, Clerke's reaction was remarkably restrained:

> . . . The Death of this Gentleman is a most unfortunate
> stroke to our Expedition altogether; his distinguished abilities as
> a Surgeon, and unbounded humanity, render'd him a most
> respectable and esteemed Member of our little Society, and the
> loss of his Superior Knowledge of and wonted attention to the
> Science of Natural History will leave a Void in the Voyage much
> to be regretted.

Anderson had not only been the doctor, he had also taken on the responsibilities of being the expedition's scientist, with duties previously carried out by Joseph Banks. His death brought about a rearrangement of the medical personnel on the two ships with John Law, Clerke's surgeon, going to *Resolution* and David Samwell, her surgeon's mate, being transferred to *Discovery*.

By the time they reached Unalaska the ban on women had been relaxed. Clerke was well enough to visit the people in their homes and found them to be kindly and happy people. 'The ladies offered their services . . . all were exceedingly clean and decent and many of them handsome . . . the compliment usually paid for a beauty's favours was a hand of Tobacco, for one of inferior Charms a few leaves of this valuable Weed.'

In 1728 the 60 year old Danish explorer Vitus Bering, a native of Jutland but working for the Russians, had been the first European to pass through the Strait named after him. *Resolution* and *Discovery* followed him on August 11th, 1778 with Asia visible to port and America to starboard. Clerke was cheerful and enjoying the clean air as the weather had cleared, giving the barren country on either side a pleasing appearance. Six days later they saw the ice blink, a lightening of the sky in the north, and soon after they came up to a very wide field of ice standing ten feet above the surface of the sea. For several days they sailed along its edge but were unable to find a way through. It was now late in the season and on 29th August, at latitude 70° 41' N. they began the return journey to the south, towards the Sandwich Islands where it was intended to spend the winter. The highest latitude reached was 70° 44' N. almost exactly the same as that *Resolution* had attained to the south in her previous voyage in the Antarctic.

While on the way back into the Pacific, three weeks were spent at anchor off the Aleutian Peninsular as the more urgent repairs were carried out. In September some natives came alongside in canoes and sold the sailors berries and dried salmon at rates which Clerke thought were very reasonable. Looking for bargains is not confined to supermarkets, for not all Clerke's crew shared his opinion and he heard one of them: 'Damning his Eyes most heartily because they gave him only two salmon for a small yellow bead'.

It was about this time that Clerke suffered another blow. Following the custom in the Navy, as a Captain he had his own servant, a man named John Mackintosh, who fell down the ship's main hatchway and was killed. He would, naturally, be sorry to lose any member of his crew but this was a hard knock because, with his health deteriorating, he must have been increasingly dependant on help from Mackintosh.

While trying to round the coast of the Hawaiian Islands in search of a suitable anchorage *Resolution* found herself off a lee shore. It was with some difficulty that she avoided being wrecked but Clerke, either by design or good fortune, kept his ship well to the north and she was never in any danger.

The anchorage they found this time was not on Kauai but at Kealakekua Bay, on the west coast of the island of Oahu. On 17th January 1779 each ship sent a boat to scout out a landing place; *Resolution*'s was in the charge of William Bligh, her Master, a man of considerable talent who was destined to make a reputation of his own in the Pacific and beyond. A host of canoes, which some on board numbered as being fifteen hundred strong, put off from the shore and it was not long before their occupants had managed to set to one side any feelings of apprehension they may have felt and enthusiastically set themselves to the task of taking whatever they could find. Any piece of metal which took the eye was removed with gusto, even the nails holding in position the sheathing over the ships' bottoms were not sacrosanct. They were levered out with stone- tipped sticks.

The island was ruled by King Terreeoboo, a man with almost absolute power, but a physical wreck. He was about fifty years old and much given to alcohol; in Clerke's opinion, and he had some experience of drink, he was totally debilitated. Once, when Terreeoboo dined on *Discovery*, he came on board barely able to stand; his hands shook so much he was hardly able to feed himself or take wine from a glass.

Again, the people treated Cook as a demi-god and Clerke was not far behind in their pantheon. The Hawaiian legend that one day God would visit them in a great canoe may have been the reason for the warmth of King Terreeoboo's welcome. Clerke was ashore one day attending a ceremony when a small pig was sacrificed in his honour 'as though I had been a being of a superior Nature'. On another occasion he was involved in a rite with an important local chief named Parea, who, with much ceremony, decorated him by placing a red cloth round his neck and a yellow feather cloak on his shoulders. Whenever the King, Cook, or Clerke was seen approaching, the people fell on their faces and barely looked up until they had gone at least thirty yards past them. Clerke found all this very distasteful and had the priests revoke the law as it applied to him. These were not isolated incidents and, finding adulation a disagreeable kind of amusement, he did his best to avoid it. It could have been worse for he noticed the Hawaiians paid their respects to dead noblemen by using human sacrifice: when a great man was buried the skulls of two men were stuck on posts each side of the corpse.

The Hawaiians were generous almost to a fault. Clerke went to dinner with Terreeoboo one evening and as he was leaving the King's house to return to his ship he was presented with thirty pigs and as much fruit as his crew could eat in a week.

The Hawaiians seemed to be an inoffensive people and Clerke recorded:

> I see no Scars of Honour about them. I believe the troublesome
> Science of War is not much studied by them.

He could hardly have been more wrong.

The crews had now been away from home for more than two years and, almost inevitably, the commanders had to deal with problems close to the heart of the sailor—women and drink.

The great volume of spirits brought from England was now running down and Cook decided to conserve as much as possible of the dwindling supplies for when they again went into high latitudes. He ordered spruce beer to be made as a substitute but the sailors had conservative tastes and it was not well received. One man expressed his dislike more forcefully. It is unlikely that the cooper who broached the cask in which it was stored did so in order to propagate his views on abstention but, whatever his motives, he was given a flogging. Cook was still mindful of the impact the arrival of Europeans would have on the life of the native people, and particularly of the spread of infection. What always worried him most was his men's spreading venereal disease in the indigenous population and it was with this in mind that he again ordered that there be no contact between the sailors and the local women. The ships were full of vigorous young men some of whom did not regard Cook's instructions with any great enthusiasm and were prepared to defy him. Clerke noticed that many of the island men and women already had V.D. which, they said, had been brought to the islands on the ship's last visit.

Even the displeasure of Cook the demi-god was incapable of stopping the thieving which went on apace. Anything removable was at risk of quickly disappearing over the side and Clerke, his patience completely drained away, had one persistent thief flogged.

* * * *

The islands were very fertile but the visit of the strangers had put a severe strain on the economy. Nevertheless, when the ships left on 4th February, after a stay lasting two and a half weeks, the people showed all the signs of regret at seeing them go.

They were sailing north again, to be in position for an earlier foray that year through the Bering Strait, when they were struck by a gale lasting a day and a half and _Resolution_ sprang a foremast. Clerke and Cook consulted together. They were anxious not to return to Hawaii, for they knew how their visit had depleted supplies there, but their knowledge of the geography of the area was sketchy in the extreme. They knew of no other safe anchorage along the planned route where repairs could be carried out and it was with some reluctance that they decided there was no alternative to turning back to Kealakekua Bay.

This time they had a very different welcome; to the Hawaiians Cook may have been God descending from Heaven but the Second Coming was a different matter. The resources of the island were not limitless and the return of nearly 200 uninvited visitors, perhaps for an indefinite period as far as they knew, could not fail to put a strain on the food supply. Theology had to take second place to practicality. The arrival of the two ships on 11th February must have been greeted with a silent, collective groan from the islanders and very few canoes came out from the shore. Eventually, King Terreeoboo went on board each ship in turn but his visit coincided with one of the days when Clerke was feeling more unwell than usual and he was unable to greet his Majesty.

It was an inauspicious start but it was only the first of a series of events which ended in the death of Cook.

The trouble began, of course, with a theft. On the morning of the 13th _Resolution's_ foremast was lifted out and the heel was found to have rotted away. The spar was taken ashore so that repairs on it could begin and in the afternoon a crowd of natives gathered not far from where the carpenters had set up their workplace. Shortly afterwards there were the first signs of violence when a watering party from _Discovery_ was threatened with stones. Cook happened to be nearby and he ordered Lieutenant King, who was in charge of the operation, to open fire with ball if any more stones were thrown at his men. A few minutes later Cook was watching his carpenters at work when shots were heard coming from *Discovery*. A party of Hawaiians had come over the side into *Discovery* and when the ship's armourer turned around he found one of his chisels and a pair of tongs were missing. Clerke was very unwell and had come to the end of his tether. The thief was caught and, uncharacteristically, he ordered that the culprit be severely punished by being given forty lashes and held until the tools were returned. They came back within half an hour but Parea, the local chief who had been with Clerke in *Discovery*'s Great Cabin when the theft took place, protested vigorously about the treatment of his subject and added the warning: 'You will bring violence on yourselves'.

At about 5.00 p.m. Parea and Clerke were talking in the Great Cabin when another man in Parea's party evaded the sailors on the deck, grabbed the recently returned tools and leaped over the side. The theft was premeditated because, as he swam for the beach, he was picked up by a canoe which was waiting for him. As soon as he heard the disturbance Clerke acted swiftly and he ordered his men to open fire on the thieves but they failed to hit them. Clerke saw Cook running along the beach from the place where he had been watching the carpenters towards where he thought the canoe would land. The hue and cry was now well and truly up and Clerke ordered Edgar, *Discovery*'s Master, to set off in pursuit in the ship's cutter and this officer was soon joined by the pinnace from *Resolution*. Cook had been misled, probably deliberately, by the natives who had offered to be his guides and he was taken to a different place on the beach from that reached by the ships' boats. Edgar succeeded in getting back the tools and, thinking some punishment was called for, he tried to seize the canoe. Unfortunately, it proved to belong to Parea, who had now landed from *Discovery*. A crowd of people two or three hundred strong had gathered and began to throw stones at the sailors; in the melee which followed Parea was hit by an oar. *Resolution*'s pinnace had to be abandoned by her crew, the men were picked up by *Discovery*'s cutter and they returned to the ships with their tails between their legs. The sailors had not been armed with muskets and the Hawaiians had taken note of how vulnerable they were when without their firearms.

It was the practice each evening to moor *Discovery*'s cutter to a buoy and fill it with water to prevent the sun's heat from splitting the timbers. At dawn on the fateful day of Sunday 4th February 1779,

Clerke was wakened by Lieutenant Burney to be told that the 4 inch rope attaching the cutter to the bouy had been severed and the boat had gone. Clerke had himself rowed over to *Resolution* where he conferred with Cook. It was to be the last time they met. They decided to send *Resoution's* boats to the north-west point of the bay and *Discovery's* to the south-east with the object of preventing the escape of any canoes which might be trying to avoid being held against the return of the cutter.

It was between 6.00 a.m. and 7.00 a.m. when Clerke got back to his ship and ordered away a mixed force of sailors and marines in two boats, the launch and the remaining small cutter, under the command of Lieutenant Rickman, to the position in the bay he had agreed with Cook. The boats had not been long gone when Clerke thought he should talk further with Cook and went over to *Resolution* in his Jolly Boat but as he came nearer Gore shouted to him that Cook had gone ashore to negotiate with King Terreeoboo.

He was rowed back to *Discovery* from where, at about 8.00 a.m., he heard shots coming from the direction of Rickman's boats; his lieutenant's men had opened fire and a native chief had been killed. Shortly afterwards there was another volley, this time from Cook's party, and Clerke, who was watching through his telescope from his position on the forecastle, saw a confused tumult on the beach and the ships' boats pulling away from the shore. *Resolution*, which was closer inshore, fired her cannon and the men in the boats kept up a fire towards the land. All of Clerke's boats were committed and he had no more to send to give help. He knew only what he had seen, that there had been a fight caused by an incident of which he had no knowledge, and he had to wait for John Williamson, the lieutenant from *Resolution* who had been in one of the boats, to come aboard *Discovery* to tell him what had happened. The news was dreadful for Cook was dead, four marines had been killed and three were badly wounded.

Cook had decided that the quickest way to resolve the situation was to revert to his old custom of hostage taking. Intending to seize the King and hold him against the good behaviour of his subjects until the time came to sail, he landed near the native town with a force of nine marines which included their commander, Captain Phillips, a twenty-four year old Irishman. They went to Terreeoboo's house to find him waking from his sleep. The King and Cook talked for a little while and when Cook proposed that he go aboard *Resolution* Terreeoboo accepted the invitation without hesitation. The party had begun to walk towards the beach when one of the King's wives and two of his chiefs begged him not to go any further, having heard of the death of the chief killed by Rickman's party. Cook and the marines now found themselves in the middle of a crowd estimated to be two to three thousand strong but the people were willing enough to make an avenue down which Cook set off with his marines towards the water's edge which was fifty to sixty yards away. Men had been seen collecting their weapons and when Cook was about to order his men to embark in the boats, he saw one of the Hawaiians flourish a spear and make to throw a stone he had in his other hand. The man was wearing a mat over his chest, a primitive form of armour which was used to protect the wearer from the stones often used in Hawaiian warfare, but it was enough to prevent injury when Cook fired at him with small shot. This encouraged the crowd, for it showed them that European weapons were not always fatal. They began to throw stones and knocked down one of the marines, Captain Phillips was stabbed in the shoulder and the same thing was about to happen to Cook when the Captain fired a musket, this time loaded with ball, and killed a man who was standing close to the man who had attacked him. The Hawaiians did not fall back, as did most island people when fired upon, and they began a general attack The marines were ordered to shoot into the crowd and fall back on the boats. When troops let off a volley it was the normal practice for only half the men to fire followed shortly afterwards by the others, thus giving time for the first section to reload. Because this procedure had not been followed, and perhaps because of the small number of marines who were ashore, all the muskets were empty of ball and would take a little time to be recharged. Cook's men found themselves almost defenceless and several of them began to run over the rocks towards the beach. Cook and his remaining marines again came under attack and Cook waved his hand as a signal for the boats to come inshore to take them off. The pinnace responded and began to pick up men from the water while all the boats lying offshore kept up a brisk fire on the Hawaiians in an attempt to hold them back.

Even up to this point, because of his status among the islanders, Cook may have had some small chance of survival but this now went. Lieutenant Williamson, an intelligent man but one universally despised for his violent temper, was in overall charge of the three offshore boats. Afterwards claiming to have misunderstood Cook's signal, he gave the command for the boat he was in to withdraw, abandoning the men on the beach; at first his men refused to obey him and they came close to mutiny. All those left behind were slaughtered, with the Captain being the last to die. Cook had reached the water's edge and was seen wading towards the pinnace, holding his left hand behind his head to protect it from stones and with a musket under the other arm. He was stunned by a blow to the head from a club wielded by an islander who crept up behind him and, staggering, Cook dropped the weapon into the sea. A second man then came up to him as he was trying to rise and stabbed him in the neck. Cook fell when within only a few yards of the pinnace and was then overwhelmed by the pursuing crowd, some of whom tried to hold his head under the shallow water. Cook was a strong man and somehow he raised enough of his remaining strength to temporarily throw off his assailants. He reached a rock and was seen to be trying to hold himself upright against it when he was killed by a heavy blow from a club. His attackers then hauled Cook's corpse onto the rock and, such was their frenzy, even snatched daggers from each other's hands in order to stab at it.

Cook had built up a formidable reputation in the Pacific islands and had probably been drawing on his credit with the Hawaiians during his walk through the crowd, hoping to make the boat without further violence. If this was the case he had tried one bluff too many, for his credibility had been reduced by the incident in which the protective mat had saved the Hawaiian from the buckshot.

Clerke had watched the drama unfold from his position on *Discovery*[7] but what few lingering hopes he had for Cook's survival were dashed when Williamson and Phillips returned. After listening to their story, Clerke placed little blame on the Hawaiians for Cook's death, thinking it unpremeditated and the result of a series of incidents each of which had exacerbated its successor.

Clerke assumed command of the expedition but his promotion to the leadership had come at an appalling cost. He found himself in a very difficult position, for not only had Cook been a close personal friend, a man he both admired and respected, but his own physical condition was such that he was barely able to go on deck. Nevertheless, ill as he was, he did not allow his health to disturb his judgement and he kept his head. His first move was to have himself taken over to *Resolution* while his friend John Gore, her second-in-command, took over the command of *Discovery*. The next was to order ashore a strong force under Lieutenant King to protect the small base where the astronomers were making observations and the carpenters were working on the damaged mast. A large crowd had gathered nearby and Clerke fired his four pounders to disperse them, probably without doing any damage because there were a number of stone walls nearby to give shelter to the people.

Realising that if *Resolution*'s foremast was seized by the Hawaiians it would cripple the ship and seriously hamper the next journey north, he ordered that it be immediately taken aboard and by midday it had been brought alongside. To have continued work on it ashore would have invited continual harassment, even though a strong guard had been provided. While the astronomical equipment and the spar were being ferried to the ships, King's party came under repeated attack; they fired ball and about a dozen Hawaiians were killed or wounded. Despite this interference, the foremast was hoisted aboard *Resolution* and the carpenters of both ships set to work on it.

Clerke was well aware that he was being handicapped by his physical condition:

> I cannot help but lamenting my own unhappy state of Health which sometimes is so bad as hardly to suffer me to keep the Deck and of course father incapacitates me for the succeeding so able a Navigator as my honour'd friend and Predecessor.

Monday 15th February was a fine day and during the morning Clerke and his officers gathered to discuss whether or not there should be any retaliation. The new commander wanted no more bloodshed but his position was made more difficult by a group of natives on the shore who strutted about wearing the bloody clothes of the men they had killed and waving the cutlasses and bayonets they had taken from them. When, to add further insult to injury, they presented their bare buttocks to the furious sailors the crew asked Clerke's permission to take revenge. He procrastinated, partly because he wished to avoid casualties among his crews and partly because he could not be sure that they would obey a direct refusal. He was particularly concerned that in any landing the sailors, clad in leather soled shoes, would be at a disadvantage to the sure footed natives on the slippery rocks they would have to cross. He mollified his men by saying the ships were not in a safe enough condition and that he would make a decision in a few days time when, he hoped, their anger would have cooled.

Clerke wished to be away from Hawaii as soon as he could, but before leaving there was something else he had to do; he must secure the return of Cook's remains. Relations with Terreeoboo had usually been good, but it was no use seeking his help because the King had disappeared:

> We were told that immediately after the action in which Capt. Cook was killed the old King had returned to a cave in the steep

part of the mountain that hangs over the bay which was accessible only by the help of ropes and where he remained for many days having his victuals let down to him by cords.[8]

In the evening Clerke sent two boats filled with well armed sailors to the shore, one commanded by King, the other by Burney, with orders to find out what had happened to Cook's body. Each came back with a different story. King was told it had been taken inland but would be brought back the next day, while Burney was given to understand that it had been cut up. No more could be done that day but, to avoid surprise attack, Clerke gave orders that guard boats should circle the ships during the night.

Soon after darkness fell on the evening of the next day, a priest went out to *Resolution*. The officers and men were not unduly sensitive, but they were horrified to see the contents of a bundle he carried which proved to be a human thigh from which the bone had been removed. The rest of the corpse, he said, had been burned in ceremonies held in different places on the island and the other bones, which were all that remained, were held by King Terreeoboo.[9]

The following day a man in a canoe came to within two hundred yards of the ships and, to the delight of a large group of people assembled on the shore, began waving Captain Cook's hat. This was too much even for Clerke, who was trying to keep his crews' emotions under control, and he ordered that the 4 pounders be fired at the crowd. In the evening, two priests came out and asked for peace, saying several men had been hurt that morning and that four priests and thirteen men had been killed in the affray in which Cook met his death.

Despite the proffered palm, there was more violence. A watering party under Lieutenant Rickman came under attack from a stone throwing mob, shots were fired and several men were killed:

> . . . the sailors were so much enraged that, in spite of everything, they cut off the heads of two, one of which they tied to the bow of *Resolution*'s large cutter, and the other they carried on board; but as soon as the captain was informed of the affair, he gave orders for the heads to be thrown overboard.[10]

On the 20th, repairs to the mast were complete and it was restepped. Relations with the islanders had improved over the past few days and Terreeoboo finally made his presence felt by sending a peace offering, to which Clerke responded by agreeing to re-establish good relations, providing all Cook's remains were returned. This brought an immediate response. At noon a priest named Hiapo arrived at the beach with a number of attendants and was met by

Clerke in the pinnace. Hiapo and three other priests went aboard *Resolution* and gave Clerke a carefully wrapped parcel which contained all that was left of Cook. It was taken into *Resolution's* Great Cabin and when opened was found to contain all the bones with the exception of those of the back, jaw and feet. All the flesh had been removed except from the hands which had been pickled. Later in the day Hiapo produced the jaw and feet and told Clerke the vertebrae had been burned. In the eyes of the sailors, this treatment of Cook's body was barbaric in the extreme but what they did not know was that in Hawaiian society it was considered to be a great honour, reserved for only the most important chiefs.

Cook's mortal remains were placed in a coffin and at about 5. 00 p.m. on the fine evening of Monday, 22nd February 1779 Clerke committed what was left of Captain James Cook's body to the deep with 'all the attention and honour we could possibly pay in this part of the World.'

Lieutenant Williamson, who had been in charge of the boats lying offshore during the assault on Cook's party, came in for a great deal of criticism for not having done more to save the life of his captain. He had under his command a well armed and disciplined force of between thirty and forty men and if they had landed they may well have been able to disperse the unorganised native crowd. Clerke felt compelled to hold an inquiry into his behaviour but nothing came of it. Evidently the matter was not settled to everyone's satisfaction and resentment against him must have festered on for it was rumoured that Williamson and Phillips, who had done well during the fight on the beach, fought a duel at the Cape during the voyage home.

Clerke was anxious to put Oahu behind him and at 8.00 p.m. on 22nd February his ships left Kealakekua Bay for the last time. There had been no more thefts to cause another confrontation and, amazingly, in view of what had gone before, the parting with the Hawaiians was amicable.

First they went back to Kauai where a party under the command of Lieutenant King was landed to gather water. The newly found goodwill had not reached there from Oahu and some of the people tried to snatch the muskets with which the sailors were armed; there was a scuffle and another native was hurt. *Resolution* was leaking again and the carpenters of both ships were set to work recaulking her. In early March, a lady purporting to be the new Queen of the island came out to the ships and tried to entice some of the sailors to assist her in battles which were being fought with rivals who were contesting her position. She met with little success because Cook's death had had a salutory effect on the men:

> . . . that idea of turning Indian which was once so prevalent among them as to give us a great deal of trouble is now quite subsided, and you could not inflict a greater punishment upon those who were the warmest advocates for this curious innovation in Life than oblige them to take that step which 16 or 18 Months ago seemed to be the ultimate wish of their Hearts, and which some of them went so far as to attempt at the risk of death itself.

A few days after her recruitment campaign, the Queen asked to sail in *Resolution* to a nearby island but she soon showed signs of that most unpleasant of maladies, seasickness. Anyone who has ever experienced it can have only sympathy for her but she was luckier than most for she had to hand a solution many a passenger trapped in a pitching ship longs for: 'Her good Queenship with all her Regalia emberk'd in their own Vessels and made for the shore'.

As had happened so many times before, a more lasting affliction was left behind. The gonorrhoea the visitors had introduced during their first visit, despite Cook's attempts to prevent it, had now become an epidemic. As Clerke wrote:

> Our Seamen are in these matters so infernal and dissolute a Crew that for the gratification of the present passion that affects them they would entail universal destruction upon the whole of the Human Species.

Clerke intended to make his second passage through the Bering Strait from the Asiatic side, so when he left the Hawaiian Islands he made for Kamchatka, steering first west and then north so as to cover as much unknown ocean as possible. On 11th April he crossed the route usually taken by the Spanish galleons sailing the long established route between Manila and Acapulco, and eight days later he was noting the temperature as being below freezing, having dropped 53° in nineteen days. The ships were now covered in snow and the men's miseries began anew because they were pinched with the cold. The warm clothing used during the previous voyage beyond the Strait had been put in store and it was now redistributed, for the men had been liberal in their gifts of clothing to the ladies of Hawaii. The new supplies were issued: 'to the People whose Gallantry among the isles has render'd them as naked as when they were born'.

Strong gear would soon be needed and, knowing the conditions which would have to be faced, Clerke ordered that the cables, rigging and boats be put into good order. The sails were in a bad state of repair and the sailmakers were set to work in the Captain's cabin, the only dry place in the ship. Clerke was now so ill he was rarely able to leave it, but he felt that he must share his accommodation with them.

At the end of April the chronometer was found to have stopped. Benjamin Lyon, one of the sailors, had trained as a watchmaker and he managed to get it going again after he had given it a thorough cleaning. He had to open the machine again when it was found not to be as accurate as it had previously been and it was then that he discovered the pendulum spring had broken. Lyon tried to make a new one but it was beyond his capability and the use of the chronometer had to be abandoned.

By 1st May both ships were anchored half a mile off the port of St. Peter and St. Paul, or Petropavlovsk as it was otherwise known in Kamchatka, on the Asian side of the Bering Strait. Clerke was so ill he was unable to go ashore. The sailors had expected the town to be a place of some substance but it proved to be, in Kippis' words: 'a few miserable loghouses, and some conical huts raised on poles, amounting in all to about thirty'. The Governor of the area was Major Magnus von Behm who lived in the administrative centre, Bolsheretsk, which was situated on the opposite side of the peninsular, about 130 miles from St. Peter and St. Paul. Clerke was anxious to make contact with him and he sent Gore, King, and Webber on an overland journey to present his compliments. They found him to be a rather corpulent man, very polite and affable, and one who proved to be a wonderful friend during the stay in Kamchatka, being both co-operative and generous, even though it cost him money from his own pocket. The welcome the Governor offered the sailors was infinitely warmer than was the appearance of Kamchatka.

Behm was about to set out on the long journey to St. Petersburg and he offered to take with him the journals of both Cook and Clerke for onward transmission to London. Seven months later, a remarkably short time in view of the distance involved, the documents arrived safely in England. He also carried letters from the sailors, one of which was from Clerke to the Admiralty, telling their Lordships of Cook's death. Lord Sandwich wrote to Lord Mulgrave in January 1780:

> . . . I am sure you will be concerned to hear of the death of poor Captain Cook, who with some of his people were killed in a fray with the natives of a new discovered Island; this account is brought from Petersburg and dated June last . . . Captain Clerke says that he proposes to make one more trial for a northern passage (which Captain Cook once thought he had discovered

when he was stopped by an impenetrable field of Ice) he then intends to make the best of his way home but does not know which way he shall come.[11]

The news had filtered through to the Clerke family in Wethersfield. *The Essex Chronicle* of 21st January 1780 carried this report:

> A correspondent has favoured us with the following account of the celebrated Capt. Cook . . . from the date of Capt. Clerke's account from Kamchatka of the death of Capt. Cook and his intentions to pursue his route for the discovery of the north-west passage, we must with regret conclude that he has failed in the attempt, or we should have heard of him at least in the north seas long ere this, if not have congratulated him on his safe arrival.
>
> If Capt. Clerke shall have failed in his attempt to discover the north-west passage, he will have been obliged to turn again to the southward, to make the best of his way home through the Indian Ocean, and in that case it will be at least two years before we can expect his return to England.

No one in England knew that at the time this report appeared Charles Clerke had been dead for several months.

Meanwhile, King wrote to Clerke from Bolsheretsk telling him of their reception. When he returned with Gore and Webber to *Resolution* he found the captain's health had noticeably deteriorated during the fortnight they had been away. Behm, who had delayed his departure for the Russian capital in order to travel with the officers to the ships, had been told of Clerke's condition and thoughtfully stayed on shore on the evening of his arrival, so as not to disturb him. Next morning, King took the Governor out to the ship where the Marines were paraded and the usual compliments were paid. Nothing was too much trouble for Behm and he arranged the supply of everything that was requested. His generosity seemed to know no bounds, as, for example, in the matter of tobacco. The ships' original stock had been exhausted and, although the asking price of three shillings a pound was considered outrageous, many of the sailors were swearing they could not live without it. Behm came to know of the crisis and insisted on making a gift to the ships' companies of a stock little short of 400 pounds in weight.

This was not the only piece of good fortune the men enjoyed in Kamchatka for many of them came away with a good profit in their pockets. The ships had originally been suspected of being traders, or even pirates, but the matter was cleared up during a conversation between some Germans, who dined with Clerke on 4th May, and

Webber, the expedition's artist who spoke their language. The following day a merchant appeared who knew of their purchase of Sea Beaver skins and he bought them for a good price. One sailor made £60.

Behm was not the only man who befriended them. In the village of Paratounca, which was sixteen miles away, lived a priest called Romaan Feodorwitz Vereshagin. He had heard of Clerke's condition and showed him great kindness, sending regular gifts of milk, butter, and bread, all things which would not be readily available in such a remote place.

Behm refused any cash payment for all the articles he supplied the two ships, saying it would be the wish of his Empress that a certificate be forwarded to her in St. Petersburg and she would settle the accounts. In this he was sadly mistaken for he was never reimbursed by his government for the money he had laid out. The scale of his generosity may be seen from the size of only one of several orders Clerke asked him to procure— sixteen head of cattle and 10,000 lbs of flour. Behm was eventually reduced to poverty by his generosity and went to London to beg for a pension. He was unsuccessful, and his sorry state was relieved only when he returned to Russia where the Emperor Paul took pity on him and ordered that he should have an allowance.

Clerke's letter to the Admiralty contained the sentence:

> My health has been such lately as totally to incapacitate me from drawing up an account of this place for their Lordships perusal, whom I hope on that account will excuse my deferring it. You will see by Captain Cook's letter what chance there is of a Northern passage into the Atlantic, indeed I much fear the impediments are too numerous, but whatever can be done shall be done . . .

Clerke set out on his last voyage on 16th June 1779; as he sailed out of the harbour of St. Peter and St. Paul a nearby volcano was erupting. *Resolution* and *Discovery* kept to the Asiatic side as they went towards the Bering Strait, often in fog or thick weather and firing guns to stay in contact. They passed through the Strait on 6th July and next day came upon an extensive ice field. Several times they risked damage to the ships by trying to force a way through but eventually it was decided to continue along the ice edge towards the American shore. On the 19th they turned northward again but could get no further than 70° 11' N. by 197° 4' E.

Finally, Charles Clerke had to give in and the last entry in his journal, made on 21st July 1779, records his decision to turn back:

It is now clearly impossible to proceed in the least further to the N°ward upon this Coast and it is equally as improbable that this amazing mass of Ice should be dissolv'd by the few remaining Summer weeks which will terminate this Season but it will doubtless remain as it now is a most insurmountable barrier to every attempt we can possibly make. I therefore think it the best step I can take for the good of the Service to trace the Ice over to the Asiatic Coast, try if I can find a Hole that will admit me any further North, if not see whats to be done upon that Coast where I hope but cannot much flatter myself with making better success for this Sea is now so Choak'd with Ice that a passage I fear is totally out of the question.

Although Charles Clerke's physical condition was now in a pitiful state, his body little more than a skeleton, his mind was as active as ever and he continued to command the expedition. Everyone on board both ships had given up all hope for his recovery but to the outside world he presented his usual cheerful face. But he was under no illusions as to the true situation and on 15th August he asked Lieutenant King: 'under his authority to inspect and give the necessary orders. Never was a decay so melancholy and gradual' wrote his friend.

The ships turned again towards Kamchatka and three weeks later, on 12th August, Charles Clerke drew on his small fund of remaining energy to dictate to King a last, poignant letter of farewell to his old friend Joseph Banks. It is worth reproducing in its entirety because it encapsulates so much of Clerke's character. His own condition and his suffering are dealt with almost in passing, the emphasis is upon the value he placed on old friendships and on doing what he could for men who had served him well. The letter contains not an iota of self-pity nor of regrets of what might have been; he wishes to be remembered as the honest, decent man he was:

> The disorder I was attacked with in the Kings Bench prison has proved consumptive, with which I have battled with varying success, although without one single day's health since I took leave of you in Burlington Street. It has now so far got the better of me, that I am not able to turn myself in my bed, so that my stay in this world must be of very short duration; however I hope my friends will have no occasion to blush in owning themselves such, for I have most perfectly and justly done my duty to my country as far as my abilities would enable me, for where that has been concerned, the attention to my health which I was very sensible was in the most imminent danger has never swerved me a single half mile out of the road of my duty;

so that I flatter myself I shall leave behind that character it has ever been my utmost ambition to attain, which is that of an honest and faithful servant of the Public whom I had undertaken to serve.

I have made you the best collections of all kinds of matter I could that have fallen in our way in the course of the voyage, but they are by no means so compleat as they would have been had my health enabled me to pay more attention to them; I hope however you will find many among them worthy of your attention and acceptance, in my will I have bequeathed you the whole of every kind, there are great abundance so that you will have ample choice.

I must beg you to present my warrant and most affectionate compliments to Dr. Solander and assure him I leave the world replete with the most social Ideas of his much esteemed and ever respected Friendship.

I must beg leave to recommend to your notice Mr. Will Ellis one of the Surgeon's mates who will furnish you with some drawings and accounts of the various birds which will come to your possession, he has been very useful to me in your service in that particular and is I believe a very worthy young man and I hope will prove worthy of any services that may be in your way to confer upon him.

The two Clerks of the two ships Mr. W. Dewar and Mr. Greg Bantham have I believe been very honest servants in their stations and having by Capt. Cook's and very soon my own death lost those to whom they looked up to for protection are I fear destitute of friends; if it should be in your power to render them any services I flatter myself they will be worthy of such attention.

If I should recollect anything more to say to you I will trouble my friend Mr King, who is so kind to be my amanuensis on this occasion, he is my very dear and particular friend and I will make no apology in recommending him to a share of your friendship, as I am perfectly assured of his deserving it, as is that also of the worthy Doctor's.

Now my dear and honoured friend I must bid you a final adieu; may you enjoy many happy years in this world and in the end attain that fame your indefatigable industry so richly deserves. These are most sincerely the warmest and sincerest wishes of your devoted affectionate and departing Servant /
Chas Clerke

Resolution and *Discovery* had come back south through the Bering Straits on 30th July, heading towards Kamchatka. By 17th August, realising his remaining time could be measured in hours,

Charles made a last will. He first asked his agent in London, James Sykes of Crutched Friars, to settle his debts which included the loans made by Sir Robert Ainslie and Dr. Maty. Small sums were repaid to Henry Wyate and John Ramsden, the instrument maker.

To his 'dear and honoured father' he left one guinea and a gold watch with a second hand to it; to the man who had brought so much trouble upon him 'my dear Brother and friend Sir John Clerke in his Majesty's Navy' he bequeathed ten guineas and to 'my dearest friend Lady Clerke wife of my brother Sir John Clerke' he gave five guineas. His other brothers and sisters were not overlooked, nor were various people who had sailed with him in different capacities. His friend Edward Thompson, also an officer in the Navy and the executor of the will, was to get his second watch.

At about 8.30 in the morning of 22nd August, 1779, within sight of Kamchatka, Charles Clerke died, aged 38 years.

Resolution sailed into the harbour of St. Peter and St. Paul with her colours at half mast, followed by *Discovery*. Monday, 30th August 1779 was a cloudy day with occasional rain sweeping across the anchorage, the weather matching the mood of the ships' crews. At noon, Clerke's body was put into the pinnace and the vessels began to toll their bells. The crew of the boat were dressed in white shirts and black caps and had their oars reversed and heads inclined. The pinnace was towed to shore by another boat with the officers following behind, black crepe on their arm bands, and the ships' crews came after in order of seniority. When the coffin was taken ashore it was covered with a Union flag across which was laid Clerke's drawn sword.

All the Russians in the garrison formed up, led by the priest from Paratounca who had been so kind to Clerke, and joined the sailors. To the sound of French Horns and muffled drums the procession moved off in the direction of the church where Clerke had said he wished to be buried. His request was to be denied because it was the Russians' intention to build a new church and the priest recommended a place which he thought would be at the centre of it. Sadly, the good priest met his own death a few weeks later.

His old friend John Gore picked the spot for Clerke's final resting place, under a tree in a valley on the north side of the harbour. Mr Law, the surgeon, read the burial service and the final act was a volley fired over the grave by the Marines. An inscription carved in wood was fixed to the tree and, as a mark of regard and affection for their friend and commander, the sailors planted willow trees around his resting place.

The new church was built some distance away from its intended position and when a Frenchman visited the site a few years later the cross at the head of the grave had rotted away. He replaced it with a copper plate. Finally, an obelisk was put up on the site but when Frederick Whymper visited it in 1865 it was gone, supplanted by nettles and weeds.

* * * *

It may truly be said of Charles Clerke that, in all senses of the words, he was a man of endeavour, resolution and discovery. Yet he was an uncomplicated man who from the age of thirteen years dedicated his life to the Royal Navy; as Lieutenant King wrote of him: 'He was bred to the Navy from his youth'. In his early years he pursued adventure and pleasure with equal enthusiasm but underlying his cheerful exterior was a firmness of purpose and once his allegiance was given, whether to an individual, a project or a cause, his commitment was absolute. His experiences at sea while still only a boy, particularly the two major engagements in which he took part and his narrow escape in the fall from *Bellona's* mizzen mast, seem only to have confirmed him in his choice of career.

His easy manner made him many friends from various walks of life. At one end of the social scale he was pleased to attend the weddings of people who were ordinary country folk and may well have been family servants, at the other he mixed freely with men such as Banks, Cook, and Sandwich.

Charles Clerke was fortunate to live in an age of enquiry which manifested itself in the fields of philosophy, science, and discovery. He was shrewd enough to take advantage of the last and the pivotal point of his career was when he set out on the circumnavigation of the world between 1764 and 1766. From the time that Clerke sailed with Byron his course parted from the conventional path of most naval officers because his life was then to be that of an explorer. The experience he gained of the Pacific from this voyage enabled him to join the small band of men who had knowledge of the great ocean and was almost certainly the reason for his returning from America to sail with Cook. When he decided to go with Byron, Charles Clerke's career was at a cross roads and the path he took brought him to Cook, the greatest navigator and discoverer of his age, and perhaps of any age. Cook was a first rate teacher, surveyor and commander of men who recognised the importance of looking after the health of his crews and the limits of the discipline they would tolerate, particularly in the free-living life style of Polynesia. Clerke was a willing pupil and when the time came he made good use of the knowledge that Cook had passed on to him.

The voyages to the Pacific brought Clerke into contact with men of power and influence. Joseph Banks was probably the most important, not only for his political connections which extended as far as the King, but because he and his entourage on the first voyage made up one of the most eminent scientific assemblies in Europe. During the three years he was in their company a young man still in his twenties could hardly fail to learn from a gathering of such intellects.

As he grew older, it is noticeable how Charles Clerke's judgement matured. From the many available, three examples must suffice. Firstly, when *Endeavour* was almost wrecked for the second time on the Great Barrier Reef Clerke engaged himself in taking fixes to set the position of the hazard for the benefit of future mariners. Secondly, when in Polynesia on the third Cook voyage, Clerke was using ridicule to deter thieves rather than relying entirely on armed force. Thirdly; after Cook was killed in 1779 his handling of the situation was masterly. In view of this evidence, Samwell's opinion that Clerke was better fitted to be second in command than first cannot be sustained.

Clerke was certainly the victim of an injustice, even though what happened to him was legal at the time, but even when the great disaster of his life befell him he was quite without rancour. The actions of his irresponsible brother John brought forth no word of complaint, Charles offered no recriminations to him or to his unhelpful father and to the very end of his short life his affection for his family was undiminished. This was despite contact with his family having become more perfunctory from 1764 onwards because he was away from England for much longer periods than were most naval officers.

Charles Clerke had many of the appealing human virtues and few of the vices. One of the former was modesty since he never recorded his courage, which was undoubted. It combined with his sense of duty when, together with Dr. Anderson, he decided against taking the only small chance he had of surviving the tuberculosis which had so cruelly afflicted him and went on to the high latitudes which he knew would kill him.

Throughout his life, in all his writings, Charles Clerke's most obvious characteristic continually shone through. He observed people and events closely and recorded what he saw with wry humour— laughter is never far from the surface. It would be a dreary person who did not recognise his sense of humour or not be amused by, for example, his account of the way in which the islanders of New Caledonia chose to decorate themselves.

One question will always remain unanswered: what would Clerke have achieved if his life had not been cut so tragically short? If he had survived the voyage, he would have found on his return that Britain was at war with France, Spain, and the American colonies and that there was a demand for experienced sea officers with consequent chances for promotion. When the Napoleonic Wars started and the Navy entered another period of rapid expansion he would have been in his full maturity, well placed for the command of a major expedition.

In the end, all speculation is of no avail for bacteria, one of the smallest forms of life, had a hand in the matter and reduced Charles Clerke to dust, as happens to all men.

15. This print of the 'town' of St. Peter and St. Paul on Kamchatka is by John Webber who was the artist on Cook's third voyage.

Quotation from Kippis:
    'At length they discovered, on a narrow point of land, a few miserable loghouses, and some conical huts raised on piles, amounting in all to about thirty, which, from the situation, they were under the necessity of concluding to be PETRO PAULOWSKA.'

Captain King:
    ' . . . for in this wretched extremity of the Earth . . . we met with feelings of humanity, joined to a greatness of mind and elevation of Sentiment, which would have done honour to any nation or climate.'

EPILOGUE

Following the death of Charles Clerke the command of the expedition was taken over by his old friend Lieutenant John Gore who returned to *Resolution*, with James King going to *Discovery*. Gore held a conference with his officers and it was decided to follow a homeward route which would allow an exploration to be made of the east coast of Japan, a country which at that time was virtually unknown to Europeans. The ships left Kamchatka on 10th October and made several sightings of Japan and of Japanese shipping but foul weather and gales prevented them from making a landing. In mid December they reached Macao where it was learned that France had joined in the American War. In nearby Canton the crews were told of a letter of recommendation sent by Benjamin Franklin to the captains of American warships:

> A ship having been fitted out from England before the Commencement of this War, to make Discoveries of new countries in unknown Seas, under the Conduct of that most celebrated Navigator and Discoverer Captain Cook; . . . recommend to every one of you that in case the said Ship, which is now expected to be soon in the European Seas on her Return, should happen to fall into your Hands, you would not consider her as an Enemy, nor suffer any Plunder to be made of the Effects contain'd in her, nor obstruct her immediate Return to England . . . but that you would treat the said Captain Cook and his People with all Civility and Kindness, affording them as common Friends to Mankind all the Assistance in your Power which they may happen to stand in need of . . .

The French (who had come into the war on the side of the American secessionists in 1778) and the Spaniards (who had joined in during 1779) acted in a similar fashion.

From China the ships sailed to False Bay, near Cape Town where repairs were carried out. They left there to begin the journey to England on 9th May, after a stay of nearly a month. When they were almost in sight of home, strong winds from the south made it impossible for the vessels to enter either the Channel or the port of Galway, on the west coast of Ireland, which was the landfall of second choice. They were forced to carry on to the north and it was at the end of August that the ships reached Stromness in the Orkneys where the sailors were able to go ashore for the first time since leaving the Cape. *Resolution* and *Discovery* then began the last leg of the voyage down the east coast before reaching the Nore, at the mouth of the Thames, on 1st October 1780.

During the four years, two months and twenty-two days they had been away, fifteen men had died— seven from illness, three in accidents, and five in the incident in Hawaii.

Several attempts were made in the years after the Cook and Clerke expedition to find the North-West Passage but it remained undiscovered until 1905. On 26th August of that year Roald Amundsen found a way into the Pacific from the Atlantic side, having sailed from Oslo two years previously in a tiny 47 ton yacht with a seven man crew. He had been lucky, because the ice that year was less formidable than usual and he was able to force a way through an area in which previous adventurers had found their path to be barred. The route he came upon was far removed from the hopes and expectations of the strategists and of the explorers who had preceded him. There was never to be a commercial seaway by the North-West Passage and the shortening of the journey to the East had to wait for the construction of the Suez and Panama Canals.

The Admiralty published a three volume book of Journals of the Cook and Clerke voyage and divided the profits between the families of the officers who had died during the expedition. Mrs Cook had a half share and Charles Clerke's beneficiaries one-eighth, amounting to about £500.

Subsequently, several of Clerke's shipmates had interesting lives. James Burney, the brother of Fanny, the novelist, had a good career and was in several actions before having to retire from the Navy because of ill health. The midshipman Edward Riou later became a successful frigate captain before being killed at Copenhagen, fighting in Nelson's fleet. John Elliot, a midshipman on *Resolution's* first voyage, was a Lieutenant on *Ajax*, a 74, and fought with Rodney on 12th April 1782 at the battle of Les Saintes in the West Indies. He was severely wounded in the action but survived and reached the rank of Commander. He died, aged 75 years, on 17th September 1834 and his memorial plaque is on the west wall of Ripon Cathedral. George Vancouver, who sailed on Cook's 1772-5 voyage and then in *Discovery*, became a famous marine surveyor and led an expedition to the Pacific where he charted the south-west coast of Australia. Later he went to the north-west coast of America and sailed round the island eventually named after him, which he had first visited with Clerke. He died in 1798, aged 41 years. Perhaps the most famous of all Charles Clerke's companions and the one whose story is best known was William Bligh who, after the mutiny on the *Bounty* in 1789, sailed an open boat on that incredible journey of more than

3,600 miles. His subsequent career was hardly less colourful and included a period as governor of the penal colony in Sydney where he was involved in another mutiny. John Gore made the rank of post captain in 1780 and was given the captain's berth at Greenwich left vacant by Cook. He died there, aged about 60 years, on 10th August 1790: 'A most experienced seaman and an honour to his profession', according to *The Gentleman's Magazine*. Edward Thompson, the executor of Clerke's will, had taken part in the blockade of the French coast and the Battle of Quiberon Bay during the Seven Years War and had become a captain in 1772. He was court marshalled for losing the Guiana colonies in 1782 but escaped the fate of Admiral Byng, being honourably acquitted. He died in 1786, aged 48 years.

Joseph Banks did best of all. For over forty years he was President of the Royal Society and had enormous influence both inside and outside the scientific community. Clerke's wish for his friend to have a long life was granted, for when Banks died in 1820 he had reached the age of 77 years.

Neither John Rickman, Second Lieutenant of *Discovery*, nor Thomas Edgar, her Master, were as fortunate. Rickman seems to have gone no further in his career while Edgar, who had been known as a hard working, conscientious man, was another to die of drink, in spite of making the rank of lieutenant in 1781. James King, the man to whom Clerke dictated his last will, reached the rank of captain, but was not destined to enjoy a long life for he died at the age of 34 years in the south of France.

A year after his return, David Samwell was in Plymouth. Let his be the last word:

> We are all hearty and in good spirits and as none of us made our fortunes in Otaheite, we are all keen hunters after Prizes. There was never such a collection of Fine Lads take us for all in all, got together as there was in the RESOLUTION and DISCOVERY.

Appendix I

Joseph Clerke Memorial Plaque,
St. Mary Magdalene Church, Wethersfield.

To the Memory of Joseph Clerke Esq
Who died July 24th 1790 AET 81
For more than half a Century an inhabitant of this Village
And in the Commission of the Peace;
he was regarded as an Useful Magistrate
and a Man of Singular Benevolence
in whom the Poor and Indigent ever found a Friend;
in the same Grave lies the Remains of Anne his wife
who died in Child-bed of her 12th child, Feb 14th 1747.
Four of their children died in their Infancy, and of those
who attained maturer Years; Sir John Clerke Knt their elder son, was a
Captain in the Royal
Navy & died in Madras September 1776.
Joseph, their 2nd Son, who died at Abington, Cambridgeshire,
April 18th 1784. William, their 3rd Son, died Jan 2nd 1753 and is
Buried near this Stone. Charles, their 4th Son, was a Captain
in the Royal Navy, who after having with equal Honour
to himself & his Country, completed three Voyages round
the World, died in attempting a fourth with Captain James Cook
and was buried at Kamtschatka August 29th 1779. Thomas
their 5th Son was sometime Chaplain to the English Factory
at Surat, and died there 1773.
Reader, in this Example of a Father living to lament over five Sons,
who had Brightened the Prospect of His
Advancing Years See the Vanity of Human Hopes and
look for permanent Felicity beyond the Grave.
Near this Stone lieth interred also the Body of Sarah Clerke
The last survivor of the family of Joseph and Anne Clerke
Who departed this Life the 16th Feb 1818; aged 74 Years
Who by Will left to the Trustees of M. Dorothy Motts School of this
Place, the Reversion of L 360 in Furtherance of this Charity.

Appendix II

Lieutenant King on Charles Clerke:

At nine O'Clock in the morning, on Sunday the 22nd of August, Capt. Charles Clerke expired, in the thirty-eighth year of his age. His death was occasioned by consumption, which he had manifestly commenced before his departure from England, and of which he had lingered, during the whole continuance of the voyage. His very gradual decay, had for a long time rendered him a melancholy object to his friends; but the firmness and equanimity with which he bore it, the constant flow of good spirits, which he retained even to the last hour, and a cheerful resignation to his fate, furnished them with some consolation. It was impossible, not to feel an uncommon degree of compassion for a gentleman who had experienced a series of those difficulties and hardships, which must be the inevitable lot of any seaman, and under which he at last sunk. He was bred to the Navy from his youth, and had been in many engagements during the war which began in the year 1756. In the action between the *Bellona* and *Courageaux*, he was stationed in the mizzen-top, and was carried overboard with the mast; but he was afterwards taken up, without having received the least injury. He was midshipman on board the *Dolphin*, commanded by Commodore Byron, when he first sailed round the world; and was afterwards on the American Station.

It would savour of injustice and ingratitude to his memory, not to mention, that, during the short time he commanded the expedition, he was most remarkably zealous for its success. When the principle command devolved upon him, his health began rapidly to decline; and he was unequal in every respect, to encounter the severity of a high northern climate. The vigour of his mind, however, was not, in the least, impaired by the decay of his body: and though he was perfectly sensible, that his delaying to return to a warmer climate, was depriving himself of the only chance of recovery; yet so attentive was he to his duty, that he was determined not to suffer his own situation to bias his judgement to the prejudice of the Service: he therefore persevered in the search of a passage, till every officer in the expedition, declared they were of opinion it was impracticable, and that any further attempts would be equally hazardous and ineffectual.

William Samwell on Charles Clerke.

William Samwell was a Welshman who served as Surgeon's Mate to William Anderson on *Resolution*. He was the son of a Parson, well liked by the crew and has been described as 'a hearty young extrovert'. The Dear Girls were his constant preoccupation. He was not without blemish, for when he sailed on this voyage he left behind a pregnant girl who died in childbirth along with the child.[1]

Capt. Clerke was a sensible man and a good sailor but did not possess that degree of firmness and resolution necessary to constitute the character of a great commander. He was ever diffident of himself and consequently wavering and unfixed in his conduct, except where a certain line of action was chalked out to him and then no man was readier to pursue it than himself; he was fitter to be second than first in command, fitter to execute than to plan. However his perseverance in pursuing the voyage after the death of Captain Cook, notwithstanding his own bad state of health will ever reflect honour upon his memory. The most remarkable part of his character was his happy convivial turn and humorous conversation in which he excelled most men; these joined to an open generous disposition made his company universally caressed and engaged him in the excesses which laid the foundation of the complaint of which he died.

.....

Samwell's Journal - Sunday 22 August 1779

. . . He was born at Wethersfield Hall near Braintree in the County of Essex, and at the time of his death was aged 38 years. His Father was a Justice of the Peace and possessed an Estate of ab^t £500 a year . . .

.....

Burney's Journal - Sunday 22nd August 1779

At 1/2 past 8 depart'd this Life Capt. Charles Clerke, he had since the 16th been entirely confined to his bed, when giving over all hopes of Recovery, he resign'd himself to his situation with an equanimity that doubtless lessen'd the sensations of the beholders. Yet who can help lamenting the death of a man in the prime of his Age, whose life had been mostly spent at Sea, with few intervals of quiet or the enjoyment of satisfactions only to be met with on land, amongst ones Relations and friends, for since the War in which he had a narrow escape he had three times encircled the World and attempted a fourth, in the pursuit of which for the last half year he commanded the expedition, nor did he swerve in any instance from persevering on account of his health, preferring his duty to his Country to even his own life.

Appendix III

Charles Clerke's Monumental Inscription at
KAMCHATKA

Gore 29th August 1779[1]

At the foot of this tree lies the body of Captain Charles Clerke Esq who succeeded to the Command of His Britannic Majesty's Ships the Resolution and Discovery, on the death of Captain James Cook Esq (who was unfortunately killed by the Natives at an Island in the South Sea on the 14th February, in the year 1779). He died at Sea of a lingering Consumption on the 22nd of August in the same year, aged 38.

* * * * *

Underneath his Escutcheon in the Church of Paratoolka is the following Inscription.

The above is the escutcheon of Capt. Charles Clerke Esq, he succeeded to the command of his Britannic Majesty's Ships the Resolution and Discovery on the death of Capt. James Cook Esq (who was unfortunately killed by the Natives at an Island in the South Sea on 14th February 1779 after having explored the Coast of America from 42° 30' to 70° 44' Latitude in search of a passage from Asia to Europe). Captain Clerke died of a lingering Consumption at Sea on the 22nd of August 1779, aged 38 years, and lies buried at the foot of a Tree near the Ostrog of St. Peter and St. Paul: he had made the Second attempt in search of a Passage from Asia to Europe, and penetrated as far to the North, within a few miles, as Captain Cook, but found any further progress that way impracticable.

APPENDIX IV

CHARLES CLERKE'S WILLS

(Will of 29th July 1776)

I Charles Clerke of his Majesty's sloop the *Discovery* do make this my last will and Testament. I give to my honoured father Joseph Clerke of Wethersfield in Essex Esquire ten Guineas and my Gold Watch to my dear Brother Sir John Clerke Captain in his Majesty's Navy ten Guineas to my Brother Joseph Clerke of Ipswich Attorney at Law one Guinea to my good Friend Sir Robert Ainslie at present his Majesty's Ambassador at Constantinople one hundred pounds to my good friend Doctor Maty of the British Museum fifty pounds to my good friend ? ? Rickman Attorney at Law in Cooks Court Castle Yard Holborn twenty pounds and the rest and residue of my Effects whatsoever or wheresoever whether real or personal that at this time or at any time hereafter belong to me I do hereby give and bequeath the same to my loving sister Sarah Clerke of Wethersfield aforesaid and I do hereby appoint Edward Thompson of Bow Captain in his Majesty's Navy and James Sykes of Crutched Friars London ?? my executors on oath of whom I bequeath a legacy of thirty pounds.
Whereof I have now unto set my hand and Seal this 29th Day of July 1776 Chas Clerke
Signed and Delivered by the testator Capt Charles Clerke as his act and deed and published as his last Will and Testament in the presence of us John Cantiloo and Robt Burney.

* * * * *

(Will of 17th August 1779)

I Charles Clerke of his Majesty's Sloop the *Resolution* having been long in a ?? state of Straiten and not knowing how soon it may please God to remove me from this life I hereby make this my last Will and Testament that all my just and lawful debts be paid and which are as follows. Mr James Sykes of Crutched Friars my agent who hath my Credentials in his hands having settled my accounts to acquit himself of the Sum I now stand indebted to him and from the remainder pay to my honoured friend Sir Robert Ainslie one hundred pounds with the interest due to the same thereof To my honoured friend Doctor

Maty or his sons the Sum of fifty pounds with the lawful interest to the date hereof To Mr Henry Wyate of Panton Street London hosier Seven pounds eleven shillings and Eight pence to Mr John Ramsden of Piccadilly Optician one pounds Sixteen Shillings To my dear and honoured father one Guinea and my Gold Watch with a second hand to it To my dear brother and friend Sir John Clerke Captain in his Majesty's Navy ten Guineas and to my dear Brother Joseph Clerke of Ipswich Attorney at Law five Guineas to my dearest sisters Hannah and Anne Clerke five Guineas each to my dearest friend Lady Clerke wife of my Brother Sir John Clerke five Guineas to my honoured friend Joseph Banks Esquire of New Burlington Street all my Curiosities Natural and Artificial which I have collected in the course of this voyage in token of my Gratitude and respect for his friendship To my good friend ?? Rickman Ten Guineas To Gregory Broutham my late Clerk of the *Discovery* the Sum which with his pay of Clerk shall make at the rate of fifty pounds a year during the time he was my Clerk in that Ship according to my agreement provided his accounts are ever as I have reason to expect they will be To William Coulston Cooper of the *Discovery* the sum of ??? being the agreement I made with him to come the voyage in that capacity to Richard Collott the Sum of thirty pounds for his faithful Services To John Fisher and John Arnobe or ? Booker five guineas each and after the above debts and Legacies are Discharged all the rest and residue of my Effects whatsoever and wheresoever real or personal that at this time or at any time hereafter shall belong to me I give and bequeath to my loving sister Sarah Clerke and I do hereby appoint Edward Thompson of Bow Captain in his Majesty's Navy to whom I bequeath my Second Gold Watch as a memorial of my friendship and James Sykes of Crutched Friars London to whom I bequeath the Sum of ten Guineas my executors are witness whereof and hereunto set my hand and Seal this Seventeenth day of August one thousand Seven hundred and Seventy nine Chas Clerke signed and sealed in the presence of James King, Alex ???

BIBLIOGRAPHY

Beaglehole, J.C., *Journals of Captain Cook on his Voyages of Discovery.* Hakluyt.

Beaglehole, J.C., *The Life of Captain James Cook.* A. & C. Black, Ltd., London, 1974.

Brown, A.F.J., *Prosperity and Poverty in Rural Essex 1700-1815.* Essex Record Office, 1996.

Chelmsford Chronicle. Chelmsford Public Library.

Clerke Journal. Public Record Office, ADM/103.

Coller, D.W., *The People's History of Essex.* Meggy and Chalk, 1861.

Dictionary of National Biography. Oxford University Press.

Edwards, A.C., *A History of Essex.* Phillimore & Co. Ltd., London and Chichester, 1958.

Ellis, W., *An Authoritative Narrative of a Voyage Performed by Captain Cook and Captain Clerke.* National Maritime Museum, London.

'Essex Countryside'. April 1960.

Feiling, Keith, *A History of England.* Macmillan, 1966.

Holmes, C., *Capt. Cook's Second Voyage: The Journals of Lts. Elliott and Pickersgill.* Caliban Books, 1984

Hough, R., *Captain James Cook.* Hodder and Stoughton, 1994.

Hughes, R., *The Fatal Shore.* Collins Harvill, 1987.

Kennedy, P., *The Rise and Fall of the Great Powers.* Unwin Hyman, 1988.

Kippis, A., *Voyages Round The World Performed By Captain James Cook.* Thomas Nelson, Edinburgh, 1837.

Knox-Johnston, R., *The Cape of Good Hope.* Hodder and Stoughton, 1989.

Little, Shelby, *George Washington.* Routledge and Sons, 1931.

London Chronicle. Guildhall Library, London.

Moorhead, A., *The Fatal Impact.* Hamish Hamilton, 1966.

National Maritime Museum, *James Cook, The Opening of the Pacific.* 1970.

Rodger, N.A.M., *Naval Records for Genealogists.* P.R.O., 1988.

Rodger, N.A.M., *The Insatiable Earl, A Life of the 4th Earl of Sandwich.* Harper Collins, 1993.

Rodger, N.A.M., *The Wooden World.* William Collins, 1986.

Sobel, D., *Longitude.* Fourth Estate, 1996.

Stamp, T. and C., *James Cook Maritime Scientist.* Caedmon of Whitby Press, 1978.

Stokesbury, James, *A Short History of the American Revolution.* Wm. Morrow & Co., New York, 1991.

Sugden, J., *Sir Francis Drake.* Barrie and Jenkins, 1990.

Survey of London, Vol XXV. London County Council, 1955.

Thomson, G.M., *The North-West Passage.* Secker and Warburg, 1975.

Trevelyan, G.M., *A Shortened History of England.* Penguin Group, 1987.

REFERENCES

THE EARLY YEARS

1 Parish Records: Essex Records Office .
2 *The Wooden World*, p. 259, N.A.M. Rodger. Fontana Press, 1988.
3 Samwell Journal.

LAND AND SEA

1 Wethersfield Vestry Records. Essex Records Office.
2 *The Insatiable Earl, A Life of the 4th Earl of Sandwich*, p. 138, N.A.M. Rodger. Harper Collins, 1993.
3 ADM 52/571, P.R.O.
4 ADM 36/3785, P.R.O.

DOLPHIN AND *ROMNEY*

1 ADM 36/7487.
2 ADM 8/42.
3 ADM 36/7487.

ENDEAVOUR

1 ADM 6/87.
2 Admin 1/1609 No 3.

RESOLUTION

1 Wethersfield Parsh Record. Essex Records Office.
2 *History of Essex.* D.W. Coller. Meggy and Chalk, Chelmsford 1861.
3 *The Opening of the Pacific.* National Maritime Museum .
4 Clerke Journal. PRO Kew, ADM 55 / 103.
5 Letter to Navy Board. Captain Cook Memorial Museum, Whitby.
6 J.C. Beaglehole, App. VIII p. 931.
7 Lady Lydia Clerke Letters. Society of Antiquaries, London.
8 Navy Board to Admiralty, 3.6.1772. Capain Cook Memorial Museum, Whitby.
9 *Captain Cook's Second Voyage. The Journals of Lieutenants Elliott and Pickersgill,* Edited by Christine Holmes. Caliban Books, 1984.
10 Banks letter to Lord Sandwich, 30.5.1772. Captain Cook Memorial Museum,Whitby.
11 Lord Sandwich to Johann Forster 20.10.1775. Captain Cook Memorial Museum, Whitby.
12 James Cook letter to William Hammond, from Madeira, 1.8.1772. Capain Cook Memorial Museum, Whitby.
13 Journals of Lieutenants Elliot and Pickersgill.

14   Ibid.

THE KING'S BENCH

1   *Journal of Captain Cook,* J.C. Beaglehole, Vol III Pt. 1.
2   *Captain James Cook,* Richard Hough, P 345, Hodder and Stoughton 1994.
3   *The Chelmsford Chronicle,* Chelmsford Public Library .
4   Lady Lydia Clerke Letters, Society of Antiquaries.
5   Ibid.
6   Ibid.
7   Surrey Records Office, Quarter Session Record, 3/2/6.
8   Geo III, Ch. 38.
9   PRO Chancery Lane, B/11 1070 and B/11 1067.
10   Lady Lydia Clerke Letters, Society of Antiquaries
11   ADM 1/1611
12   Surrey Records Office, Quarter Session Record Book 29.7.1776 .
13   Lady Lydia Clerke Letters, Society of Antiquaries .

DISCOVERY

1   Bank's Papers, Mitchel Library, Glasgow.
2   Letter from James Cook to John Walker, Captain Cook Memorial Museum, Whitby.
3   J. C. Beaglehole, *The Journals of Captain James Cook on his voyages,* Vol III, Pt. 2.
4   Letter from James Cook to John Walker, 14.2.1776, Captain Cook Memorial Museum, Whitby.
5   *London Chronicle,* 11.6.1776, Guildhall Library, London.
6   Ibid.
7   Ellis Journal.
8   Cook and King Journal, Vol II, p. 66.
9   Ellis Journal, Vol II, p.1151.
10   Ibid.
11   Captain Cook Memorial Museum, Whitby.

APPENDIX II
1   J. C. Beaglehole, Vol III.

APPENDIX III
1   ADM 55/120.

INDEX